Conducting Educatio Design Research

MW00574096

Educational design research blends scientific investigation with systematic development and implementation of solutions to educational problems. Empirical investigation is conducted in real learning settings – not laboratories – to craft usable and effective solutions. At the same time, the research is carefully structured to produce theoretical understanding that can serve the work of others.

To support graduate students as well as experienced researchers who are new to this approach, *Conducting Educational Design Research* integrates multiple perspectives of educational design research throughout this three-part book. Part I clarifies the educational design research origins, approach and outcomes. It also presents a generic model portraying the overall process. Part II discusses the constituent elements of the model in detail, these are: analysis and exploration; design and construction; evaluation and reflection; and implementation and spread. Part III offers recommendations for proposing, reporting and advancing educational design research. Through related readings and richly varied examples, *Conducting Educational Design Research* offers clear and well-documented guidance on how to conceptualize and conduct this stimulating form of inquiry.

For decades, policies for educational research worldwide have swung back and forth between demanding rigor above all other concerns, and increasing emphasis on impact. These two qualities need not be mutually exclusive. This volume supports readers in grasping and realizing the potential of educational design research. It demonstrates how rigorous and relevant investigation can yield both theoretical understanding and solutions to urgent educational problems.

Susan McKenney is Associate Professor of Curriculum Implementation at both the University of Twente and the Open University of the Netherlands.

Thomas C. Reeves is Professor Emeritus of Learning, Design, and Technology at the University of Georgia, USA.

Conducting Educational Design Research

Susan McKenney and
Thomas C. Reeves

Routledge
Taylor & Francis Group

LONDON AND NEW YORK

First published 2012
by Routledge
2 Park Square, Milton Park, Abingdon, Oxon OX14 4RN

Simultaneously published in the USA and Canada
by Routledge
711 Third Avenue, New York, NY 10017

Routledge is an imprint of the Taylor & Francis Group, an informa business

British Library Cataloguing in Publication Data
A catalogue record for this book is available from the British Library

Library of Congress Cataloging in Publication Data
McKenney, Susan E.
Conducting educational design research / Susan E. McKenney,
Thomas C. Reeves.
   p. cm.
   1. Instructional systems–Design–Research. I. Reeves, Thomas C.
(Thomas Charles) II. Title.
   LB1028.38M35 2012
   371.1007–dc23   2011041864

ISBN: 978-0-415-61803-8 (hbk)
ISBN: 978-0-415-61804-5 (pbk)
ISBN: 978-0-203-81818-3 (ebk)

Typeset in Galliard
by HWA Text and Data Management, London

Printed and bound in the United States of America

Contents

PART III
Moving forward

Figures

Tables

Acknowledgments

Writing this book has been a learning experience and a privilege. It would not have been possible without the generous support of many people. Though a brief mention here cannot do justice to their contributions, we would like to thank them, nonetheless.

Special thanks go to the University of Twente's Stimulation Fund and the Faculty of Behavioral Sciences for providing the funding to enable time away from the office for Susan to work on this book. In addition, fellow members of the Department of Curriculum Design and Educational Innovation graciously supported this endeavor through their critical comments and frequent invitations to discuss educational design research issues.

Gratitude is also due to College of Education at The University of Georgia (UGA), especially its Department of Educational Psychology and Instructional Technology, for providing Tom with space and support to work on this book, even though he is officially "retired." Much of our early writing collaboration took place during the sabbatical that Susan spent at UGA in 2009.

We are extremely grateful to our graduate students, who have questioned us and prompted us to think more deeply about educational design research. Particular recognition goes to the students in UGA's Learning, Design, and Technology doctoral program, who helped create the rubric presented in Table 8.1, and to the National Educational Research School (ICO) course participants we have been fortunate to teach together in the Netherlands. In addition, our interactions with several students, who actually applied educational design research during their doctoral studies under our guidance including Ferry Boschman, Amina Cviko, Ying Liu, Eujung Oh, David Porcaro, and Harini Raval, helped develop the ideas presented throughout these pages.

Professor Jan Herrington from Murdoch University in Australia was a dedicated, critical friend to this project. Collaborating with her helped set the stage for writing several chapters, especially Chapter 8 (Herrington, McKenney, Reeves, & Oliver, 2007). She is a true pioneer of educational design research.

Professor Janette Hill and Associate Professor Ike Choi from UGA also deserve special mention for their leadership in organizing the "Educational Design Research: Local Change and Global Impact" conference at The University of Georgia in March 2010. Timely and energizing, this event greatly helped to strengthen our resolve to write this book.

An earlier version of this book was substantially revised, thanks to the extremely generous and insightful feedback from (in alphabetical order): Jan Jaap Adema, Jacqueline Barber, Theo Bastiaens, Ferry Boschman, Barbara Bradley, Saskia Brand-Gruwel, Stan Buis, Hugh Burkhardt, Gemma Corbalan Perez, Petra Cremer, Christine Cunningham, Huub de Beer, Walter Doyle, Petra Fisser, Kim Gomez, Koeno Gravemeijer, Adam Handelzalts, Tjark Huizinga, Yael Kali, Paul Kirschner, Renske Klein, Ard Lazonder, Suzy Loper, Nienke Nieveen, Chandra Orill, Bart Ormel, Natalie Pareja, Denis Phillips, Jules Pieters, Tjeerd Plomp, Harini Raval, Richard Reeve, David Reinking, Kim Schildkamp, Alan Schoenfeld, Chris Schunn, Robert-Jan Simons, Pieter Swager, Bettine Taminiau, Annette Thijs, Jo Tondeur, Joan van Aken, Johan van Braak, Jan van den Akker, Ellen van den Berg, Ludo van Meeuwen, Irene Visscher-Voerman, Monique Volman, Joke Voogt, Amber Walraven and Brooklynn Wynveen.

Our families have kindly supported this endeavor in many ways. Pam, Dick and especially Theresa McKenney as well as Adriana Helder, Jeannette Haveman, and Roel Kok took loving care of Susan's children while much of this book was written. Skyler, Logan and Mitchell provided highly valuable grounding and distraction when needed. Most of all, we want to express our deep and sincere thanks to our spouses, Kevin McKenney and Trisha Reeves, for understanding why we undertook this project and for supporting us along the way.

There is one person whose contribution to this book stands out, among all others. The steps he took to enable and prioritize the time for writing were instrumental in bringing it to fruition.

We therefore dedicate this book to Professor Jules Pieters.

Introduction

We entered the field of education because of our passion for working with young people and commitment to facilitating their learning as well as our own. We grew into educational research because we enjoy the challenge and wanted to investigate ways to support others in teaching and learning processes. We gravitated to design research because of its naturally close ties with the practice that is dear to us, and in response to disillusionment with too much educational research that does not, in the short or long term, serve to improve practice. Finally, we have taken up the torch of educating and supporting design researchers because of our conviction that this approach, alongside others, can yield valuable results for both theoretical understanding and educational practice. To introduce this book, we briefly discuss our intentions, the book structure, and the limitations of its linearity.

Intentions

Design research is a multi-faceted, complex endeavor and, while we do attempt to present some useful ideas about how it can be undertaken in this book, we recognize that this resource cannot speak to every researcher's needs. In fact, given the rich variation with which educational design research is conducted, we stress that this book is not an attempt to provide "the" authoritative guide to this type of inquiry. In fact, we are not convinced that educational design research has evolved to the point that a definitive guide could be written.

Instead, we share our experiences and views of educational design research in this book, and have made an effort to show where they converge with others in the field. In working with researchers, especially doctoral students, we have grown accustomed to the kinds of questions people often ask about design research. As laid out in the following chapters, we have also found our ways of answering them.

We view undertaking the enterprise of design research, particularly for the first time, as a kind of educational intervention in itself. We know from our own research and experience that sustainable use of new ideas does not come when an intervention focuses on using new resources or changing overt behaviors. Real change can come when we focus not only on what and how things can be done, but when we also work to understand why. For a new idea to be taken up and used – in a form that is true to its intent – people need to see and identify with the rationale behind it. This is also true when that new idea is conducting educational design research. In keeping with an audience of practicing researchers and especially doctoral students, this book endeavors to offer accessible, usable guidance which does not compromise clarity and depth in the portrayal of the theoretical underpinnings from which these ideas grew.

This volume was written to support graduate students as well as experienced researchers who are new to educational design research. We also relish the notion that the ideas presented in this book spark dialogue between graduate researchers and their mentors. Finally, we hope that the issues raised and the perspectives offered here provide useful fodder for continuing discussion among the educational design research community and for moving this exciting genre of inquiry forward.

Three parts

This book is divided into three main parts. Part I, "Foundations," lays the groundwork for the rest of the book and contains three chapters. Chapter 1, "About educational design research," defines and describes educational design research. Chapter 2, "Contributions to theory and practice: concepts and examples," discusses the dual outcomes of design research and gives several – very different – examples of how these dual outcomes were achieved through brief portraits of four actual studies. Chapter 3, "Toward a generic model for educational design research," illustrates how core ideas from the fields of instructional design and curriculum development, as well as different models for educational design research, shape our view of the process; it then presents a generic model of educational design research. That model forms the backbone of the next part of the book.

Part II, "Core processes," describes each main process depicted in the generic model. Chapter 4, "Analysis and exploration," concerns the establishment of a research focus and centers on understanding the problem to be addressed, with inputs from both theory and practice. Chapter 5, "Design and construction," describes the process of mapping and actually building creative solutions that are informed by theory, empirical findings and craft wisdom. Chapter 6, "Evaluation and reflection," describes ways to consider and shape the field testing of interventions, from early design ideas to full scale tryouts. Chapter 7, "Implementation and spread," discusses the interaction with practice that is present from the very start and tends to increase throughout the entire design research endeavor.

Part III, "Moving forward," builds on the discussions throughout Parts I and II to offer recommendations for proposing, reporting, and advancing educational design research. Chapter 8, "Writing proposals for educational design research," offers guidelines for addressing the same basic elements of any strong research proposal, but from the perspective of integration with an iterative design process. Chapter 9, "Reporting educational design research," presents some practical guidelines for tackling the daunting task of reporting on design studies. Chapter 10, "Looking back and looking ahead," reflects on the chapters of this book, discusses new directions for educational design research, and issues a call to action to existing and new members of the educational design research community.

The impetus for this book came primarily from the needs of the numerous doctoral students we have worked with over many years. For this reason, we anticipate that all chapters will be relevant to them. For masters students, we suspect that Part I will be of interest; and for those actually conducting design research for their thesis work, Part II may also be useful. For experienced researchers new to educational design research, Parts I and II are likely to be of greatest interest. This is especially the case for experienced researchers who are mentoring graduate students interested in this kind of inquiry. Part I may also be valuable to anyone concerned with knowing about design research but not actually conducting it themselves, such as research program officers. In terms of advancing discussion among the existing educational design research community, Chapter 3, Part II, and Chapter 10 may be the most relevant.

Books are linear, educational design research is not

There are many ways to put the generic model (Chapter 3) to use, and the sequence of chapters in this book shows but one. As stated earlier and illustrated throughout this book, educational design research is a genre of inquiry – not a fixed method. As such, there are myriad approaches to conducting the enterprise. We cannot provide a comprehensive picture of that variation, but do explicitly attempt to demonstrate it by way of examples. The differences in problems being tackled and the contexts in which solutions are to be implemented require a repertoire of approaches, not one. Such a repertoire is influenced by experience, as well as methodological preferences, domain-specific traditions, and areas of expertise. Though our rational hindsight descriptions may suggest otherwise, serendipity often plays a role in the pathways studies actually take. Very often, different design research processes are concurrent. While greater scales of intention and larger project teams can expand the orchestration required, even small projects often require that researchers juggle multiple demands at once. We thus stress here that the ideas, and especially the sequence in which they are presented in this book, are offered as springboards to assembling useful pathways for design research projects and not as ready-made formulae.

Part 1

Foundations

Chapter 1

About educational design research

What sets educational design research apart from other forms of scientific inquiry is its commitment to developing theoretical insights and practical solutions simultaneously, in real world (as opposed to laboratory) contexts, together with stakeholders. Many different kinds of solutions can be developed and studied through educational design research, including educational products, processes, programs, or policies. This chapter provides an introduction to educational design research. After a definition and brief description of the main origins of educational design research, characteristics and outputs of this approach are discussed. Following attention to the rich variation in educational design research (e.g. in focus, methods and scope), two prevailing orientations are described: research conducted on interventions, and research conducted through interventions. The chapter concludes with considerations of what distinguishes educational design research from educational design, and from other genres of inquiry.

Motives and origins for educational design research

Educational design research can be defined as a genre of research in which the iterative development of solutions to practical and complex educational problems also provides the context for empirical investigation, which yields theoretical understanding that can inform the work of others. Its goals and methods are rooted in, and not cleansed of, the complex variation of the real world. Though educational design research is potentially very powerful, it is also recognized that the simultaneous pursuit of theory building and practical innovation is extremely ambitious (Phillips & Dolle, 2006).

Educational design research is particularly concerned with developing what Lagemann (2002) referred to as usable knowledge, thus rendering the products of research relevant for educational practice. Usable knowledge is constructed during the research (e.g. insights among the participants involved) and shared with other researchers and practitioners (e.g. through conference presentations, journal articles and the spread of interventions that embody certain understandings). Because educational design research is conducted in the naturally occurring test beds of school classrooms, online learning

)nments, and other settings where learning occurs, these studies tend to be
ıııcrnọdologically creative. Multiple methods are often used to study phenomena
within the complex systems of authentic settings, thus possessing high degrees
of ecological validity. In an ecologically valid study, the methods, materials, and
setting of the study approximate the real life situation that is under investigation
(Brewer, 2000). The external validity of a study (the ability of a study's results
to be generalized) stands to be increased when conducted under real world
conditions. The remainder of this section provides a brief historical perspective
of the two main motives of relevance and robustness. Later in this chapter,
additional attention is given to the notion of generalizability (see "Main outputs
of educational design research").

Linking basic and applied research

Research is often classified as being either basic or applied. In *basic research*,
the quest for fundamental understanding is typically shaped by using scientific
methods to explore, to describe, and to explain phenomena with the ultimate
goal of developing theory. Basic research generally follows what has been
characterized as an empirical cycle. De Groot (1969) described this cycle through
five phases: observation (data collection); induction (formulating hypotheses);
deduction (making testable predictions); testing (new empirical data collection);
and evaluation (linking results to hypotheses, theories and possibly new studies).
In contrast, *applied research* features the application of scientific methods to
predict and control phenomena with the ultimate goal of solving a real world
problem through intervention. Applied research generally follows what has been
characterized as a regulative cycle, described by van Strien (1975, 1997). The
five phases of the regulative cycle are: problem identification; diagnosis; planning;
action; and evaluation. Although fundamental and applied research approaches
have historically been considered mutually exclusive, many argue that this is not
the case, as described next.

For over a hundred years, social science researchers and research critics,
including those in education, have struggled to define the most appropriate
relationship between the quest for fundamental understanding and the quest for
applied use. Psychologist Hugo Münsterberg (1899) and educational philosopher
John Dewey (1900) both spoke of a linking science, which would connect
theoretical and practical work. Taking these ideas further, Robert Glaser (1976)
laid out the elements of a psychology of instruction, calling for a science of design
in education. More recently, Donald Stokes (1997) provided a fresh look at the
goals of science and their relation to application for use, in his highly acclaimed
book, titled *Pasteur's Quadrant: Basic Science and Technological Innovation*.

Use-inspired basic research

Stokes (1997) lamented the artificial separation of basic and applied science,
suggesting instead a matrix view of scientific research as illustrated in Figure 1.1.

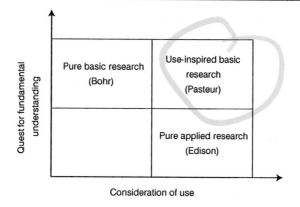

Figure 1.1 Pasteur's quadrant
Source: Stokes, 1997

Whether particular researchers are seeking fundamental theoretical understanding or whether they are primarily concerned about practical applications of research determines their placement within the matrix. To illustrate, Stokes described the research conducted by Niels Bohr as typical of pure basic research. Bohr was a Nobel Prize winning Danish physicist who sought basic knowledge about the structure of the atom; his work was not concerned with practical application of that knowledge. In sharp contrast, Stokes described the research conducted by Thomas Edison as typical of pure applied research. Edison was an American inventor who sought to solve practical problems by creating innovative technologies; he expressed little interest in publishing his research findings or contributing to a broader scientific understanding. Linking the motives of these two scientists, Stokes described the research of Louis Pasteur as typical of use-inspired basic research. Pasteur was a French chemist and microbiologist who sought fundamental knowledge within the context of solving real world problems such as the spoilage of milk and treatment for rabies. Stokes left the quadrant which represents research that neither seeks fundamental understanding nor considers practical use blank. However, critics of educational research have argued that too much educational research belongs in this sterile quadrant because it contributes little to understanding or to use (cf. Reeves, 2000).

Stokes (1997) called for much more focus on "use-inspired basic research" of the kind conducted by Pasteur. Stokes also questioned the popular assumption that basic research inevitably leads to the development of new technologies. He argued that technological advances often permit the conduct of new types of research, thus reversing the direction of the basic to applied model. For example, the development of powerful computers and sophisticated data analysis software has allowed scientists as diverse as astronomers and neuroscientists to apply computational modeling as an effective method for advancing their research agendas (Shiflet & Shiflet, 2006). As discussed in the following section, others have argued that the relationship between basic and applied research is interactive.

Robust and relevant educational research

Schoenfeld (2006) pointed out that the advancement of fundamental understanding and practical applications can be synergistic. Using the Wright brothers' work to develop a flying machine to illustrate, he described how theory influenced design and vice versa (p. 193):

> Theory and design grew in dialectic – nascent theory suggesting some improved design, and aspects of design (even via *bricolage*) suggesting new dimensions to the theory. As they matured, aspects of each grew independently (that is, for example, theory was capable of growing on its own; at the same time, some innovations sprang largely from their inventors' minds rather than from theory.) Yet, the two remained deeply intertwined (emphasis in original text).

Educational design researchers have characterized their work as belonging to Pasteur's quadrant (cf. Roschelle, Bakia, Toyama & Patton, 2011). Indeed, educational design research is a form of linking science, in which the empirical and regulative cycles come together to advance scientific understanding through empirical testing during the development of practical applications. Through such a synergistic process, educational design research stands to increase both the robustness and the relevance of its products.

Robust design practices

The need for increased, reliable, prescriptive understanding to guide robust design of educational products, processes, programs, and policies has been stressed in the literature for several decades, most notably in the field of curriculum (e.g. Stenhouse, 1975; Walker, 1992; van den Akker, 1999). Several reasons for this can be identified. First, research is needed to provide grounding that can inform initial or subsequent design decisions. Edelson (2002) refers to three classes of decisions that determine a design outcome: design procedure (how the design process will proceed); problem analysis (what needs and opportunities the design will address); and design solution (what form the resulting design will take). Decision making within each of these classes can be greatly facilitated by research, conducted within the project, and/or through reports of other studies. Second, planning for interim testing that allows designs to respond accordingly is needed to increase the chances of ambitious and complex interventions to succeed. Innovative design is typically ill-specified, and cannot be conceived of at the drawing table alone (van den Akker, 1999). Planning for and embedding formative research into design trajectories emphasizes the principle that design decisions should not all be made up front, and acknowledges the expectation that research findings will responsibly inform the development. Third, embedding substantial research into the design process can contribute greatly to the professional development of educational designers. Given that huge numbers of the world's learners are exposed to the products of educational designers (e.g. from curriculum institutes and textbook publishers), their levels of expertise are not inconsequential. Burkhardt's (2009) article describing important considerations of strategic design stressed that designers must learn from mistakes (as he says, "fail fast, fail often") and that research is essential to feed such learning. Burkhardt also stated the need for more people trained in educational design research (he used the term "engineering research") to design and develop robust solutions.

Relevant and robust from a scientific perspective

A symposium titled "On Paradigms and Methods: What To Do When the Ones You Know Don't Do What You Want Them To?" was held at the 1991 American Educational Research Association annual meeting to examine how relevant theoretical understanding can be obtained, including the design experiment. Building on that discussion, Collins (1992) and Brown (1992) each published landmark papers, which have often been credited as primary catalysts for launching the genre of educational design research. Brown (1992) recommended design experiments based on the convictions that: theory informs design and vice versa; research on learning must be situated in the contexts where that learning actually takes place; and multi-pronged approaches are needed to influence learning (e.g. teacher expertise, learner activities, classroom materials, formative assessments) because educational settings are inherently complex systems. Collins (1992) persuasively argued for a design science of education, where different learning environment designs are tested for their effects on dependent variables in teaching and learning. This view emphasizes the interactive relationship between applied and basic research, by stressing the role of theory in informing design, and the role of design testing in refining theory. Collins (1992) also highlighted the problem inherent in much educational research whereby an innovation as designed in a laboratory and the innovation as implemented in real classrooms is – more often than not – quite different.

Brown (1992) offered a rich description of her work on metacognition, reciprocal teaching and reading comprehension, which points to the importance and challenges of developing theoretical understanding that is based on relevant findings. She described the tensions that she had experienced between the goals of laboratory studies and the goals of educational innovations, as well as the challenges inherent in integrating innovations in real world classrooms. In addition, she described how the laboratory work informed her classroom observations and vice versa. She stressed the value of cross-fertilization between laboratory and classroom settings for enriching understanding of the phenomenon being studied, and clarified that "Even though the research setting has changed dramatically, my goal remains the same: to work toward a theoretical model of learning and instruction rooted in a firm empirical base," (Brown, 1992, p. 143). Since these papers were published in 1992, increasing attention has been given to the need for theory to inform design and vice versa (Cobb, Confrey, diSessa, Lehrer & Schauble, 2003); the need to understand learning as it naturally occurs and, specifically, what that means for how we shape education (Bransford, Brown & Cocking, 2000); and the need for classroom interventions to fit into the dynamic and the complex system in which they are implemented (Evans, 2001; Hall & Hord, 2010).

Relevant from a practical perspective

The relevance of educational research has to do with its connection to practical applications. Educational research has long been criticized for its weak link with practice. This may be a function of the fact that educational theories are only rarely confirmed by evidence that is unambiguous and/or thorough (Kennedy, 1997). Some have argued that educational research has not focused on the problems and issues that confront everyday practice (Design-Based Research Collective, 2003). Others have lamented the lack of useful knowledge produced by research that could help inform the development of new innovations and reform (van den Akker, 1999). The different languages spoken and values held by researchers and practitioners, respectively, have also been the topic of empirical investigation as well as critique (de Vries & Pieters, 2007). Further, the weak infrastructure supporting the research-based development function in education has been cited as problematic (McDonnell, 2008). In addition, the reward systems in place for both researchers and practitioners are generally incompatible with meaningful researcher–practitioner collaboration (Burkhardt & Schoenfeld, 2003). Based first on literature review and later validated through research, Broekkamp and Hout-Wolters (2007) clustered these issues into four main themes: (a) educational research yields only few conclusive results; (b) educational research yields only few practical results; (c) practitioners believe that educational research is not conclusive or practical; and (d) practitioners make only little (appropriate) use of educational research. The last decade has borne witness to a renaissance of concern surrounding the research–practice gap, in which scholars are systematically studying how policy makers and educators access, value and use research; various modes through which knowledge is generated and shared; and what aspects of evidence-based practice and research utilization in other fields can be applied to education.

We do not argue that educational design research alone will solve the issues described here. However, we, and others (e.g. Burkhardt, 2009; Schoenfeld, 2009a; van den Akker, 1999) do contend that this form of inquiry is one promising avenue to improving both the robustness and the relevance of educational research. In the publications that have appeared since the ground-breaking papers of Brown and Collins in 1992 (cf. Kelly, Lesh, & Baek, 2008; Plomp & Nieveen, 2009; Reinking & Bradley, 2008; Richey & Klein, 2007; van den Akker, Gravemeijer, McKenney & Nieveen 2006b; and special issues of journals including *Educational Researcher, Journal of the Learning Sciences, Educational Psychologist,* and *Educational Technology*), many differing perspectives and priorities have been promoted. This is only natural for a nascent research genre. Nonetheless, it would seem that striving toward robust and relevant outputs are two core values shared by the educational design research community. The following section examines additional aspects of design research, including both convergent and divergent views described by educational design researchers.

Characterizing educational design research

Portraying the process

In the same way that engineering design melds creative insights with pragmatic understanding and follows the best available theoretical principles derived from physics, materials science, aesthetics, and other disciplines, educational design research is a complex and multi-faceted endeavor. The educational design research process has been described as: adaptive, collaborative, contextual, flexible, goal-oriented, grounded, integrative, interactive, interventionist, iterative, methodologically inclusive, multilevel, pragmatic, process-focused, theoretical, transformative and utility-oriented (cf. Cobb, Confrey, diSessa, Lehrer & Schauble, 2003; Kelly, 2003; Reinking & Bradley, 2008; van den Akker, McKenney & Nieveen, 2006a; Wang & Hannafin, 2005). It is easy to agree with all these as characteristics of educational design research. Here, features of the design research process which we consider to be both defining and universal across the genre are briefly discussed: theoretically oriented, interventionist, collaborative, responsively grounded, and iterative. For each feature, examples from (among others) Physics Education Research (PER) are given, drawing on the review conducted by Hake (2008), who presented evidence that serious progress in improving physics education has been accomplished in recent years by forms of, using his terms, design-based research.

Theoretically oriented

A defining feature of most disciplined research is that it uses existing theory to frame inquiry, the results of which ultimately help construct or further elaborate theoretical understanding. In this regard, educational design research is no different from most research. What is unusual about the theoretical orientation in educational design research is that scientific understanding is used to frame not only the research, but also (alongside craft wisdom and creative inspiration) to shape the design of a solution to a real problem. Empirical testing is used to validate, refine, or refute hypotheses and conjectures that are embodied in the design. The development of theoretical understanding in design research thus evolves through consideration of not only empirical findings, but also consideration of their implications for specific dimensions of the design in question. As illustrated in the many examples throughout this book, and especially in Chapter 2, design research may draw upon and contribute to theoretical understanding related to many themes, including learning in specific subject areas (e.g. domain-specific instructional theories), classes of learning problems (e.g. learning theories), and principles for guiding other design efforts (e.g. innovation theory).

For example, Hake (2008) described research supporting several innovative approaches to physics education that have resulted in more and deeper learning than traditional didactic methods. These approaches center on "interactive engagement" methods such as Socratic dialogue, collaborative peer instruction, and hands-on experiments with physical models. A wide range of principles derived from diverse learning theories such as developmental learning theory

(Piaget & Inhelder, 1969) and situated cognition (Brown, Collins, & Duguid, 1989) have informed innovative approaches to physics education. In turn, design studies have allowed the refinement of these principles within this specific domain.

Interventionist

In tandem with the production of new theoretical understanding that can serve others, outside the immediate context of the study, educational design research strives to positively impact practice, bringing about transformation through the design and use of solutions to real problems. Throughout this book, the term "intervention" is used broadly to encompass the different kinds of solutions that are designed. Interventions can include educational products (e.g. learning materials), processes (e.g. teaching repertoires), programs (e.g. professional development scenarios), or policies (e.g. protocols for school evaluation). Educational design research starts with identification of significant educational problems in need of innovative solutions and appropriate for scientific inquiry, followed by clarification of their causes. It is interventionist because, over the long term, educational design research teams engage in the creative activity of developing solutions informed by existing scientific knowledge, empirical testing, and the craft wisdom of project participants. While the scope can vary (ranging from one researcher and one teacher, to hundreds), the intention is – alongside the development of theoretical understanding – to make a real change on the ground.

Peer instruction (Mazur, 1997) is one of the interventions described by Hake (2008) as having been developed through a design research approach. Crouch and Mazur (2001) explained in detail how the collaborative peer instruction model evolved over 10 years of iterative design, testing, and redesign. Peer instruction involves classroom "activities that require each student to apply the core concepts being presented, and then to explain those concepts to their fellow students" (Crouch & Mazur, 2001, p. 970).

Collaborative

Educational design research is conducted – to varying degrees – in collaboration with, not solely *for* or *on*, practice. It requires collaboration among a range of actors connected to the problem at hand. Starting with identification and exploration of a problem together with the problem owners (cf. Ejersbo, Engelhardt, Frølunde, Hanghøj, Magnussen, & Misfeldt, 2008), the craft wisdom and ground-level instincts of research partners in schools and other design research contexts are valued, studied, and put to use. Researchers learn from practitioners, e.g. through adaptations of interventions that meet the same basic goals in ways different from those conceived of by its designers (cf. Clarke & Dede, 2009), and vice versa.

Within the PER community described by Hake (2008), collaborative design and research have been integral to the progress made to enhance both secondary and undergraduate physics instruction. For example, Mazur (1996) explained how instructor disillusionment with the ineffectiveness of traditional lectures led him, together with colleagues at Harvard University, to develop the Peer

Instruction model. Collaborative evolution of this instructional inno
rendered it suitable for a wide spectrum of educational contexts (cf. La$
& Watkins, 2008).

Responsively grounded

The products of educational design research are shaped by participant expertise, literature, and especially field testing. The emerging theoretical and practical insights and in some cases, even the research design, adjust course based on the empirical data, which are collected in real world settings. Educational design research is structured to explore, rather than mute, the complex realities of teaching and learning contexts, and respond accordingly. For example, Kali and Ronen-Fuhrmann (2011) described how their intervention (in this case, a teaching model) evolved over four iterations of enactment and refinement. For each iteration, student learning processes were characterized in terms of learning challenges encountered by students. For each challenge, they made design decisions yielding a refinement to the teaching model, which was enacted in the next iteration. Then, they examined the effects of the refinements on students' learning, searching for both outcomes that confirmed resolution of the challenges as well as for additional learning challenges. Through this responsively grounded process, they were able to fine-tune their understanding of student learning processes while also attuning their teaching model accordingly.

Hake (2008) described how design research within the PER community responded to the problem of students coming to undergraduate physics education underprepared for sufficiently high levels of learning. After discerning that a major cause could be traced to the inadequate learning opportunities of high school physics teachers during their pre-service learning in undergraduate physics, a collaborative movement was launched across the PER community to develop and refine educational interventions to address this problem. This led to innovations such as active learning problem sets (van Heuvelen, 1995), Socratic dialogue inducing laboratories (Hake, 2008), and collaborative peer instruction (Mazur, 1997).

Iterative

The insights and the interventions of educational design research evolve over time through multiple iterations of investigation, development, testing, and refinement. Within one larger study, several sub-studies often take place, each with its own complete cycle of inquiry and sound chain of reasoning. Gravemeijer and Cobb (2006) describe their design research process in terms of longer macro-cycles and daily mini-cycles. McKenney and van den Akker (2005) used cycles within phases to portray the overall process of a study on computer-based support for curriculum designers. Shown in Figure 1.2, the study comprised a total of eight cycles distributed across three phases. The example demonstrates how several sub-studies can be incorporated into one study, and that sub-studies can also be clustered into intermediate stages.

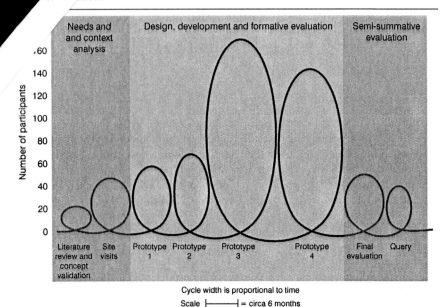

Figure 1.2 Process display of a design study
Source: McKenney and van den Akker, 2005

Conducting what he identified as design research, Hake (2008) iteratively developed, explored, confirmed, and disseminated an intervention he called Socratic dialogue inducing laboratories. He tested and refined this intervention in a range of different classrooms with: undergraduates in introductory physics classes; premedical students; and pre-service science teachers. His iterative testing and (re)design has lasted nearly two decades (Hake, 2008).

Project catalysts: design, research or both

In educational design research, empirical investigation and intervention development are intertwined. While both are core goals, it is not uncommon for one to provide the main catalyst for a project. Often due to the streams of funding behind the work, some design studies are attached to existing development efforts. For example, the Lawrence Hall of Science design research on the Seeds of Science/Roots of Reading curriculum (cf. Pearson, Moje, & Greenleaf, 2010) was set in motion after development work had already commenced. In other cases, development efforts are undertaken to facilitate inquiry. This was the case with Bradley's (2004) formative experiment to enhance verbal interactions in a preschool classroom, where the research goal provided the impetus to undertake the study and create the intervention. It is also not uncommon for both research and development to be conceived of together. The Computer Assisted Curriculum Analysis, Design and Evaluation (CASCADE) series of investigations at the University of Twente are examples of design studies initiated with balanced research and development motives within one project (McKenney, 2001; Nieveen, 1997; Wang, 2001; Zulkardi, 2002).

Reciprocity between research and practice

In this book, references to "practice" are done so in a broad sense. Here, practice refers not only to the work conducted in classrooms and schools, but also to the work that *directly affects* classrooms and schools. This can include the work of supportive professionals (e.g. educational coaches and consultants); intermediaries (e.g. regional centers and in-service educators); or others in the educational system. Consequently, use of the term "practitioner" throughout this book refers to many kinds of educational professionals including, but not limited to, teachers.

Different views of research as well as personal preferences and local conditions strongly influence the researcher–practitioner cooperation in educational research. This is true of many genres of inquiry, and particularly relevant for educational design research, where meaningful cooperation between researchers and practitioners is essential. Along with Wagner (1997), who refers to shaping the researcher–practitioner relationship as the "social design of research projects," we have noted that the social elements in forming relationships between researchers and practitioners commonly get short shrift in graduate courses (on the researcher side) as well as in pre-service education (on the practitioner side). Both researchers and practitioners could be better prepared than is often the case to actively shape the cooperative relationships they undertake. One important step in that direction is acknowledging that there are different forms of cooperation, and that the form should be chosen based on the research questions being asked, the people involved, and the context in which the study is being carried out.

Wagner (1997) identifies three different forms of researcher–practitioner cooperation: data-extraction agreements; clinical partnerships; and co-learning agreements. As these distinctions are particularly useful to start discussions, they are presented in Table 1.1 in an excerpt from Wagner's (1997, p. 17) description. Reflecting on the social aspects of the design research literature we have studied so far, we suspect that much of existing design research has been a combination of "data extraction agreements" and "clinical partnerships," although the model of change underpinning many studies has characteristics of all three forms.

The many names of educational design research

We use the term "educational design research" to describe a family of approaches that strive toward the dual goals of developing theoretical understanding that can be of use to others while also designing and implementing interventions to address problems in practice. This family of approaches has been described under various names, the most common of which are *design-based research* (DBRC, 2003; Kelly, 2003), *development research* (van den Akker, 1999), *design experiments* (Brown, 1992; Collins, 1992; Middleton, Gorard, Taylor, & Bannan-Ritland, 2008), *formative research* (Newman, 1990; Walker, 1992), and *educational design research*

Table 1.1 Excerpt from Wagner's three forms of researcher–practitioner cooperation

	Data extraction agreement	Clinical partnership	Co-learning agreement
Research process	Direct, systematic inquiry designed, conducted and reported by researcher	Systematic inquiry, cooperatively designed and reported by researcher and practitioner	Reflexive, systematic inquiry, stimulated in part by ongoing collegial communication between researchers and practitioners
Context and stance	Researcher is outside the schools and engaged in reflection; practitioners are inside the schools and engaged in action	Researcher is outside the schools and engaged in reflection; practitioners are inside the schools and engaged in action and reflection	Researchers and practitioners both participate through action and reflection in processes of education and systems of schooling
Model of change	Knowledge generated through research can inform educational policy and contribute to improved instruction	Researchers and practitioners conduct cooperative research on problems of practice to help practitioners improve their own effectiveness	Drawing on knowledge gained through cooperative research, researchers and practitioners are responsible for initiating complementary changes in their own institutions
Expert roles	Researcher as researcher; practitioner as practitioner	Researcher as researcher and collaborator; practitioner as practitioner and collaborator	Researcher as researcher–practitioner and practitioner as practitioner–researcher in their home institutions

Source: Wagner, 1997

(van den Akker, Gravemeijer, McKenney, & Nieveen, 2006b). We have adopted the term educational design research for two main reasons. First, as have others (Kelly, Lesh, & Baek, 2008; Plomp & Nieveen, 2009; van den Akker, Gravemeijer, McKenney & Nieveen 2006b), we incorporate *education* in the term to denote the field in question to avoid confusion with design research from other fields (e.g. Laurel's 2003 book, *Design Research*, that concerns the field of human computer interface design and industrial engineering). Second, although we like the term "design-based research," we have found that it seems to engender more frequent misconceptions, often being equated with research-informed design, thus under-representing the theoretical output. Of course, the term educational design research is not completely immune to the same affliction.

Main outputs of educational design research

As previously stated, the educational design research process advances both theory and practice simultaneously, even synergistically. It is important to note that theoretical understanding in design research: (a) underpins the design of an intervention; (b) frames the scientific inquiry; and (c) is advanced by findings generated through empirical testing of the intervention. These theoretical and practical outcomes, the generation of which is intertwined, are briefly presented in the remainder of this section. They receive more in-depth treatment in the following chapter. This section concludes with comments on the generalization of both theoretical and practical outputs of educational design research.

Theoretical contributions

In addition to a practical contribution in the form of the intervention, design research also yields theoretical understanding. That is, understanding about the phenomenon in question that is abstracted from empirical findings, and contributes to a body of knowledge that is useful to others outside the research setting. Educational design research can contribute to the development of theories that are used to describe, explain or predict certain phenomena. In addition, educational design research can yield theoretical insights of a prescriptive nature. These are often referred to as design principles, as they recommend how to address a specific class of issues in a range of settings. Theoretical understanding developed through educational design research can range from locally to more broadly applicable understanding, although the latter tends to be less common. Chapter 2 describes the theoretical contributions of design research in greater detail.

Practical contributions

An essential feature of educational design research is the development of solutions to problems of practice. While testing of these solutions provides the context for scientific inquiry, they are also valuable in their own right. These interventions, inputs into educational environments that are fine-tuned through empirical testing, constitute the main practical contribution of educational design research. This is because they are designed for actual use. The interventions created through educational design research are not merely hypothetical concepts; they are implemented (adopted, enacted, and – we hope – sustainably maintained) in authentic settings with the goal of solving real problems. In addition, the design research process itself can also make a practical contribution, for example, by providing opportunities to those involved for reflection and learning. Our own preference is for substantial elements of the intervention to be co-constructed by researchers and practitioners working closely together, to the degree that is feasible and effective given the situation at hand. Different kinds of design research interventions are described throughout this book. The examples given in Chapter 2 illustrate the wide range of possibilities: strategies for developing preschooler oral language skills; para-teacher professional development in Indian slums; technology-rich learning in middle school mathematics; and an integrated curriculum for primary school science and literacy.

A few words on generalization

About generalization

Generalization is important because it allows insights from one situation to advance understanding not only of that specific instance, but of other, similar, instances. Though typically thought of as the extent to which research findings and conclusions from a study conducted with a sample population can be applied to the entire population, generalization has other meanings as well. In logic, it can refer to reasoning from detailed facts to general principles (induction). In psychology, it can refer to transferring the response learned to one stimulus to a similar stimulus. In educational design research, generalization concerns being able to transfer theoretical insights and/or practical interventions to other settings. As Brown (1992, p. 143) put it, "We must operate always under the constraint that an effective intervention should be able to migrate from our experimental classroom to average classrooms operated by and for average students and teachers, supported by realistic technological and personal support."

Replication within and across contexts

Generalization can, to some extent, be boosted by replication. This has been done, for example, through the multiple micro- and macro-cycles of testing within a limited range of contexts as carefully described in the work of Gravemeijer and Cobb (2006); Cobb and Gravemeijer (2008). In addition, studies have also tested the boundaries of underlying theories by implementing relatively stable interventions across differing contexts, as have Nelson, Ketelhut, Clarke, Bowman, and Dede (2005). Since there are so many factors at play when interventions "go live," replication in design research is different from replication in the laboratory sense. As Reinking and Bradley (2008, p. 42) note:

> When formative and design experiments are replicated across diverse instructional contexts, they may reveal generalizations and theoretical findings that transcend the complex variability across classrooms and the teachers and students that inhabit them. Thus, generalizations in scientific experiments treat variability as a collection of random factors. In formative and design experiments, generalizations are derived from careful consideration of that variability.

Being sensitive to contextual factors and working systematically can enable researchers to make cautious inferences, and propose theories to explain their observations. But "when we give proper weight to local conditions, any generalization is a working hypothesis, not a conclusion" (Cronbach, 1975, p. 125). The need to explicate the "local conditions" as an integrated element of the results of design research has been addressed in the literature, along with ideas about how to do so (cf. Hoadley, 2004; McKenney, Nieveen & van den Akker, 2006; Reinking & Bradley 2008; Tabak, 2004; van den Akker, 1999). More is presented about the role of context in Chapter 7.

Forms of generalization

In design research as well as other genres of research, the onus of generalization can be seen as two-sided. On the one side, the producer of theoretical and practical contributions is obligated to explicate how the specific instance studied compares to other instantiations of the phenomenon. In so doing, description of salient characteristics of both the intervention and the context in which it is enacted are essential. But on the other side, when it comes to putting the outputs of design research to use, it is the consumer who must make the transfer to other specific contexts.

Firestone (1993) critiqued different approaches to generalization. Two forms of generalization, analytic generalization and case-to-case generalization, seem particularly useful in light of educational design research. Each form helps in finding ways to ascertain which lessons learned in one context might be of value in a particular (different) setting.

Analytic generalization, according to Yin (1989, p. 44), is a process through which "the investigator is striving to generalize a particular set of results to a broader theory." Firestone (1993, p. 17) elaborates:

> When one generalizes to a theory, one uses the theory to make predictions and then confirms those predictions. In a specific study, predictions hold under specific conditions. If the predictions hold only under those conditions, they become scope conditions that limit the generalizability of the theory...[or clarify] the scope of a theory – that is, the conditions under which it applies.

For example, Janssen, Tigelaar and Verloop (2009) developed and tested a domain-specific heuristic intended to assist student teachers in designing biology lessons that emphasized comprehension. They concluded that their design heuristic was useful for assisting student biology teachers in developing problem-posing biology lessons, but they cautioned that different design heuristics should be developed for other subject domains.

In contrast, case-to-case generalization refers to the transfer of ideas that takes place when a person in one setting considers adopting an intervention, or its underlying ideas, for use in another setting. Firestone (1993) supports and elaborates the arguments of Kennedy (1979) by comparing this to the notion of precedent, used by judges in court. To establish precedent, four criteria are applied: (a) material facts (how comparable the cases are, externally, e.g. kind of intervention, kind of schools, kind of learners); (b) appropriateness (value judgments about the fairness of the comparison); (c) the reason for the decision made in the original case (what were the arguments then, and are they applicable here?); and (d) grounds for the original decision (based on a technicality or on more fundamental grounds). Case-to-case generalization has been seen in the way design researchers incorporate ideas from other interventions into their own designs. For example, Nieveen's (1997) study on Computer Assisted Curriculum Analysis, Design and Evaluation in The Netherlands served as a springboard for three related design studies in southern Africa (McKenney, 2001), China (Wang, 2001) and Indonesia (Zulkardi, 2002), respectively.

What works is necessary but not sufficient: how, when and why warrant attention

While scientific research seeks understanding that can, even modestly, inform other situations, it is important to note that a premature quest for generalizability can even be counter-productive. Similar to premature closure or false clarity, attempting to generalize before the functional mechanisms are fully understood can waste valuable resources. This can be especially detrimental when broader replication of innovations is attempted too soon.

Premature scaling is widely recognized as the most frequent cause for failure among startup companies, but this lesson seems less acknowledged when it comes to educational innovation, perhaps because there are often political pressures involved. For example, the One Laptop Per Child (OLPC) project is an innovation that holds great potential for improving access to information and education on a global scale, if implemented well. Its founder, Nicholas Negroponte, encouraged governments of developing nations to take sweeping action by buying and implementing the $100 XO laptop on a national scale. Due to insufficient pilot experiences worldwide, his stance has been criticized as both irresponsible and unethical because, "if the grand national experiment fails, it is developing countries and their children that are least able to manage the consequences of this failure or recover from the expended costs" (Kozma, 2007). Instead, experts have called for long-term testing (several months to a school year) in classrooms, to understand not only if, but also how, when and why the XO laptops can contribute to pupil learning, so that implementation efforts can be attuned accordingly.

The pursuit of understanding concerning how, when and why things work has prompted researchers to dig deeper, investigate more carefully and make exciting new discoveries. Hippocrates and centuries of other physicians understood how and when to use salicylic acid, the active ingredient in aspirin, but did not understand why it worked. Decades of studies persisted until researchers in the mid-1960s finally identified the basic mechanisms of its effects; this understanding has, in turn, helped lead to new discoveries. In education, for example, researchers and practitioners alike know that teacher involvement in intervention design can facilitate its implementation. What is less known is: Does it help because of

increased ownership? Or does it have more to do with improved un
of the intervention? Under what circumstances does this approac
The need to structure the quest for "what works" such that it is ui
by a concern for how, when, and why (cf. Cobb, Confrey, diSessa,
Schauble, 2003) is evident in the two orientations to educational design research
described in the next section.

Rich variation across two orientations

Two orientations: research on and research through interventions

Educational design research may be conducted in many ways, to study many
different kinds of phenomena. Across the wide variety of intellectual domains
upon which educational design research may focus, two basic orientations to
the inquiry may be identified. The difference between these orientations has
primarily to do with the role of the designed intervention itself during empirical
investigation. In some design cycles, the intervention serves more as the research
context or as a complex treatment, whose primary purpose is to provide a means
for studying specific phenomena that are related to, but not the same as, the
intervention itself. We refer to this orientation as design research conducted
through interventions. In contrast, design research may be conducted directly
on interventions. This orientation features research focusing explicitly on
characteristics of the design of the intervention, and how the intervention works,
with whom, under what conditions.

In educational design research conducted *through* interventions, the inquiry is
focused on understanding the responses the intervention engenders. Unraveling
the multi-faceted interaction between intervention and context is taken into
consideration, if not an explicit focus of the research. Here, the intervention
may be viewed more as a means through which deeper insight can be gained
into certain phenomena related to teaching and learning in authentic settings.
For example, a question that might guide research with this orientation could
be, "What are the effects of instructional prompts, when given individually and
collectively, on student comprehension of fluid dynamics?" This orientation
is concerned with generating and testing theory that is not directly related to
interventions of a specific type, although the work is highly contextualized, and
is also used to inform the intervention at hand. The theoretical contributions
emerging from this kind of work may relate to (among others): teaching (e.g.
patterns in how teachers develop pedagogical content knowledge); learning (e.g.
factors influencing pupil motivation); and design (e.g. models describing ideal
and actual instructional design trajectories).

Sandoval (2004) provided a rich example of this kind of orientation when
describing how learning theory can be developed by conjectures that are
embodied in educational designs. Through studying use of a computer-based
intervention, his research tested the theoretical conjecture that "conceptual and
epistemic scaffolds for scientific inquiry should be integrated such that they can

help students understand the epistemic goals of their inquiry [while providing] conceptual guidance that supports students as they try to make sense of particular problems in specific domains" (Sandoval, 2004, p. 216). In this example, learning theory was refined through a decade of design research within the Biology Guided Inquiry Learning Environments (BGuILE) project. In general, research conducted through interventions tends to seek fundamental understanding, which is used to describe and explain specific phenomena that the interventions engender.

Research that focuses primarily *on* interventions, on the other hand, strives to generate knowledge about characteristics and functions of particular intervention types. It views the intervention as one manifestation of a particular phenomenon (e.g. serious games), and inquiry focuses on qualities of the intervention, as an end to meet certain goals. For example, a question that might guide research with this orientation could be, "How practical and effective are the scaffolds and prompts embedded in this serious game about computational chemistry and why?" This orientation is concerned with testing how (well) design ideas have been embodied or enacted in specific instantiations of the intervention. Findings from this orientation contribute to theoretical understanding, which can be used to underpin the designs of certain same-type interventions relating to (among others): curriculum (e.g. features of educative curriculum materials); professional development (e.g. environments and processes to support teacher reflection); and instructional tools (e.g. frameworks for serious games). Herrington and Oliver (2000) conducted research with this orientation. They identified characteristics of situated learning; designed and tested a multimedia environment; and used the aggregate insights to develop an instructional design framework for authentic learning environments. In general, research conducted on interventions tends to serve applied use, with findings being used to predict what will happen when interventions are shaped in prescribed ways.

While individual cycles of design research often emphasize one orientation or the other, across the long term, design studies often reflect each of these orientations, at some point. This demonstrates the interaction previously discussed, between fundamental and applied aspects of use-inspired basic research. Whether the intervention is the means of inquiry or the immediate object of study is directly tied to the particular research questions in a cycle of inquiry, the goals of an intervention and especially the kind of information necessary to feed its subsequent development. Other important factors shaping the orientation of the research include the epistemological beliefs of specific researchers; their methodological paradigms; and the research traditions in which the studies are rooted. Middleton, Gorard, Taylor and Bannan-Ritland (2008, p. 27) additionally acknowledge the roles of personal biographies, experiences, ideologies and "perhaps even serendipity" in establishing the research focus of those who engage in educational design research.

Rich variation

In addition to the two orientations described above accounting for some of the variation among design studies, the field is rich with variation in interpretations and applications of this general approach. Some of the differences stem from the grain size of analysis, scope of implementation, nature of the subject areas addressed, or from the research domains and methodological traditions in which studies originate. Other differences can be attributed to the wide range of motives, catalysts or goals of design research projects. Some authors have described that variation primarily in terms of research focus. For example, in advocating that we embrace the theoretical and methodological pluralism within this genre, Bell (2004) delineated the following theoretical modes of design research: developmental psychology design-based research; cognitive science design-based research; cultural psychology design-based research; and linguistic or cognitive anthropology design-based research. Cobb, Confrey, diSessa, Lehrer, and Schauble (2003) identified various classes of design experiments, which differed in both focus and scope: one-on-one (teacher–experimenter and student) design experiments; classroom experiments; pre-service teacher development studies; in-service teacher development studies; and school and school district restructuring experiments.

Other scholars have described variation less in terms of focus or scale, and more in terms of processes. For example, Nieveen, McKenney, and van den Akker (2006) speak of validation studies, development studies, and effectiveness research. Validation studies yield learning theories as scientific output. These theories may feed development studies, which aim to produce interventions and design theories supporting them. In turn, the interventions (and thereby the learning and design theories embodied in them) may be subjected to large-scale effectiveness research. With a similar process orientation, Schoenfeld (2009a) described three stages: (I) generating promising ideas or products; (II) exploring the conditions under which they seem to work and what they look like in practice (including unintentional results); and (III) large-scale testing for effectiveness. In assessing the state of educational research today, Schoenfeld (2009a) argued that the rush toward Stage III studies (e.g. randomized controlled trials), has given short shrift to the kind of theoretical developmental work conducted in Stage I studies, and has omitted the essential investment in studies on designing and using educational interventions in different contexts (Stage II studies).

To be sure, very little current, large-scale research can be characterized as design research. And research focusing solely on after-the-fact effectiveness usually has little relationship to educational design. However, as have others (e.g. Burkhardt & Schoenfeld, 2003), we see opportunity for and wish to encourage more design research to take on the challenges of designing for scale, and testing at scale. Studies of interventions conducted at advanced stages and on large scales can yield more than effectiveness insights alone. It is possible to conduct large-scale studies that examine not only what happens, but also how and why implementation takes place across a range of contexts. Design research that tackles, head on, the challenges of scale is aligned with Burkhardt's description of engineering research (2006), and stands to contribute much to further understanding of what Burkhardt (2009) refers to as "strategic design." For related discussion, please refer to Chapter 7.

Variation exemplified: three design studies

In this section, the rich variation described above is illustrated through three very different reports of design research conducted recently (Barab, Gresalfi, & Ingram-Goble, 2010; Clarke & Dede, 2009; Swan, 2007). For each one, summarized in Table 1.2, the theoretical contributions, methods used, the scope of the intervention involved, and its practical contributions are highlighted. All of the examples indicate that the different reports cover sub-components within larger projects. All of them were designed and tested with a small number of participants but eventually used on a wider scale. They are presented in brief here for the purpose of illustrating variety. We refer readers to the original sources for additional information. Chapter 2 describes four other educational design research projects in greater detail.

Published in the *Educational Researcher*, the Barab, Gresalfi, and Ingram-Goble (2010) article represents one of a series of journal papers in which Barab and colleagues describe their efforts to refine a theory of transformational play while at the same time seeking to develop advanced forms of interactive learning games. This paper summarizes the results of two specific studies, but is primarily an attempt to summarize the status of a long-term educational design research agenda focused on demonstrating the value of transformation play in learning science. Quest Atlantis, a 3D multiplayer virtual environment (MUVE), serves as the primary vehicle for instantiating the transformational play learning theory and allowing it to be refined through iterative design-based research (Barab & Squire, 2004).

Published in the *Journal of Mathematics Teacher Education*, Swan (2007) described a multi-year project to enhance student learning related to mathematics as well as the capacity of students for active and reflective learning through the development and refinement of teacher professional development (PD) resources. These resources include a multimedia CD-ROM and a workshop. The paper provides considerable detail about the nature and components of the professional development resources as well as the design studies that were carried out to refine the PD resources and demonstrate their effectiveness. Evidence related to changes in teacher beliefs and teaching practices as well as evidence of enhanced student learning is provided in this paper.

Published in the *Journal of Science Education and Technology*, Clarke and Dede (2009) described a framework for how to design for scale in education, using an approach they label as "robust design." Scalability involves extending the methods and results of an innovative treatment with demonstrated efficacy in a certain context to larger and more diverse contexts. In particular, this paper focuses on sustainability as one aspect of a five-dimensional framework (based on Coburn, 2003) that also includes depth, spread, shift, and evolution. The River City Curriculum, a multi-user virtual environment (MUVE), serves as the primary vehicle for testing and refining design and implementation heuristics related to scalability. This paper provides summaries of several iterations of design research, but is primarily a presentation of the heuristics that others might consider in efforts to develop scalable innovations.

Table 1.2 Three examples demonstrating educational design research variation

	Swan, 2007	Clarke and Dede, 2009	Barab, Gresalfi and Ingram-Goble, 2010
Main focus	Demonstrating how failing students can become more active and reflective learners through enhanced teacher professional development (PD)	Demonstrating how a curricular innovation can be designed and implemented to achieve "scalability" by accounting for local needs and contexts	Demonstrating the value of transformational play as a means of enhancing students' capacity to construct scientific understanding
Intervention developed	Professional development activities and resources	River City: A multi-user virtual environment (MUVE) curriculum	Quest Atlantis: A 3D multiplayer virtual environment
Primary theoretical contribution	Design principles for teacher PD focused on beliefs about teaching, learning, and mathematics	Large-scale design and implementation heuristics	Theory of transformational play
Research methods used	• Observations • Interviews • Surveys • Oral reports • One quasi-experimental study	• Classroom observations • Interviews • Surveys • Artifact analyses • Several quasi-experimental studies	• Observations • Interviews • Surveys • Document analyses • Two quasi-experimental studies
Research scope	The design research study described in this paper was conducted over a two-year period	This design research initiative has been underway for nearly a decade	This design research initiative has been underway for more than a decade
Primary practical contribution	As of 2007, the multimedia PD resources were being used in further educational institutions throughout England	As of 2009, the River City Curriculum had been used by 250 teachers and 15,000 students in the USA and Canada	As of 2010, Quest Atlantis had been used by 50,000 students in more than a dozen countries

While these examples are provided to highlight variety among design studies, two issues should be clarified. First, the purpose of this discussion is to demonstrate that design research is indeed a "manifold enterprise" (cf. Bell, 2004) and to offer some insight into the variation within this genre. Second, the specific accounts of research summarized above are static, snapshots in time. But the examples given refer to scholars and their projects, both of which are dynamic. Design researchers and the interventions they study evolve over time, and a shift in orientation is not only possible, but also likely.

How is educational design research different?

Despite the variation among design studies, as described above, Larson and Dearing (2008) maintained that design research is a unique and innovative approach to conceptualizing scientific inquiry. Earlier in this chapter, defining and universal characteristics of educational design research were discussed (theoretically oriented, interventionist, collaborative, responsively grounded, and iterative). Many of these characteristics are shared by other approaches to design as well as research. The last section of this chapter clarifies how design research is different from both educational design and other forms of research.

Educational design research is different from educational design

There are many similarities between educational design research and (research-based) educational design. They can both be scientific disciplines. Often, they both have attitudes that value a rational approach. In many cases, they both embrace systems thinking and benefit from creative inspiration. And they are both shaped by iterative, data-driven processes to reach successive approximations of a desired intervention. The fundamental difference lies in the fact that educational design research strives explicitly to make a theoretical contribution – of value to others outside the research/design setting – whereas (even research-based) educational design does not. In educational design research, issues related to the design task are problematized, characterized and investigated with an external orientation; that is, in such a way that they exemplify a case of the phenomenon to be studied and could therefore be informative to others interested in that phenomenon. While educational design may use theoretical, empirical or colloquial evidence to create educational interventions (demonstrating theory as input for design), it does not explicitly contribute to understanding a particular phenomenon through study of one or more instances of it (demonstrating theory as output). This fundamental difference has implications for the entire process. The main differences are italicized in the overview shown in Table 1.3.

Explicit design and development goals

Bereiter (2002, p. 321) wrote that "Design research is not defined by its methods but by the goals of those who pursue it. Design research is constituted within communities of practice that have certain characteristics of innovativeness, responsiveness to evidence, connectivity to basic science, and dedication to continual improvement." Understanding research goals, as different from research approaches and methods, is important for any study. We find ourselves regularly responding to questions about methodologies to even advanced

Table 1.3. Educational design compared to educational design research

Research-based educational design	Parameters	Educational design research
Internal users (e.g. teachers, learners) Internal clients (e.g. schools, districts)	Main audiences	Internal users (e.g. teachers, learners) Internal clients (e.g. schools, districts) *External educational researchers* *External educational professionals*
Product or program	Goals	Product or program *Usable knowledge/theories* *Professional development*
Problem exploration Largely informal	Analysis	*Detailed* problem exploration *Formally documented* *Based on a framework informed by literature*
Previous organizational practices Designer expertise	How design and development are predominantly informed	*Scientific research* *Research and development projects in a variety of settings*
Formative Summative evaluation less common	Evaluation	Formative *Summative*
To make decisions	Reflection	To make decisions *To produce new knowledge*
Limited Primarily for internal use	Documentation	*Extensive* *Aims to make project work transparent*

graduate students with the rather simple observation, "That really depends on the research question you are trying to answer." And often, discussion ensues in which the confusion between research goals and methods is untangled.

Inspired by previous work (Plomp, 2009; Reeves, 2000), five types of research goals are briefly discussed here: descriptive, interpretive, predictive, development, and action. Researchers with descriptive goals are focused on portraying specific aspects of education, such as the engagement of learners in a specific type of learning environment. Researchers with interpretivist goals not only describe, but also attempt to explain, the meaning or implications of phenomena related to teaching, learning, performance, assessment, social interaction, leadership, and other educational factors. Educational researchers with both descriptive and interpretivist goals often draw upon naturalistic research traditions borrowed from other sciences such as anthropology and sociology. Researchers with predictive goals are focused on testing hypotheses related to theories of teaching, learning, performance, assessment, social interaction, instructional design, and so forth.

Predictive research is usually what lay people think of first when they think of research because it often involves the experimental designs used in classic sciences such as physics and chemistry. Predictive research has dominated educational research for decades. Researchers with development goals conduct their studies through the design, development, and testing of interventions that speak to human teaching, learning, and performance problems. Educational researchers with action goals most often seek to improve professional practice, usually their own, and sometimes in collaboration with others.

The theoretical understanding emerging from design research can be descriptive, explanatory, or predictive in nature; it can also be more prescriptive, aiming to guide future development efforts. But embedding the pursuit of theoretical understanding in the design and development of educational interventions is what sets educational design research apart from others. Researchers with action goals are focused on a particular program, product, or method, usually in an applied setting, for the purpose of describing it, improving it, or estimating its effectiveness and worth. While action researchers may contribute to knowledge production, they are not fundamentally concerned with constructing and testing theory, models, or principles to describe, explain, or predict certain phenomena, nor to deriving prescriptive heuristics that could guide the design initiatives of others.

In reviewing any research genre, including educational design research, "The serious question to be considered is not, 'is this research of one type or another' but 'what assumptions are being made, and how strong is the warrant for the claims being made?'" (Schoenfeld, 2007, p. 103). High-quality educational design research yields usable knowledge and interventions, both of which are built upon sound reasoning and robust evidence. When conducted well, one can experience the powerful gratification that comes with solving real problems and seeing new insights prove useful to others. But the appeal of design research is not limited to what it can produce; the educational design research process can be extremely invigorating and inspirational. In the next chapter, the dual products of design research are further discussed. Thereafter, four different examples are given of how the process yielded both theoretical and practical contributions.

Chapter 2

Contributions to theory and practice

Concepts and examples

Educational design research produces two main contributions: one to fundamental understanding (theory), and the other to applied use (an intervention that solves a problem in practice). This chapter aims to clarify the outputs of educational design research. The first section of this chapter addresses the nature of the theoretical contributions of educational design research. These can be used to describe, explain, predict, or prescribe. Such fundamental understanding can range from being locally to more broadly applicable. The second section of this chapter discusses its contributions to practice. Attention is especially given to the main practical contribution of educational design research: the interventions developed. Thereafter, both the theoretical and practical contributions of four design studies are described, along with the processes that led to them.

Theoretical contributions of educational design research

What is theory?

Theories are explanations of real world phenomena substantiated by scientific evidence. They provide models or schemes for understanding the nature and causes of certain phenomena. Theories describe or explain things that happen, and can be used to predict or steer future occurrences. Some theories, e.g. grand theories like the Big Bang theory, cannot be tested directly, although they may withstand the test of time. Other theories are subject to empirical scrutiny, to be verified, falsified, or refined. Theories are powerful and important mental tools because they help us make sense of the world, and can be used to inform our manipulations of it.

Developing theoretical understanding

Theories are not developed from single studies. Rather, they are built over time upon hypotheses, conjectures, evidence, and other theories. Educational design research investigations may, ultimately, lead to theories. In the interim, however, they contribute the building blocks of theory, by yielding various forms of theoretical understanding: conjectures (unproven propositions that are thought to be true), evidence (verification of an assertion), or theoretical principles (from nascent to mature) about how the world works and what is likely to happen when we tinker with it in certain ways.

Theoretical understanding is developed through reflection (discussed more in Chapter 6) and especially through reasoning. Reasoning is a rational thought process by which existing ideas give rise to new ones. Because reasoning is central to the development of theoretical understanding, three forms of reasoning are briefly described here: deduction, induction, and abduction. Deduction is the process of deriving a conclusion that logically and necessarily follows from a set of premises. For example, a deductive argument could be: learners stay engaged when given personalized feedback; that learner is being given personalized feedback; therefore, that learner will stay engaged. This argument is valid because the conclusion follows necessarily from the premise, but it may not be sound, because the premise "The learners stay engaged when given personalized feedback" may not be true. Induction is the process of deriving a reliable generalization from multiple observations. An inductive argument could be: each of these learners stayed engaged; each of them was given personalized feedback; therefore, personalized feedback contributes to engagement. An inductive argument suggests some degree of truth, but does not ensure it. Another kind of reasoning generates hypotheses about relationships between observable phenomena: abduction. An abductive argument could be: this learner was given personalized feedback; this learner stayed engaged; therefore, a relationship may exist between feedback and engagement. Through different forms of reasoning, more or less supported by existing theories, conjectures, and evidence, new theoretical understanding is developed.

Theories categorized by purpose

As mentioned in Chapter 1, the theory developed through research can serve various purposes: to describe, explain, predict, or even prescribe how to change or affect certain phenomena. Theoretical contributions serving each of these purposes can be developed through a range of approaches, including educational design research. In educational design research, it is common and possibly even necessary for multiple types of theoretical understanding to be sought within the lifespan of one, long-term project – sometimes concurrently, sometimes sequentially. Often, the educational design research conducted through interventions is more fundamental, yielding understanding that can be used to describe and explain certain phenomena; whereas educational design research conducted on interventions is frequently more applied, yielding understanding that can be used to predict and prescribe how to manipulate certain phenomena. The discussion below shows how each purpose of theory builds on the previous one. To illustrate the connection between research in general and educational design research, each description contains multiple examples: the work of a famous scientist; that of educational theorists and researchers; and a design research example.

Descriptive

Theories can describe real world phenomena. Derived from empirical observation, the particular contribution of theories that portray phenomena often lies in the unconventional lens used to study the world. The theoretical understanding produced through Jane Goodall's research was largely descriptive. She studied how chimpanzees live and socialize, and uniquely described parallel traits that humans and chimps share in terms of intelligence, group behavior, and emotion. Many educational theories are descriptive. For example, Howard Gardner's theory of multiple intelligences primarily describes eight, relatively autonomous intelligences: language, music, emotional, logical–mathematical, spatial, kinesthetic, creative, and interpersonal. DeVaney's (1998) analysis of the field of educational technology in relation to race, gender, and power is an important example of descriptive postmodern research. Comparative research also describes educational realities, but focuses on differences and similarities among phenomena, such as pupil achievement, math curricula, or teacher education structures in different contexts. The Trends in International Mathematics and Science Study (TIMSS) is one of the world's largest comparative studies in educational achievement. Drent, Meelissen, and van der Kleij (2010) conducted an extensive literature review which concluded that TIMSS results were contributing to theories of educational effectiveness, albeit modestly. Joseph and Reigeluth (2005) used educational design research (though they call it formative research) to develop theoretical understanding that describes a school district's readiness for change.

Explanatory

Some theories are used not only to describe reality, but to also offer credible explanations as to why or how certain phenomena exist. These theories attend to relationships between concepts. Darwin's theory of evolution through natural selection is explanatory. Many learning theories are also intended to be explanatory: they describe how learning takes place and provide reasons for why learning does or does not occur. For example, constructivist theory argues that, because each individual is unique, humans create their own knowledge and meaning from interaction between their experiences and ideas. Enright (2011) employed case study methods to describe and explain the language and literacy experiences of bilingual and monolingual high school seniors. Based on this theoretical understanding, Enright argued the need for reframing how the concept of mainstreaming is used in schools. Through design research, Lehrer and colleagues (cf. Lehrer, 2009; Lehrer & Schauble, 2004) contributed to explaining domain-specific learning processes, such as how modeling, a form of knowing critical to scientific progress, can also be used in education to help students learn.

Predictive

Theoretical understanding can also include using descriptions of phenomena, and explanations of how and why things work to predict effects. Using theories for predictive purposes attends to what will happen under certain circumstances. Edward Jenner used theory to predict the work of vaccines. Observing that patients exposed to a milder disease, cowpox, did not contract the deadly smallpox disease, Jenner theorized that mild exposure to a disease could protect humans from contracting it. In education, theoretical understanding can be used to help make predictions in a host of areas, such as: effective characteristics of multimedia learning (e.g. Mayer, 2009); behavior problems among elementary school students based on the quality of teacher–child relationships (e.g. O'Connor, Dearing, & Collins, 2011); and factors that influence student retention in higher education (e.g. Tinto, 2010). Palincsar, Magnusson, Collins, and Cutter (2001) conducted a two-year design study, which yielded insights that help predict the learning requirements of special needs learners engaged in guided inquiry science instruction.

Prescriptive/normative

Theories can also be used for prescriptive, or normative, purposes. In these cases, understandings of certain phenomena, how they work, and cause–effect relationships are used to recommend certain activities that will yield certain effects. The purpose of this kind of theoretical understanding is to identify and articulate promising plans or decisions to make.

Long after they died in the 1800s, the work of Oliver Holmes and Ignaz Semmelweiss continues to influence hospital care around the world. They were the first to hypothesize and test the relationship between dirty hands and infection. This theoretical understanding has led to the hand washing and sterilization protocols that have become standard medical practice. Many pedagogical theories serve prescriptive purposes. For example, Maria Montessori identified the concept of sensitive periods in children. She theorized that children should learn through exploration in an environment that is socially engineered by the teacher, based on pupil learning needs during their sensitive periods, and prescribed methods for doing so. In educational design research, studies conducted on specific types of interventions yield theoretical understanding of a prescriptive nature. An example of prescriptive understanding produced by educational design research can be found in the work of Kim and Hannafin (2008), who developed principles for the grounded design of web-enhanced case-based activity. Generated by empirical tuning and study of existing literature, their recommendations help instructional designers recognize what works (or not), how, why, under which conditions, and with whom.

Although the terms "intervention theory" (Plomp, 2009) and "design theory" (Reigeluth & Frick, 1999) have been introduced, "design principles" is probably the most prevalent term used to characterize the kind of prescriptive theoretical understanding developed through educational design research (cf. Kali, 2008; Kim & Hannafin, 2008; Mishra, & Koehler, 2006; Quintana, Reiser, Davis, Krajcik, Fretz, Duncan, et al., 2004; van den Akker, 1999). This kind of theory integrates descriptive, explanatory and predictive understanding to guide the design of interventions.

Some experts suggest that the integrated theoretical understanding encompassed in design principles can be conveyed through heuristic statements. For example, van den Akker (1999, 2010) recommends the following formula for conceptualizing design principles:

> If you want to design intervention X [for purpose/function Y in context Z]; then you are best advised to give that intervention the characteristics C1, C2, ..., Cm [substantive emphasis]; and do that via procedures P1, P2, ..., Pn [procedural emphasis]; because of theoretical arguments T1, T2, ..., Tp; and empirical arguments E1, E2, ... Eq.

Though this formula has been used to actually present design principles (e.g. Stoof, Martens, & van Merriënboer, 2007), van den Akker's work has been used more often to describe the nature of design principles or to focus rich, detailed descriptions of the outcomes of design research (e.g. Herrington, Herrington, & Mantei, 2009). There are, of course, other ways to portray theoretical understanding of a prescriptive nature (e.g. Bers, 2001).

Theories categorized by level

Theories that are used to describe, explain, predict, or even prescribe how to engender certain phenomena can be closer to or more removed from specific manifestations of those phenomena. The discussion below presents three levels of educational theories, each of which can be produced by educational design research: local theory; middle-range theory; high-level theory. Examples of how educational design research can yield theoretical understanding that is used to describe, explain, or predict are given for each level. Based on the framework originally described in Linn, Davis and Bell (2004) and elaborated by Kali (2006) together with Linn (Kali & Linn, 2008), design principles (serving predictive purposes) are also characterized for each level. The distinctions between these levels are not precise; rather, we view them as three locations on a continuum.

Local theory

Because educational design research is conducted in practice, together with various actors connected to the problem at hand, much of this work contributes theoretical understanding that is closely tied to the specifics of the investigation, yielding local theory. In educational design research, local theory is produced when limited manifestations of a certain phenomenon are studied (e.g. several iterations of one basic intervention are studied in just a few classrooms). Because this kind of work results in understanding of learning within specific ecological contexts (and not across a wide range of settings), these kinds of theories are, in the words of Cobb, Confrey, diSessa, Lehrer, and Schauble (2003, p. 9) "relatively humble." Local theories can be used to describe, explain, or predict. For example, Bannan-Ritland (2003) described how parent literacy facilitators developed awareness and skill in implementing reading activities. Local theories can also be prescriptive. "Encourage students to come to consensus on shared criteria for decisions and products," is a "specific design principle" (Linn, Davis & Bell, 2004) that was generated from one design research project (Clark, 2004) but also offers starting points for similar design studies. Specific design principles are usually derived from abstraction of empirical findings from a limited range of contexts and contain the rationale behind the design of a specific feature of an intervention.

Middle-range theory

Especially as interventions begin to mature, educational design research may strive to develop middle-range theory. Sociologist Merton (1957) introduced the concept of middle-range theory in his argument for the need to link the low-level interpretations of empirical findings produced by individual studies with high-level, unifying theories. Such theories are "...intermediate to the minor working hypotheses evolved in abundance during the day-by-day routine of research, and the all-inclusive speculations comprising a master conceptual scheme" (Merton, 1957, p. 5). In educational design research, middle-range theories are developed when the enactment and effects of multiple manifestations of an intervention are studied in several settings (e.g. several iterations of one basic intervention are studied across a range of classrooms). Middle range theories can be used to describe, explain or predict phenomena. For example, Oh (2011) explains how and why different time zones limited effective communications among students engaged in online group work. Synthesized from several empirical studies and therefore cutting across contexts, "pragmatic principles" (Linn, Davis & Bell, 2004) constitute middle-range theories that serve prescriptive purposes. These are validated, refuted or refined with subsequent investigations. For example, "build on student ideas" is a pragmatic principle derived from the conjectures and empirical findings from several different design studies.

High-level theory

High-level theory synthesizes middle-range theories and may be, in part, derived from a wide range of manifestations of a certain intervention type across many different settings. High-level theories are based on paradigms, sets of assumptions, and epistemologies. This kind of theory development is less common in general; it is also less common when it comes to educational design research. Briefly described in Chapter 1, the theory of transformational play is an example of a high-level theory derived from educational design research (Barab, Gresalfi, & Ingram-Goble, 2010). High-level theories can be used to describe, explain or predict certain phenomena. For example, theoretical understanding based on the work of Lewis, Perry, and Murata (2006) predicts that science lessons will be more effective if teachers introduce them with a real world problem relevant to the lives of the learners. High-level theory can be also be prescriptive. For instance, the meta-principle "help students learn from others" (Linn, Davis & Bell, 2004) is derived from a socio-cultural theoretical stance on learning and connects several pragmatic principles (which are forms of middle-range theories).

Theoretical spaces of (educational design) research

As discussed previously, individual studies do not yield rich, detailed theory. Rather, individual studies contribute to theoretical understanding by providing scientific insights which constitute the building blocks of theory. In this book, we use the term "theoretical understanding" to refer to the broad range of scientific insights that, on varying levels, contribute to describing or explaining phenomena, or are used to predict or prescribe the achievement of certain effects.

Table 2.1 demonstrates how educational design research can contribute to various kinds of theoretical understanding. The examples in the table do not present specific theories. Rather, they identify several important themes in the theoretical understanding that has emerged from one line of inquiry, and link them to the purposes and levels of theoretical understanding described above. The examples draw on over a decade of McKenney, Voogt and colleagues' experience studying teachers designing and implementing technology-rich curricula for early literacy (Boschman, McKenney & Voogt, 2011; Cviko, McKenney & Voogt, 2011; McKenney & Voogt, 2009, 2010, in press). This multi-year design study addressed the question, "How can a technology-supported learning environment contribute to helping four and five year old children understand the nature and functions of written language?" Some insights portray basic observations, often simultaneous ones (describe); while others offer data-driven reasons for why certain – sometimes simultaneous – observations are made (explain). Building on these, and refined by empirical testing, expectations are described (predict) and recommendations are given (prescribe).

The theoretical contributions of educational design research used for descriptive and explanatory purposes are often, but not exclusively, produced by exploring and analyzing the existing problem, needs, and/or context. The theoretical contributions which are used for predictive and prescriptive/normative purposes are often, but not exclusively, produced by iterative cycles of design, empirical testing, and refinement of interventions that address the problem. Not all educational design research endeavors strive to make contributions for all purposes, at all levels. However, in the wake of increasing emphasis on evidence-based practice, it has been argued that descriptive theories alone are insufficient to solve complex problems (Green, 2000). The explanatory and predictive power of theory is especially needed to design interventions that solve real problems; and theories that serve normative/prescriptive purposes are required to transplant and refine interventions.

Table 2.1 Theoretical spaces of (educational design) research: an example

Purpose	Level		
	Local theory	**Middle-range theory**	**High-level theory**
	e.g. applicable to a few teachers, using multiple iterations of the same information and communications technologies (ICT)-rich curriculum	*e.g. builds on local theories, applies to multiple schools using varied but similar ICT-rich curricula*	*e.g. builds on middle-range theories, applies to many contexts using the same class of curricula*
Describe e.g. how teachers implement ICT-rich curricula	Teachers integrate on-computer activities with off-computer activities to varying degrees	Higher degrees of integration are found in schools where teachers co-design the activities	Curricular ownership is positively related to the level of technology integration
Explain e.g. why teachers behave as they do in implementing ICT-rich curricula	Teachers integrate on-computer activities with off-computer activities to varying degrees not only due to differences in knowledge, skills and attitudes about early literacy, but also because of their perceived role as nurturers first, and educators second	Teachers value and prioritize certain aspects of early literacy (e.g. vocabulary and comprehension; technical (pre-) reading and writing; communicative functions of language) in different ways, often because of different pre-service education and/or school cultures	Kindergarten teachers tend to limit new initiatives in the classroom (even if they support them) until a safe, trusting, routine and predictable classroom climate has been firmly established
Predict e.g. which level of involvement in ICT-rich curriculum design is needed to sufficiently improve enactment and thus pupil learning	Teachers designing curriculum materials will be more likely to implement them, but may not be up to the task (due to lack of time, expertise, interest)	Personal interest (not time, remuneration, expertise, or authority) most powerfully determines which teachers will prefer higher levels of design involvement	If well-structured, even modest degrees of design involvement will foster curricular ownership, which facilitates implementation
Prescribe e.g. how to facilitate collaborative design of ICT-rich curriculum for optimum integration and thus learning	Scaffold teacher planning of the design process to help participants focus more creative effort on the design task, without stifling ownership of the product	Provide teachers in different contexts need-based variation in expertise and support; together with teachers, identify and define areas of freedom	Provide tailored support to build teacher understanding and endorsement of core ideas; encourage freedom and creativity to develop different manifestations of those core ideas

Theoretical understanding: described in literature, embodied in interventions

Educational design research *uses* theory, along with empirical findings, craft wisdom, inspiration, and experience as *inputs* to create interventions that solve real problems. In this book, we refer to the theoretical understanding that goes *into* design as design propositions. Through the research embedded in the intervention development process, educational design research *produces* theoretical understanding as an *output*. Most theoretical understanding is described in words, some in visual models. Because it is undertaken to develop solutions to problems, ostensibly because satisfactory solutions do not exist, design research often explores novel theoretical spaces. Several design researchers have also argued that the designed interventions themselves are important vehicles for sharing theoretical understanding. In Chapter 1, we briefly introduced Barab's theory of transformation play as an outcome of education design research. This is a complex theory that is not easily communicated in words alone. Barab, Dodge and Gee (2009) suggest the use of worked examples to portray instantiations of the theory of transformational play. They, and others, share examples openly at: http://workedexamples.org/. In the next section, the practical contributions of design research, including but not limited to the interventions created, are discussed.

Practical contributions of educational design research

What are practical contributions?

The primary practical contribution of educational design research is the intervention developed to solve a real problem in practice. These vary tremendously in scale, scope, type of intervention and field to which they are related. Interventions are primarily useful for the solution that they offer to a specific problem, but they can also be of value by setting a powerful or inspiring example. Another practical contribution of educational design research is the development of expertise among project participants (e.g. researchers, teachers, administrators, other educational professionals). Indeed, most of the design research endeavors we have encountered do yield powerful insights for participants, fed by data and enhanced by the mutual exchange among educational researchers and practitioners. We feel that this role has been under-represented in most of the literature on design research to date.

Developing practical contributions

Developing the practical contributions of educational design research takes time, measured more in months and years than in days and weeks. Problems to be addressed are identified and explored through a process that gathers insights from both literature and the field. Potential solutions are considered and, ultimately, a design pathway is established. As development commences, empirical testing is conducted to fine-tune understanding of the problem, elements of the design, and/or the development process. The intervention is not realized in one fell swoop. Rather, it evolves through successive approximations of the desired solution. During different stages of an educational design research project, different practical contributions can be made. For example, during problem identification and exploration, researchers may become more sensitive to classroom realities (e.g. teacher authority to enact change is more limited than anticipated); through the testing of interventions, practitioners may become aware of certain learner concerns formerly unbeknownst to them (e.g. children reveal pertinent aspects of their home lives); and of course, the use of more mature interventions should help solve the specific problems identified.

Practical contributions characterized by intervention type

Educational design research interventions can be characterized by different types, including educational products, processes, programs, or policies. Educational products include resources that support learning and instruction, such as teacher guides, learning software, manipulatives or books. Educational processes are strategies, tactics, or sequences that support teaching and learning; these can include instructional approaches, learning support strategies, behavior management repertoires, or communication exercises. Programs often combine products and processes to meet an educational goal, in the form of, for example, a seminar series, learning unit, course, or professional development program. Policies indicate a commitment of intent; may be more or less strict (some are more guidelines, others are more rules); and guide subjective and/or objective decision making. Examples include state curriculum standards, performance review structures, school evaluation procedures and learner assessment protocols. While interventions may focus on one specific type, few are developed in isolation. For example, while the primary focus of an intervention may be to develop a product, such as a learning environment for science education, that product will most likely aim to: engender certain processes, be embedded in a certain kind of program, and align with certain policies. Furthermore, developing the product may prompt adjustments to any of these (processes, programs, or policies).

Practical contributions characterized by field

Van den Akker (1999) discussed four fields in which educational design research has been particularly active in the last two decades: curriculum; media and technology; learning and instruction; and teacher development. A few examples, and not a comprehensive portrayal, are given for each here. Practical contributions to the field of curriculum have included the development of courseware, design standards for corporate training, and district-wide curriculum reform. Media and technology design research teams have made practical contributions by creating technology-rich learning resources, technology-supported professional networks, and digital platforms to support teaching. In the field of learning and instruction, educational design research has made practical contributions in the form of specific learning strategies, instructional sequences, and learning materials. Finally, educational design research has made contributions to both the pre-service and the in-service learning of teachers through professional development programs, induction strategies, and domain-specific learning resources. The examples given above demonstrate that the field distinctions are not mutually exclusive. To illustrate, a technology-supported professional network for teachers could be associated with both teacher development and with media and technology. Understanding that educational design research has been active in these fields can be useful when it comes to identifying, learning from, and building on the work of others. In contrast to the broad overview presented here, the following section includes descriptions of the interventions developed through four very different design research projects.

Educational design research examples

The remainder of this chapter contains four examples of educational design research, highlighting their contributions to theory and practice, as well as the process that led to those contributions. Given that they have to be condensed for a book of this nature, what follows are merely brief impressions of each project. The projects were selected with the aim of highlighting some of the variety in: design research approaches, focus of inquiry, and pathways to developing both theoretical understanding and solutions to problems in practice. Each of the example descriptions contains recommended resources for additional reading. To facilitate comparison, each one is presented using the same structure: (1) problem, context, and approach; (2) analysis, design, and evaluation processes; and (3) practical and scientific outputs. The four interventions concern: teacher strategies for the oral language development of young children; professional development of para-teachers across subject areas; a rich technology resource for middle school mathematics; and curriculum materials for integrated teaching of science and literacy, respectively.

The first and second examples demonstrate two differing ways in which doctoral students have engaged in design research. The first project was conducted through a North American university offering a course-driven PhD program, which allots approximately 3 years for courses and one year for a dissertation project. The second was conducted through a European university, which structures its PhD program around a single, four-year study and offers about two courses per year alongside the research. The third and fourth examples were larger projects involving teams of designers and researchers. Both of these involved close collaboration of multiple types of experts working on multidisciplinary research and development teams, and each had strong university connections. The third example was initiated primarily by researchers and teacher educators. In contrast, the fourth one was promulgated by the desire of curriculum developers to increase the robustness of their design work. Taken together, these examples illustrate both commonalities across design research and some of the rich variation in research approach, topics addressed, and pathways to developing theoretical understanding and interventions.

Example 1: strategies for developing preschooler oral language skills

Problem, context, and approach

The development of oral language skills in the first 5 years of life lays an essential foundation to subsequent development of language skills in general and reading achievement in particular (including comprehension, which is needed across the curriculum). Preschool teachers play an important role in the oral language development of young children, offering them a wide range of opportunities to be exposed to and engage with language in many forms; this is especially important when children's home environments provide little stimulation for language development. For example, Bryant, Burchinal, Lau, and Sparling (1994) studied 32 Head Start classrooms with children from a range of poor quality to more stimulating home environments, and found that – regardless of the home environment quality – children in higher quality Head Start classrooms performed better on measures of achievement and pre-academic skills. Yet research has shown that current teacher–child language interactions are frequently below minimal standards. In the study mentioned above, only 3 out of 32 classrooms received scores on the Early Childhood Environment Rating Scale (Harms, Clifford, & Cryer, 1998 in Bradley, 2004) that would classify them as "developmentally appropriate," though three others appeared close; and scores on language interactions were particularly poor.

Based on literature review, Bradley (2004) described several interrelated factors that account for the low quantity and quality of teacher–child interactions, including high degrees of (a) talk relating to routine and/or organizational matters (e.g. "Jessey, would you like to be in charge of passing out the napkins today?"); (b) talk involving low-level cognitive skills (e.g. "We just looked at lots of blue things. Are you wearing anything blue right now?"); and (c) that are often group-directed instructions (e.g. "Okay class, it is time to put our coats on and go outside"). While these causes are understood, and many initiatives have been launched to introduce new strategies into early childhood classrooms to promote oral development, limited work has been done on finding ways to increase the quantity and quality of existing language interactions.

Bradley's (2004) dissertation study was carried out during a 23-week period in one rural preschool classroom, involving one teacher and one para-professional. The teacher and whole class participated, which included 20 four- and five-year-old children (10 boys and 10 girls). The class was ethnically diverse; and 19 out of 20 children received a free or reduced lunch, indicating that their households are classified as being of low socioeconomic status. The teacher and para-professional used a well-known curriculum and appreciated its core principles, but indicated before the start of the project that they considered attending to individual pupil needs more important that adhering strictly to the curriculum. This meant that they felt willing to make their own instructional decisions and would be open to exploring other strategies.

The pedagogical goal and research question guiding this study was: *How can the quantity and quality of teacher–child language interactions be increased during several common preschool activities to enhance children's oral language skills?* The study entailed three main phases: baseline, intervention, and retrospective analysis. First, a seven-week baseline phase was conducted to gain a thorough understanding of the context. Data were collected through interviews, informal discussions, observations, field notes, and video recordings. At the end of the baseline phase, the researcher discussed what she had learned from the baseline and shared her ideas (informed by theory and literature review) about an intervention with the two educators. Across the next 16 weeks, the practitioners implemented the intervention strategies (described below). During this phase, as in the baseline phase, the researcher was in the classroom two–three days per week. Throughout the intervention phase, data were collected through observations, field notes, and weekly discussions; in addition, semi-structured interviews were held at the conclusion. The third phase involved retrospective analysis. During this phase, all data sources were reviewed and lenses for data analysis were refined. Thereafter, they were used to examine the findings and draw conclusions.

Analysis, design, and evaluation processes

This study used both literature and experience to identify existing opportunities in preschool classrooms during which the quantity and quality of language interaction could be enhanced. Based on the literature review, book sharing, semi-structured group activities, and mealtimes were identified as common events occurring in preschool classrooms in which children are engaged in talk, which could be potential focal points of the intervention. Findings from the baseline study confirmed that these moments did offer some possibilities, but also revealed some challenges. For example, teachers were quite concerned about children's nutrition, and this had led to a system whereby children were required to remain quiet for 10-minute periods during mealtimes, as the teachers believed this would help them concentrate more on eating. While there were mealtime moments for discourse, these were limited. The quality of teacher–child language interaction was defined based on literature and research in this area. Based on this definition, a framework for assessing teacher–child oral language interaction quality was created and used during the baseline phase to measure the existing quality of interactions during book sharing (only done in large groups at the start of the study), small-group activities, and mealtimes.

The quality of interaction was defined by the presence of two types of teacher behaviors: semantically contingent responses and decontextualized demands. Semantically contingent responses engage children in extended conversations (defined in this study as six or more sequential exchanges) by eliciting clarification or sharing new information. For example, responding to a child showing new shoes with "Can you tell me about your shoes?" is semantically contingent and invites dialogue; whereas "Oh how nice!" invites little more than a smile. Decontextualized demands invite children to make connections to concepts or ideas abstracted from the immediate context and often require more complex linguistic abilities. For example, responding to a dispute among children by saying, "What could have been done differently?" is a decontextualized demand; whereas "What did you do?" requires recall, not abstraction. (See Snow [1983] for detailed discussion on both types of interactions.) The baseline phase thus measured the presence of these behaviors during book sharing, small-group activities, and mealtimes.

Before the start of the intervention phase, the researcher discussed development of children's oral language with the two educators emphasizing (a) its importance; (b) salient insights from research; (c) potential benefits; (d) the pedagogical goal of the intervention; and (e) strategies that might enhance their current practice, specifically, using more semantically contingent responses and decontextualized demands. In a supportive role (but not through direct instruction), the researcher was also active in the classroom. In meetings outside the classroom, she acted as an instructional coach. She offered ideas about how teachers could enrich their language instruction through increased use of semantically contingent responses and decontextualized talk, especially during book sharing (which, she pointed out, could also be done in small groups), semi-structured group activities, and mealtimes. Increased use of these two kinds of talk was the goal of the intervention.

Because the researcher was the vehicle through which these processes were introduced to the teachers, her presence and advice on how to meet those goals was, essentially, the intervention in this study. While she did use other resources and processes (e.g. reflective interviews, sometimes stimulated by review of a classroom video), these were to support the coaching task. It was the researcher's involvement as an instructional coach that was introduced into the classroom with the goal of improving practice. Bradley used prolonged engagement, persistent observation, and triangulation (cf. Lincoln & Guba, 1985) as well as mixed methods to mitigate the considerable threats of bias in this study. She also described her personal stance and how her own background revealed certain subjectivities that influenced this investigation. She wrote (Bradley & Reinking, 2011a, p. 372):

> I respect teachers' professionalism, and their values and beliefs, in making pedagogical decisions, and I understand and accept the challenges they face in meeting the needs of children and their families. Thus, although invested in the strategies and activities that defined the intervention, I did not take the stance of an unrelenting advocate for them, nor did I romanticize their potential for achieving the pedagogical goal.

During the intervention, data were collected to explore if, indeed, the instances of semantically contingent responses and decontextualized talk increased, especially during book sharing, semi-structured group activities, and mealtimes. During the baseline phase only whole-group book sharing took place, whereas the practitioner and para-educator decided about midway through the intervention phase to try out small-group book sharing as well. For both the teacher and the para-educator, the quantity of interactions with children increased notably between the baseline phase and the intervention phase (mostly during book sharing). In terms of quality, the teacher's use of decontextualized demands was already rather high to start with, but still increased during the intervention phase. Semantically contingent responses increased as well, but so did the number of teacher-led interactions, especially during small-group activities. The para-educator showed some increases, but those that were present were considerably less dramatic. Teacher appreciation of the existing (play-based) curriculum and classroom management styles set limits on the interaction possibilities especially during small-group activities. It was clear that both educators grew more accepting of encouraging conversations with children during mealtimes than was the case during the baseline, but nutrition concerns and group management issues severely limited opportunities in this regard.

Practical and scientific outputs

Several changes took place in the classroom that made clear contributions to practice. First, the teachers were sensitized to the importance of language development and they indicated that they both increased their awareness of children's vocabulary knowledge and other linguistic aspects, particularly during informal conversations. Second, the teachers indicated that they believed they had gotten to know the children better because of increased conversations with them. Third, the children were exposed to more frequent conversations than before, and while not all conversations may have been considered ideal, they were often of a higher quality than had been the case previously. Finally, the intervention also led to unanticipated effects. While it did not come as a complete surprise that increased conversations would yield better understanding of children's lives, no one had anticipated the degree of distressing information that the teachers would acquire about the home environments of the children. While responsive and empathetic, the teachers were also somewhat unnerved by information about family violence and abuse to which the children had been exposed. The increase in conversations gave more opportunities for sharing home stories; perhaps it also increased the children's security, so they were more inclined to share home stories.

The results of this study revealed factors that enhanced, inhibited, and sometimes prevented the integration of enriching language interactions during the school day. The findings suggest that drawing teacher attention to language interactions through joint review of video clips can contribute to increased understanding about how and when to use decontextualized demands; this, in turn, can increase the frequency of these kinds of interactions. The study supports previous research by emphasizing the determining role of curriculum and beliefs in teacher choices, as well as the role of skills (e.g. orchestration of multiple small groups where only one or two are directly supervised). These findings, together with the extended contextualized look at specific moments in the regular preschool routine that would be ripe for increasing the quantity and quality of interactions, give implications for professional development (e.g. working together with teachers to merge new instructional strategies into a curricular framework; or reflecting jointly on own behavior through video analysis).

This study also demonstrated some of the benefits of design research. For example, the focus on the pedagogical goal yielded an approach featuring open investigation of moments to engage children in extended conversations across the preschool day (book sharing, semi-structured activities, and mealtimes). While it is true that other forms of inquiry, not just design research, can allow for this, the interventionist nature of this study (and different from most other research genres) is what facilitated a gradual process of integration and change.

Additional information about this study

- Dissertation describing the entire study: Bradley, B. (2004). *A formative experiment to enhance verbal interactions in a preschool classroom*. Doctoral dissertation. University of Georgia.
- Article focusing on the content and findings of the study: Bradley, B., & Reinking, D. (2011a). A formative experiment to enhance teacher–child language interactions in a preschool classroom. *Journal of Early Childhood Literacy, 11*(3), 362–401.
- Article focusing on the design research process using this study as a case example: Bradley, B. & Reinking, D. (2011b). Enhancing research and practice in early childhood through formative and design experiments. *Early Childhood Development and Care, 181*(3), 305–319.

Example 2: para-teacher professional development in Indian slums

Problem, context, and approach

In developing countries like India as well as in some developed nations, para-teachers generally lack any formal qualification related to teaching and learning, but nonetheless supplement regular classroom teaching. Para-teachers usually come from the deprived communities in which they work, and are often better able to establish rapport with the local community and with the children than outsiders. While para-teachers have become recognized as valuable assets to the educational workforce in developing countries, and especially in India, very few empirical studies have been conducted on feasible and effective ways to provide professional development opportunities to these important participants in the (Indian) educational system. Through an iterative process of analysis, design, evaluation, and revision, educational design research was conducted by Raval (2010) to gain insight into desirable characteristics of a professional development program for Indian para-teachers.

This study was situated in an organization called Maitri, a non-governmental organization (NGO) in India that provides educational support to children in under-served urban communities, most of which are best characterized as slums. While Maitri is active throughout India, this study took place in the western state of Gujarat, where Maitri implements Urban Learning Centers (ULCs) provide remedial education for public school children. Originally, Maitri implemented free remedial services for students who lagged behind in basic competencies of reading, writing, and arithmetic. Later it modified its strategy and para-teachers were required to teach additional subjects including Gujarati (first language), English, math, science, history, geography, and civics, up to age 14 (which is up to about grade 7) in a learner-centered way, as well as charge fees for their services. It was Maitri's wish to support para-teachers, working independently in their own classrooms to deliver the remedial programs, that provided the impetus for this study.

The main question shaping evolution of professional development activities for para-teachers was framed as: *What kind of professional support can help para-teachers adopt and develop teaching strategies with a learner-centered orientation?* This question was answered through a series of sub-studies which took place across a four-year period. A literature review was conducted to help frame the first phase of the study, which featured analysis of problems currently encountered by Maitri's para-teachers, and their managers. In addition, a strengths, weaknesses, opportunities and threats (SWOT) analysis was carried out to establish options and boundaries for a sustainable professional development program. Based on the findings from the needs and context analysis, a second, more focused literature review was conducted to inform the design of a professional development program that would speak to participant needs and also fit in the organization. This resulted in a research-based framework for design that was tailored to the context in question.

The para-teacher professional development program was developed and implemented in three iterations. First, the main researcher facilitated a pilot program, which took place under circumstances that were slightly more favorable than usual. Based on the pilot experiences, the program was revised and adopted by the organization. During the second iteration, the main researcher was available as a resource, and co-facilitated the professional development sessions, together with location managers. After the second cycle of implementation and analyzing the results, one last round of revisions was made to the program, and it was implemented again. During the third cycle, the researcher no longer facilitated during the program – the managers were fully in charge. A final study was conducted 2 years later (no additional support was given in the interim) to study any long-term impact of the program. Finally, the research team reflected systematically between but also across all cycles of the design study to distill design heuristics for shaping the professional development of para-teachers in similar settings.

Analysis, design, and evaluation processes

The theoretical framework for the needs and context analysis study was derived from literature and centered around four main contextual factors that were considered likely to influence para-teacher learning: the para-teacher, the instructional setting, the organizational setting, and policy. Data were collected to understand the initial status of each of these factors in Maitri, and the fostering or inhibiting influences of their current characteristics on classroom enactment and the para-teachers' own learning. Results revealed that there was a high level of motivation and commitment on the part of para-teachers towards their job that could play a crucial role in fostering professional development. At the time, it also revealed that the para-teachers had (by objective assessment as well as their own personal assessment) substantial gaps in their knowledge and skills related to teaching in general and learner-centered environments in particular. Moreover, factors related to the other three (non-individual) elements in the model also posed substantial challenges that could not be ignored in designing a solution (e.g. classroom situation extremely heterogeneous; severe lack of educational leadership in the organization; and policies that privileged time for fee-collection above lesson preparation). Guidelines for designing a professional development program were articulated based on the findings from the analysis phase. In addition, exploration was conducted into how similar solutions had been devised in similar settings, though the range of inspiring examples proved quite limited.

A conceptual model was developed to guide the design of the professional development program. The model served as a framework for design and was informed by the findings from the needs and context analysis, the practical wisdom of those involved, and especially by relevant literature. The conceptual model was inspired by critical attributes of professional development, including: a situated instructional focus which connects learning to actual problems of practice; ongoing and sustained rather than isolated one-shot events; a self-directed and collaborative focus. The conceptual model emphasizes the development of three core cyclical practices as a part of the daily routine of para-teachers: lesson planning, lesson enactment, and reflection on the lessons. In addition, each of the core activities is supported by workshops, micro-teaching, and coaching, respectively. The conceptual model shows that this all takes place within an organizational context that must first create the necessary pre-conditions (e.g. sufficient time to prepare for teaching tasks, or support of leaders and peers) for these activities to flourish.

Initially, the conceptual model may seem hardly new or innovative, because it incorporates well-known concepts of professional development. However, it adds to existing understanding of para-teacher professional development by emphasizing the importance of embedding learning with routine activities of lesson planning, enactment, and reflection. It pays close attention to the cultural and contextual realities of these practitioners and offers a professional development route that is viable amidst these challenges. The conceptual model emphasizes that professional support interventions must entail designing tools or processes required to develop this cyclical approach in the professional routine of the para-teachers. Finally, it provides a concrete structure that views teachers as active learners who individually and collectively try to address their classroom problems and reflect regularly on both their solutions and their own learning.

The conceptual model described above served as a design framework, to guide the development of the professional development program for Maitri's para-teachers. Three iterations of the professional development program were studied. First, the main researcher piloted the program (in the role of facilitator, also consulting with the program-leader), in which para-teachers were introduced to the core activities of planning, enactment, and reflection of daily lessons using tailor-made templates for lesson planning and reflection. Supportive strategies were also implemented. Research conducted alongside the pilot implementation concluded that para-teachers had acquired knowledge about and high proficiency in systematic lesson planning with learner-centered strategies. Classroom enactment changes towards well-structured teaching with a learner-centered orientation were also perceived by the para-teachers. Difficulties were experienced in planning for and implementing pupil management strategies. Particularly related to this last point, revisions were made to both the program and to the organizational structures (e.g. new rules for enrolling children in class to ensure more stable pupil populations), especially to enable the next study: a tryout under normal conditions. During the second iteration, the researcher and local managers co-facilitated the activities. The findings from this sub-study indicated that the professional development program led to successful adoption of systematic, learner-centered, lesson planning and enactment practices even during a regular term, as well as improved competencies such as collaboration during, and ownership of, core activities. The organizational adjustments that were made to enable the program proved to be important for the smooth and effective functioning of the core and supportive strategies. In particular the insights on how the organization learned from the experience were capitalized on in making the final (minor) adjustments to the program before it underwent a summative evaluation. During the third iteration, improvements in lesson planning and enactment led to the conclusion that para-teachers were able and willing to gain from lesson planning, enactment, and reflection on daily lessons, through the facilitation in the organizational units alone, without additional support from the researcher. The large effect sizes in pupil learning gains clearly indicated that learning took place, strongly suggesting that the professional development enhanced teaching proficiency.

Practical and scientific outputs

Two years later, an impact study was conducted and revealed that – without any external support – the program had been retained, along with Maitri's capacity to sustain the professional development of its para-teachers. While all teachers evidenced substantial aspects of learner-centeredness, it is clear that improvements can still be made in this area. This five-year study has helped to highlight how para-teachers can be afforded opportunities to gradually make transitions during their professional development, and how organizational learning within educational NGOs can be stimulated by this process. For example, earlier on in the study, support was especially focused on adopting healthy planning routines, transitioning from what they were accustomed to (limited, individualized, and drill-based planning) to more extensive plans based on learning needs and using more active learning strategies. Later, as the planning became more natural, the focus turned to expanding para-teacher pedagogical repertoires, improving subject matter knowledge, and sharing ownership of the intervention across the organization. This study also emphasizes the value of a contextual stance toward learner-centeredness, viewing certain strategies as effective ways of teaching even though they may not meet the criteria for a full-fledged, learner-centered approach. These strategies are considered meaningful since they move away from overly didactic practices, are achievable within the constraints of the classroom, and also prepare teachers for developing capacity towards more refined learner-centered teaching.

Two sets of design heuristics have been distilled to inform the professional development of un(der)-trained teachers with similar goals in poorly resourced contexts. One set of guidelines is substantive, describing salient characteristics of professional development that have emerged as desirable over the course of the study. The other set is procedural, indicating useful ways of implementing professional development programs like this one, or the procedures that contribute to the effectiveness of the program. The substantive design guidelines describe five main characteristics of professional development: guided by individual as well as contextual (organizational) requirements; guided by an instructional focus; guided by realistic choices; guided by attributes of teacher learning; and supported by a systemic approach. The procedural heuristics suggest that professional development should involve: promoting the plan–enact–reflect cycle; supporting the plan, enact, and reflect cycle; using templates to scaffold planning and reflection; emphasizing the role of teacher-heads in designing and implementing learning activities (for the para-teachers); and carefully implementing changes in the organizational conditions. For each of these themes, the heuristic set presents relevant theoretical and empirical evidence that lead to the specific design heuristics from this study. For example, one theme points to the role of individual and organizational requirements that influence the professional development agenda. The heuristic cites ideas from previous research (Kubitskey & Fishman, 2005; Loucks-Horseley, Hewson, Love, & Stiles, 1998) and relevant empirical data from this study (e.g. on learning requirements of para-educators; enactment gaps identified in practice; and organizational constraints). Both these validate the main substantive design guideline that plans about professional development must be informed by perceived learning needs of teachers, the actual status of their classroom practices, and the actual, not idealized, strengths and weaknesses of their work context. The descriptive, explanatory, predictive, and prescriptive theoretical understandings derived from this study have been shared through workshops and conferences, as well as the publications listed below.

Additional information about this study

- Dissertation describing the entire study, based largely on the articles below: Raval, H. (2010). *Supporting para-teachers in an Indian NGO: The plan–enact–reflect cycle*. Doctoral dissertation. Enschede: Twente University.
- Needs and context analysis: Raval, H., McKenney, S., & Pieters, J. (2011a). A needs and context analysis for teacher learning in an Indian

NGO. *International Journal of Training and Development.* Advance online publication. Doi: 10.1111/j.1468-2419.2011.00393.x
- Conceptual model and design framework: Raval, H., McKenney, S., & Pieters, J. (2010). A conceptual model for supporting para-teacher learning in an Indian NGO. *Studies in Continuing Education, 32*(3), 217–234.
- First design: Raval, H., McKenney, S., & Pieters, J. (under review). Supporting para-teachers by regularizing and strengthening planning, enactment and reflection of daily lessons.
- Second design: Raval, H., McKenney, S., & Pieters, J. (2011b). Institutionalizing planning, enactment and reflection of daily lessons through appropriate organizational restructuring. *The Asia-Pacific Educational Researcher, 20*(3), 438–455.
- Third design: Raval, H., McKenney, S., & Pieters, J. (under review). Summative evaluation of para-teacher support for remedial teaching in Indian slums.

Example 3: technology-rich learning in middle school mathematics

Problem, context, and approach

The genesis of the *Adventures of Jasper Woodbury* problem-solving series project can be traced back to a group of cognitive scientists, educational researchers, and teacher educators working at Vanderbilt University in Nashville, Tennessee, in the mid-1980s. What came to be known as the Cognition and Technology Group at Vanderbilt (CTGV) eventually expanded to include a cadre of 70 design researchers, including collaborating practitioners and graduate students. Members of the CTGV were concerned with a major problem in education, namely that students are often unable to solve real world problems as opposed to the ones found in their textbooks. This is related the phenomenon of inert knowledge, i.e. students can often show that they possess certain kinds of knowledge when they are given tests shortly after a unit of instruction or even asked to apply it to situations identical or very similar to the contexts in which it was taught, but these same students cannot recall or use the knowledge to solve never-seen-before problems that are somewhat removed from the original context even though the knowledge is directly relevant to the new problems. This problem resides at virtually every level of education and training. In fact, one major distinguishing factor between experts and novices is that the former have usable knowledge that they can readily access to solve novel problems whereas the latter possess poorly organized inert knowledge that they usually fail to apply when it is needed (Bransford, Brown, & Cocking, 2000).

Analysis, design, and evaluation processes

The CTGV conducted educational design research for more than 10 years to help students in fifth grade and above develop their problem-solving capabilities and reduce the problem of inert knowledge. Two of the major products of this large-scale design research project were a teaching model called anchored instruction and the *Jasper* video "anchors" (videos available in linear video, interactive videodisc, and eventually CD-ROM formats).

Anchored instruction represents an "attempt to overcome the inert-knowledge problem by creating meaningful problem-solving environments that permit sustained exploration by students and teachers" (Cognition and Technology Group at Vanderbilt, 1997a, p. 24). Proponents of anchored instructional theory (cf. Bransford, Sherwood, Hasselbring, Kinzer, & Williams, 1990) argued that students as young as 10 can learn by trying to solve problems that are much more complex than the simplistic word problems that are typically presented to them in classrooms or instructional materials such as textbooks. These complex problems encourage students to identify, represent, and solve problems in the same ways that experts such as scientists and engineers do in the real world beyond the classroom.

The video anchors used in the *Adventures of Jasper Woodbury* problem-solving series are based on interesting vignettes that present middle school-age students with challenging problems to solve. For example, in one episode called "Rescue at Boone's Meadow," a hiker finds a wounded eagle in a remote mountain site that can only be reached by personal aircraft. The students must figure out the best route to fly the lightweight plane to rescue the eagle while dealing with variables such as wind conditions and fuel capacity. Students work in small teams to solve these complex problems. There are multiple possible solutions, and conditions such as wind speed can be changed to alter the nature of the problems and extend learning into multiple disciplines.

Numerous small- and large-scale design studies were conducted to guide the development of the *Jasper* series. Extensive observational studies allowed the Vanderbilt team to derive design and implementation guidelines such as "…there are multiple ways to use *Jasper*," and "… teachers need the freedom to adapt it to their own teaching styles" (Cognition and Technology Group at Vanderbilt, 1997a, p. 62). Many small-scale, quasi-experimental intervention studies allowed the researchers to examine issues such as near and distant transfer from the problem sets in the *Adventures of Jasper Woodbury* problem-solving series to other types of complex problems. Eventually, the research team moved to large-scale field trials of the *Jasper* materials. For example, one year-long research project was conducted with the *Jasper* program in 16 schools in nine US states (Pellegrino, Hickey, Heath, Rewey, Vye, & the CTGV, 1991). Comparing students in *Jasper* classes with those in traditional math classes using quasi-experimental designs, the researchers investigated effects in terms of mathematical problem-solving and reasoning skills, specific mathematical knowledge and skills, standardized achievement test scores, and attitudes toward mathematics. The study used both quantitative and qualitative data collection methods. The results were generally favorable for the *Jasper* students. With respect to problem solving, the *Jasper* students were more skilled in identifying problems and breaking them down into smaller components that would lead to solutions. Regarding specific knowledge and skills, the *Jasper* students outperformed the control students in areas such as decimals, fractions, and calculations of area, perimeter, and volume. The *Jasper* students also were better in solving three different types of word problems. Results were less positive in the attitude and achievement areas. Although the *Jasper* students had more positive attitudes toward mathematics at the end of the school year, they expressed no greater desire to study math than the control students. On standardized achievement tests, *Jasper* students tended to perform better than the others, but these particular results were not statistically significant.

Practical and scientific outputs

Anchored instruction as an instructional theory is still being studied and refined (cf. Dickinson & Summers, 2010; Pellegrino & Brophy, 2008; Prado & Gravoso, 2011; Sanny & Teale, 2008). Many of the members of the CTGV have left Vanderbilt University for other universities, but they continue to pursue design research related to the design principles inherent in the anchored instructional model and/or relevant theories (cf. Bransford, Vye, Stevens, Kuhl, Schwartz, Bell, et al., 2005). The CTGV also left behind an important legacy of design heuristics that these and other researchers and practitioners continue to apply and refine in their research and development initiatives. A few examples include:

- An "anchor" based on a contextualized case study or problem situation that learners can actively explore should be a key feature of effective learning and teaching activities focused on higher order outcomes such as problem solving.
- Teachers adopting learning innovations like the *Jasper* series should form a learning community that actively supports the adoption and implementation process.
- Scaffolding is needed (e.g. visualizations, models, and worked examples) to support learner engagement in a problem-based learning environment as complex and challenging as the *Jasper* series.

A major practical outcome of the design research conducted by the CTGV is that the *Jasper* series became a viable commercial product used by hundreds of teachers and thousands of students. It is available from Vanderbilt University via this website: http://jasper.vueinnovations.com/. Additional information can be found at the original project website: http://peabody.vanderbilt.edu/projects/funded/jasper/. As listed below, there are numerous publications that describe this long-term educational design project, including a book and articles in both refereed journals and magazines aimed at teachers.

Additional information about this study

- Bransford, J., Sherwood, R., Hasselbring, T., Kinzer, C., & Williams, S. (1990). Anchored instruction: Why we need it and how technology can help. In D. Nix & R. Spiro (Eds.), *Cognition education and multimedia: Exploring ideas in high technology* (pp. 115–141). Hillsdale, NJ: Lawrence Erlbaum.

- Cognition and Technology Group at Vanderbilt. (1990). Anchored instruction and its relationship to situated cognition. *Educational Researcher, 19*(6), 2–10.
- Cognition and Technology Group at Vanderbilt. (1992a). The Jasper experiment: An exploration of issues in learning and instructional design. *Educational Technology Research and Development, 40*(1), 65–80.
- Cognition and Technology Group at Vanderbilt. (1992b). The Jasper series as an example of anchored instruction: Theory, program description and assessment data. *Educational Psychologist, 27*, 291–315.
- Cognition and Technology Group at Vanderbilt. (1993). The Jasper experiment: Using video to provide real-world problem-solving contexts. *Arithmetic Teacher, 40*, 474–478.
- Cognition and Technology Group at Vanderbilt. (1997a). *The Jasper Project: Lessons in curriculum, instruction, assessment, and professional development.* Mahwah, NJ: Lawrence Erlbaum Associates.
- Cognition and Technology Group at Vanderbilt. (1997b). The Jasper series: A design experiment in complex, mathematical problem solving. In J. Hawkins & A. M. Collins (Eds.), *Design experiments: Integrating technologies into schools.* New York: Cambridge University Press.

Example 4: integrated curriculum for primary school science and literacy

Problem, context, and approach

For many children, primary school science class marks initial encounters with scientific concepts, relationships and skills. In addition to learning content, science teaching at this age level is undertaken to nurture curiosity about the world and to develop positive attitudes toward science. Contributing to the development of well-rounded citizens, an understanding of and appreciation for science is important for the development of a society. Yet current educational policies in many countries, especially the US, have marginalized nearly all subject areas, except language and mathematics. This "back to basics" stance is not without reason. However, it does appear to demonstrate insufficient understanding regarding (a) the importance of disciplinary curricula for the advancement of society; and (b) the need for high(er) level language and literacy learning (e.g. comprehension, critical literacy) to be contextualized through embedding in disciplinary learning. To address both of these concerns, increasing work has been undertaken to explore the science–literacy interface (Cervetti, Pearson, Barber, Hiebert, & Bravo, 2007). Advancements have been made in theorizing about the common cognitive demands of science and literacy (e.g. Baker, 1991; Carin & Sund, 1985; Padilla, Muth, & Lund Padilla, 1991); in addition, specific models of integration have been constructed and tested (Anderson, West, Beck, Macdonell, & Frisbie, 1997; Guthrie & Ozgungor, 2002; Palincsar & Magnusson, 2001; Pappas, Varelas, Barry, & Rife, 2002). The basic approach of integrating science and literacy seems promising both in terms of balancing out early years curricula that risk imbalance and providing rich contexts for literacy learning. However, very few curriculum materials are widely available for teachers in schools to use such an approach.

In 2003, with the aim of developing high-quality integrated science and literacy curricula that could be used by teachers throughout the USA, science educators from Lawrence Hall of Science (LHS) and literacy educators from the Graduate School of Education (both from University of California at Berkeley) came together to create something new and needed: the Seeds of Science/Roots of Reading program (Seeds/Roots). The team drew on existing previous LHS-developed inquiry science curriculum and worked to embed opportunities for literacy learning, including explicit instruction, practice, and a gradual release of responsibility to students. At the same time, team members were anxious to embed new research into the endeavor, saying it was time to move beyond the promising and provocative conversations about the science–literacy interface based on theories and models, to empirical study on putting the ideas to work in the classroom (Cervetti, Pearson, Bravo, & Barber, 2006). Over the next 4 years, the Seeds/Roots team created instructional models, instantiated them in curriculum units, and refined both the models and the curriculum through insights gleaned from the craft wisdom of the developers, the theoretical inputs from experts, and the empirical findings from field investigation.

The Seeds/Roots curriculum was created for use in a range of classroom settings. Therefore, it was designed for the most common usage pattern: out-of-box, with optional professional development. That is, in designing the materials, the developers acknowledged that professional development to learn about the ideas underpinning the approach and how to use the materials was preferred but not always possible under normal circumstances.

Analysis, design, and evaluation processes

Early stages of the Seeds/Roots investigation were aimed at developing a platform of ideas that could serve as a design framework and also advance a broader understanding of the science–literacy interface. Two main questions were central at the outset: (a) How can reading and writing be used as tools to support inquiry-based science learning?; and (b) What skills, strategies, and processes are shared by these two curricular domains? Detailed answers to these questions were derived primarily from literature review; these reviews are available (Cervetti, Pearson, Bravo & Barber, 2006; Cervetti, Pearson, Barber, Hiebert & Bravo, 2007), but highlights are given here. The team built on field knowledge of how literacy can support inquiry-based science learning, by creating model text roles: (a) to provide context (inviting learner engagement; introducing the topic/content; connecting firsthand investigations from outside the classroom); (b) deliver content (offering information; describing phenomena); (c) to model phenomena (inquiry processes; literacy processes; the nature of science); and (d) to support second-hand inquiry by providing experience with data; and/or (e) to support firsthand inquiry (by providing information that facilitates firsthand investigations; by helping pupils make sense of firsthand investigations; and by inspiring firsthand investigations) (Cervetti & Barber, 2008). With regard to the skills, strategies, and processes shared by both curricular domains, the team identified certain functions (metacognitive regulation; acquisition of information; problem solving; and connection-making); and strategies (activating prior knowledge; establishing purposes/goals; making/reviewing predictions; drawing inferences and conclusions; making connections/recognizing relationships) that are shared in both science and literacy. In addition, they reached the conclusion that science, as an academic language for communicating about the natural world, is a form of specialized discourse. Finally, based on the insight that, particularly in science, text refers to more than words on the printed page but also includes visual representations, they concluded that in this context, literacy means visual literacy. Based on these insights, a design framework was constructed which features a Do-it, Talk-it, Read-it, Write-it approach to learning.

Through the iterative process of development and testing, additional research questions were posed, notably: *What benefits accrue to reading and writing when they are embedded in inquiry-based science?* In addition to feedback from teachers on other factors (e.g. usability), data were collected on student learning to inform designers about features and activities in the curriculum that were comparatively more or less powerful.

The design, development, and evaluation process employed by the Seeds/Roots team evolved throughout the project. Over the years, they have refined a basic process that is well understood in the team, which enables them to put most of their energy into developing and testing the materials, and not into developing and refining the development-testing process at the same time, which is often the case with innovative design projects (Corrigan, Loper, & Barber, 2010). Many LHS developers have also taught in school and conducted research at the graduate level; they draw on developer, teacher, and researcher mindsets in their work.

Most of the Seeds/Roots materials have evolved through three prototypes: global prototypes are piloted; full prototypes undergo a tryout under normal classroom conditions; and then the final version is created. Leading to the first global prototype are two main processes: content orientation and backwards design. During the content orientation, developers look at standards from all states to identify the common content in the required curriculum; this is especially important to render the modules congruent with the needs and curricular autonomy of teachers and schools. Next, they ask working scientists for advice on content refinement; the scientists help discern core versus related issues, as well as which concepts are key, especially for depth and enrichment. Finally, a literature review is conducted to look for important content issues, misconceptions, learning progressions, pedagogical content knowledge, and any other sound guidance on how to teach the content at hand. Once the content has been mapped out, a backwards design process ensues. First, the content is deconstructed, and designers distinguish between the main idea and composite ideas. Second, initial modules are created, based on the content orientation and the deconstruction outputs. Third, a skeleton design – more resembling shorthand than a book or guide – is created for each module.

The skeleton design is piloted by a pair of LHS developers in a school. One developer teaches while the other developer observes and takes notes, as does the regular classroom teacher. During the pilot, data are collected through a debriefing discussion afterwards and field notes, as well as periodic assessments of student understanding. Each of the pilot sessions is driven by a question, e.g. "Are children able to use evidence from text to support their understanding of dissolving?" Where possible, the pilot is conducted in two classes, one immediately following the other, so that the insights can be applied and tested immediately. This might not be possible if developers did not also possess the researcher and teacher mindsets and skillsets. The developer pair uses the insights from the pilot to write a full version of the materials, which is then refined by a second pair of developers.

The first full prototype is tested through a tryout. The materials are sent to schools around the US. During the course of the Seeds/Roots development from 2003–2009, over 300 teachers and 6,000 learners located in diverse settings across the US participated in full prototype tryouts. Teachers use the materials as they arrive, right out-of-the-box. Data are collected through various sources: (a) preliminary survey (about the teacher and about the context); (b) daily survey during use (contains five general questions asking about how the lesson went; the learner engagement; how close teachers stayed to the instruction that was recommended in the materials; what they changed; why; and one unique session-specific question, often zeroing in on a design challenge that may not have been completely resolved to the team's satisfaction); (c) end of unit survey (more expansive questions about teacher reflections on the materials as a whole); (d) learner notebooks; and (e) pre/post test data (LHS-made assessments are administered by teachers). Concurrent with the tryout, the full prototype is also sent to the scientists for expert appraisal, which usually focuses on core/related issue distinctions and content accuracy. Also at this stage, the state standards are revisited to determine if the emerging curriculum is still in line with what is required. If deemed necessary, pilot testing is repeated on some modules. Thereafter, a final version is constructed.

Production of the final version begins with long meetings. The data from the tryout and expert appraisals are examined, and the entire developer team weighs findings and options, making the fundamental steering decisions, collectively. Thereafter, a new pair of developers (not the original pair responsible for outlining, piloting, and drafting) use the data, discussions, and steering decisions to create the final version. This phase entails revision of the pupil book text and supportive materials for the teacher, which are then polished by yet another developer before publication. Concurrent with or sometimes after tryouts, data are collected on effectiveness (achievement) but also to inform new development efforts, such as subsequent modules on related topics; or formative assessment (cf. Tilson, Billman, Corrigan, & Barber, 2011).

Practical and scientific outputs

Now commercially published, the Seeds/Roots program is being used in classrooms and schools in 42 states plus the District of Columbia, with systematic, larger-scale implementation beginning to take hold in portions of over a dozen different school districts, including Cleveland, Ohio; Minneapolis, Minnesota; Houston, Texas; and Fresno, California. For different grade levels there are units focused on different areas of science content (e.g. soil habitats or designing mixtures); each area relates to life science, physical science or earth science. All units are based on their Do-it, Talk-it, Read-it, Write-it approach. Learning goals addressed in each one pertain to science (science knowledge; science inquiry; and the nature and practices of science) as well as literacy (reading, writing, listening, and speaking). For example, students use an "Into the Soil" book as part of the soil habitats unit, in which children learn about decomposition, plant and animal adaptations, habitats, and the properties of soil. Children also learn to make predictions, pose questions, use text features as they read, and to write descriptions and scientific explanations, using new scientific vocabulary, such as organism, adaptation, evidence, and observation.

In addition to offering support online for families and home investigations, teachers are offered assistance in various ways. First, a powerful and flexible assessment system is available for each unit in the form of formative and/or summative assessment systems. The summative assessment system includes the assessments themselves, scoring guides, answer keys, and sample pupil work. The formative assessment system recommends formal and informal assessment options, as well as detailed scoring guides. The assessment opportunities are also signified in the teacher guide, which supports not only teacher monitoring of pupil progress, but also adjustment of instruction based on results.

Second, for teachers using only a few books (and not the teacher guides), strategy guides are available for them to become familiar with powerful instructional strategies that can be used with the multiple Seeds/Roots books and other books as well. Scores of strategy guides are available for reading (e.g. interpreting visual representations); writing (e.g. teaching explanation writing); listening/speaking (using roundtable discussion); and the nature of science/inquiry (e.g. analyzing part–whole relationships).

Third, the Lawrence Hall of Science in Berkeley offers periodically scheduled workshops at their location. In addition, custom training sessions can be arranged at schools; their extended network of facilitators has led professional development and curriculum implementation support sessions in multiple locations. They hold a three-day workshop every summer; this is sufficient to gain a better understanding of the Seeds/Roots philosophy, experience the activities from multiple units, learn about the benefits of this curriculum, and become familiar with the assessment system.

Finally, the main support is available in the teacher guides. The structure of these guides has been refined over years of development and testing. The left-hand pages give procedural specifications that teachers can use during classroom enactment. The right-hand pages provide teaching support and recommendations relevant to the content on the opposite page, including just-in-time notes as well as suggestions for differentiation. The guides include key questions and issues teachers can expect their students to present.

The Seeds/Roots work has produced different kinds of theoretical understanding. This team has developed rare and rich expertise in creating scientifically valid, practically relevant, and highly usable materials for a nation as diverse as the US. Much can be learned from their work in terms of development process, the characteristics of teacher materials, and shaping concomitant teacher professional development given the limited opportunities that are available. The Seeds/Roots embedded research has also contributed to better understanding of the potentials, limitations, and nuances of the science–literacy interface. Some of their studies have been conducted directly on the Seeds/Roots materials, e.g. using systematic variation of design features to test pieces of the underlying Do-it, Talk-it, Read-it, Write-it model (Wang & Herman, 2005); and to explore the comparative benefits of Seeds/Roots as opposed to business-as-usual curricula (Goldschmidt, 2010). In addition, the Seeds/Roots curriculum has set the stage for inquiry into: the role of text in supporting inquiry science (Cervetti & Barber, 2008); supporting English language learners (Lawrence Hall of Science, 2010); formative assessment for practice (Tilson, Billman, Corrigan, & Barber, 2011); and the role of genre in learning science content (Cervetti, Bravo, Hiebert, Pearson, & Jaynes, 2009). Current investigation continues, e.g. on constructing and critiquing scientific arguments.

Additional information about this study

- Cervetti, G. N., & Barber, J. (2008). Text in hands-on science. In E. H. Hiebert & M. Sailors (Eds.), *Finding the right texts: What works for beginning and struggling readers* (pp. 89–108). New York: Guilford.
- Cervetti, G., Barber, J., Dorph, R., Goldschmidt, P., & Pearson, D. (under review). The impact of an integrated approach to science and literacy in elementary school classrooms.
- Cervetti, G., Bravo, M., Hiebert, E., Pearson, D., & Jaynes, C. (2009). Text genre and science content: Ease of reading, comprehension and reader preference. *Reading Psychology 30*,(6) 487–511.
- Cervetti, G., Pearson, D., Bravo, M., & Barber, J. (2006). Reading and writing in the service of inquiry-based science. In R. Douglas, P. Klentschy, & K. Worth (Eds.), *Linking science and literacy in the K-8 classroom* (pp. 221–244). Arlington, VA: NSTA Press.
- Cervetti, G., Pearson. D., Barber, J., Hiebert, E., & Bravo, M. (2007). Integrating literacy and science: The research we have, the research we need. In M. Pressley, A. Billman, K. Perry, K. Reffitt, and J. Reynolds (Eds.), *Shaping literacy achievement: Research we have, research we need* (pp. 157–174). New York: Guilford.
- Corrigan, S., Loper, S., & Barber, J. (2010). *Cui bono? How learning progressions stand to benefit curriculum developers and education researchers.* Paper presented at the annual meeting of the American Educational Research Association, April 30–May 4, Denver, Colorado.
- Goldschmidt, P. (2010). *Evaluation of Seeds of Science/Roots of Reading: Effective tools for developing literacy through science in the early grades.* Los Angeles, CA: National Center for Research on Evaluation, Standards, and Student Testing (CRESST).

- Lawrence Hall of Science (2010). *Seeds of Science/Roots of Reading: Research and development for accommodation of English language learners.* Berkeley, CA: Lawrence Hall of Science.
- Pearson, D., Moje, E. & Greenleaf, C. (2010). Literacy and science: Each in the service of the other. *Science 328*, 459–463.
- Tilson, J., Billman, A., Corrigan, S., & Barber, J. (2011). Two for one: Assessing science and literacy using writing prompts. In P. Noyce & D. T. Hickey (Eds.), *New frontiers in formative assessment* (pp. 159–174). Cambridge, MA: Harvard Education Press.
- Wang, J., & Herman, J. (2005). *Evaluation of Seeds of Science/Roots of Reading Project: Shoreline Science and Terrarium Investigations.* Los Angeles, CA: National Center for Research on Evaluation, Standards, and Student Testing (CRESST).

Chapter 3

Toward a generic model for educational design research

The understanding of educational design research purveyed throughout this book has been shaped by our exposure to various fields, especially instructional design and curriculum development. In addition, existing models and frameworks for educational design research have influenced our conception of the process. As a backdrop, this chapter first shares key ideas from instructional design and curriculum development that have shaped our views, before discussing lessons learned from existing models and frameworks for educational design research. Building on those ideas, a generic model for conducting educational design research is then presented. The framework presented in this chapter sets the stage for the elaborated discussions in Part II of this book.

Lessons from instructional design

Our ideas about educational design have been strongly influenced by the field of instructional design and, within that, especially the development of educational media. Instructional design has a historical tie to educational design research because many of the proponents of this genre of inquiry were originally trained in instructional design. Even more importantly, theories, methods and tools developed by instructional designers are useful throughout the process of educational design research.

What is instructional design?

Informed by psychology

Instructional design is a field concerned with systematic processes for developing instruction to reliably yield desired learning and performance results. In the field and throughout this discussion, the term "instruction" is used in a very broad sense: to include intentionally created processes, resources, environments, or programs for learning. The design of instruction is naturally influenced by our evolving understanding of learning, how it takes place, and what can facilitate or hamper it. For this reason, instructional design has always held strong ties to psychology; and, more recently, it shares commonalities with the learning sciences.

Though the field has evolved dramatically since its inception more than a half century ago, instructional design has its roots in the behaviorist movement led by renowned psychologists such as Edward L. Thorndike, John B. Watson, and Benjamin F. Skinner. Behaviorist perspectives gave early instructional designers a heavy focus on observing, planning, measuring, and evaluating instruction. The instruction that resulted demonstrated these influences as well, e.g. by emphasizing reinforcement, feedback, and practice. Over time, the importance of additional factors, such as internal information processing in learning, became better understood and were incorporated into instructional design. "Stimuli became inputs; behavior became outputs. And what happened in between was conceived of as information processing" (Driscoll, 2005, p. 74). The instruction that resulted demonstrated attention to the stages of memory – sensory memory, working memory, and long-term memory. The field of cognitive psychology continues to inform instructional design; a recent example is the development of cognitive load theory. Sweller, van Merrienboer, and Paas (1998) recommended specific strategies that can be incorporated into instructional programs or materials to reduce extraneous cognitive load, such as worked examples and partially solved problems. For extended discussion of the psychological foundations of instructional design, please refer to Driscoll (2007). Influences of European learning psychologists (e.g. Vygotsky, Galperin, and Carpay), whose theories, for example, emphasize the dialogical and social nature of constructing meaning, remain visible in the field of instructional design today.

Objectivist and constructivist influences on instructional design

It has been said that positivism has been "the cornerstone epistemological perspective of the [instructional design] field, laying the foundation for many current instructional design practices" (Hannafin & Hill, 2007, p. 55). This is clearly evident in earlier work where the underlying assumption was that learning involves acquiring some universal truths about the world, which exist external to the learner, and that instruction was viewed as the primary means for transmitting them. When it comes to designing instruction, this view has been referred to as objectivist (Hannafin & Hill, 2007; Jonassen, 1999).

But across the field of education, researchers and practitioners alike have borne witness to the rapidly growing appreciation of the notion that knowledge is uniquely constructed by the individual, rather than transmitted; and instruction should therefore provide the conditions and materials to facilitate that construction. This has brought about a relativist epistemological perspective, which may be seen at odds with (though we think of it more as productively counter-balancing) the positivist one. When it comes to designing instruction, this view has been referred to as constructivist. Among other influences, this perspective has contributed to a new paradigm of instructional theory (cf. Reigeluth, 1999).

While it has been acknowledged that these perspectives may be fundamentally incompatible (Hannafin, Hannafin, Land, & Oliver, 1997), others suggest that – at least from a pragmatic perspective – they constitute complementary design tools (Hannafin & Hill, 2007; Jonassen, 1999; Young, 1993). Indeed, Merrill's

(2007) First Principles of Instructional Design were derived from a study on common elements shared across different instructional design models and theories, representing a range of approaches across an objectivist–constructivist continuum. Using Merrill's (2007, p. 63) concise versions, these principles are:

1   Learning is promoted when learners are engaged in solving real world problems.
2   Learning is promoted when existing knowledge is activated as a foundation for new knowledge.
3   Learning is promoted when new knowledge is demonstrated to the learner.
4   Learning is promoted when new knowledge is applied by the learner.
5   Learning is promoted when new knowledge is integrated into the learner's world.

Though the treatment of Merrill's work here is extremely brief, the point is to illustrate that instructional design theory can incorporate ideas that are consistent with theoretical perspectives as different as objectivism and constructivism.

Instructional design theories and models

The field of instructional design is rich with literature that includes, even combines, elements of learning theories (e.g. the learning processes we hope to engender); instructional design theories (the external conditions that can enable those processes); and instructional development processes (efficient, effective, and reliable ways to create those external conditions). Instructional design literature contains many *models*, often using flowchart-like diagrams, which describe what actions need to be undertaken to create instruction or instructional resources. Yet it is the instructional design *theories*, which explain how the process should be undertaken and why (cf. Merrill, 1994).

Nearly all instructional design models and theories attend to implications for both what instruction should look like and how to create it. However, instructional design work can differ in its respective emphasis on *instruction* or *design*. Acknowledging that they are inextricably intertwined, we distinguish between work that focuses more on the instruction – that which is concerned with shaping the *output* of instructional design; and work that focuses more on the design – that which is concerned with shaping the *process* of instructional design. Across these two perspectives, the field of instructional design has a history of seeking both fundamental understanding and applied use. The body of literature emphasizing the instructional design outputs tends to be derived primarily from (often use-inspired basic) research. In contrast, most of the literature emphasizing the instructional design process is based on craft wisdom and experience.

To illustrate how instructional design theories and models have influenced our thinking about educational design research, the following section briefly presents representative contributions made toward understanding instructional design outputs and processes, respectively. For each one, we consider the two goals of design research: fundamental understanding and applied use. An overview of the

Table 3.1 Representative instructional design models and theories

Primary emphasis	(Fundamental) understanding	Applied use
ID output	Gagné's theory of instruction	van Merriënboer's 4C/ID model
ID process	Gustafson and Branch's ADDIE elements	Posner and Rudnitsky model of course design

examples is provided in Table 3.1. For detailed discussions of the development and status of instructional design theories and models, please refer to Reigeluth and Carr-Chellman (2009) and Reiser and Dempsey (2012). See also the *Handbook of Research on Educational Communications and Technology* (Spector, Merrill, van Merriënboer, & Driscoll, 2008) for descriptions of current approaches to instructional design.

Gagné

Trained as a psychologist and an experienced designer of instruction for U.S. Air Force pilots, Gagné (1965, 1997) developed an integrated and comprehensive theory of instruction based largely on cognitive information processing theory, as well as observations of effective classroom teachers. Driscoll (2005) described Gagné's theory of learning in terms of three elements: a taxonomy of learning outcomes; conditions necessary to achieve the learning outcomes; and nine events of instruction designed to guide the instructor through the process of designing for learning. The taxonomy of learning outcomes defines the five types of capabilities humans can learn, each of which requires its own type of instruction: verbal information, intellectual skills, cognitive strategies, attitudes, and motor skills. Different internal conditions (i.e. a learner's prior knowledge and/or skills) and external conditions (i.e. the instruction and resources presented to the learner) are necessary for each type of learning. For example, practice in solving problems is necessary for developing cognitive strategies, and role models or persuasive arguments are necessary for developing attitudes. Gagné suggestsed that learning (e.g. of intellectual skills) can be organized in a hierarchy according to complexity, which can help to identify prerequisites that warrant sequencing consideration when designing instruction. Gagné's nine events of instruction each facilitate specific processes during learning and delineate steps instructors must take to meet learning outcomes. These are: gain attention; inform learner of objectives; stimulate recall of prior learning; present stimulus material; provide learner guidance; elicit performance; provide feedback; assess performance; and enhance retention and transfer (Gagné, Wager, Golas, & Keller, 2004). The work of Gagné (1965, 1997) constitutes one example of instructional design theory that can be used for prescriptive/normative purposes, in this case, to shape instruction. Its widespread and effective use has shown us the power and value of working to develop high-level theory that serves prescriptive/normative purposes in designing instructional interventions.

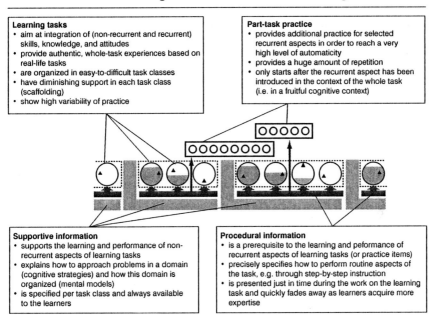

Learning tasks
* aim at integration of (non-recurrent and recurrent) skills, knowledge, and attitudes
* provide authentic, whole-task experiences based on real-life tasks
* are organized in easy-to-difficult task classes
* have diminishing support in each task class (scaffolding)
* show high variability of practice

Part-task practice
* provides additional practice for selected recurrent aspects in order to reach a very high level of automaticity
* provides a huge amount of repetition
* only starts after the recurrent aspect has been introduced in the context of the whole task (i.e. in a fruitful cognitive context)

Supportive information
* supports the learning and performance of non-recurrent aspects of learning tasks
* explains how to approach problems in a domain (cognitive strategies) and how this domain is organized (mental models)
* is specified per task class and always available to the learners

Procedural information
* is a prerequisite to the learning and peformance of recurrent aspects of learning tasks (or practice items)
* precisely specifies how to perform routine aspects of the task, e.g. through step-by-step instruction
* is presented just in time during the work on the learning task and quickly fades away as learners acquire more expertise

Figure 3.1 4C/ID model
Source: van Merriënboer and Kirschner (2007)

van Merriënboer

Particularly interested in designing instruction and learning environments to acquire and develop complex skills (e.g. those used by pilots or air traffic controllers), van Merriënboer created and later refined the Four-Component Instructional Design (4C/ID) Model (van Merriënboer, 1997; van Merriënboer, Clark, & de Croock, 2002); this work continues to evolve substantially (van Merriënboer & Kirschner, 2007). The 4C/ID model offers a holistic approach to designing instruction that: integrates development of knowledge skills and attitudes; coordinates development of qualitatively different skills; and yields learning that can be transferred to daily work or life settings. The model presupposes that complex skills are best learned by carrying out whole tasks which are authentic and contextualized. Whole learning tasks therefore are integral to the model (e.g. a pre-service teacher learns how to cope with an emergency during a school field trip). Learning to perform whole tasks may be enabled through supportive information (background information that is generic to a whole class of problems that clarify or lay the basis for the solution of the problem, e.g. teachers should first always orient themselves to the environment where a field trip is planned so they are prepared to seek help if an emergency situation arises) or just-in-time information (information specific to the particular field trip site, e.g. emergency exits in a particular museum). Connected to the whole task, part-task practice may also be included to learn how to automate recurring aspects of complex tasks (e.g. training in first aid protocols). Shown in Figure 3.1, this model demonstrates how instructional design models can provide guidance to designers of complex learning environments. The systematic, rigorous, research-based development of this model has especially influenced our understanding about how to develop and test theoretical understanding that is used for prescriptive/normative purposes.

Gustafson and Branch

Gustafson and Branch (1997, 2002) surveyed instructional design models and concluded that nearly all were shaped around five core elements of the instructional design process. Those core elements are commonly referred to with the acronym, ADDIE: Analysis, Design, Development, Implementation, and Evaluation. While the ADDIE acronym is linear and the elements constitute basic elements of instructional design, they do not represent the overall process sequence; different models vary in this regard. Analysis generally involves gathering information, mostly aimed at defining the problem and understanding its origins; in instructional design, the problem is defined as the gap between the existing and the desired situations. Design entails planning the instruction, and generally results in some kind of blueprint for developing the solution. Development refers to creating the actual solution, which may evolve through a series of prototypes whose development is informed by formative evaluation. Implementation means "going live" with the solution – using it in the target context with the target audience. Evaluation is an essential characteristic of any systematic approach to problem solving. Formative evaluations seek information to improve the designed instruction whereas summative evaluations judge its overall worth or applicability in a certain context. The core elements of ADDIE have influenced our understanding of essential processes within the design trajectory of educational design research.

Posner and Rudnitsky

Posner and Rudnitsky (1978, 2005) produced a classic text, *Course Design: A Guide to Curriculum Development for Teachers,* which is now in its seventh edition. The book centers on a model for course planning (see Figure 3.2), which emphasizes the main processes (arrows) and their major products (boxes) contributing to course design. The book provides detailed guidance on: setting the direction (e.g. understanding the existing situation and determining the intended learning outcomes); developing a course rationale (e.g. probing values and assumptions); refining the learning outcomes (e.g. clarifying, categorizing, prioritizing them); chunking (e.g. forming units) and organizing (e.g. setting the scope and sequence of the units); developing teaching strategies (e.g. instructional approaches and resources); and evaluation (planning and gathering evidence). Posner and Rudnitsky (2005) stressed that the model is a conceptual overview and not a process flowchart. For example, they indicated that it is incorrect to insist that goals and values must be specified before curriculum development commences, and mentioned that, often, abstract concerns (e.g. values, goals) only begin to take shape after consideration is given to more

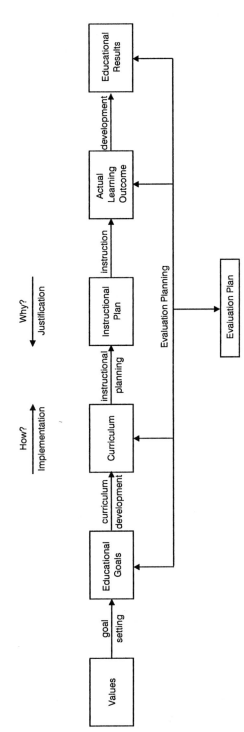

Figure 3.2 The Posner and Rudnitsky Model (2005)

concrete matters (e.g. instructional strategies). They also stress that, while their model highlights important elements of course design, it should not be misconstrued as a linear process, and emphasize that a final design results from a series of successive approximations. They explicate how the work of course design is influenced by other important matters, (e.g. group deliberation, teacher thinking) as well as how course design is conducted to align with curriculum standards. The work of Posner and Rudnitsky has influenced our understanding of the design trajectory of educational design research in several ways, especially by: emphasizing the importance of attending to values and goals in a holistic manner; demonstrating a systematic yet natural approach; and exemplifying how instructional and curriculum design converge.

Implications for educational design research

The field of instructional design has developed its own conceptualization of and appreciation for conducting research alongside the design and development of instruction (e.g. Richey & Klein, 2007; Richey & Nelson, 1996). Richey and Klein (2007) distinguished between research focusing on instructional products and tools (this aligns with instructional design *output* work, described above) and research on design and development models (this aligns with instructional design *process* work, described above). In design research, once we understand a problem and its causes, we use theories, practical wisdom, and inspiring examples, along with formative testing, to steer the development of solutions. While some procedural aspect(s) of a design research project are likely to be different, instructional design literature emphasizing the output perspective can provide solid foundations for the design of many kinds of new instructional interventions. This is also a body of knowledge to which educational design research can contribute. Instructional design literature emphasizing the process perspective has given us the systematic problem-solving mentality that is emphasized throughout this book. It has helped us see the value of planned, but flexible, iterative approaches, the importance of context, and the need to anticipate implementation complexities throughout the entire process. However, gaps between instructional design literature and real world practices are well known (Kirschner, Carr, van Merriënboer, & Sloep, 2002; Visscher-Voerman, 1999) and researchers have called for new, more realistic, integrative instructional design models (Ross et al., 2008). To date, there has been surprisingly little theory development concerning the instructional design process (Branch, 2009); we see exciting opportunities for educational design research to make a much-needed contribution in this regard.

Lessons from curriculum development

In addition to the field of instructional design, the field of curriculum has substantially shaped our understanding of educational design research. Curriculum development has a natural connection to design research, as most design research interventions somehow touch, if not directly alter, curricula. The field of curriculum offers useful lenses for viewing teaching and learning processes, and frameworks for understanding what influences them. As the following pages show, models and theories for curriculum planning can be extremely useful to a wide range of design research projects, even if the intervention being designed is not considered curriculum. This section highlights only a few key themes from the field of curriculum before examining how curriculum is developed, and describing how these issues are relevant to educational design research. Comprehensive works with more extensive overviews of the field are available (e.g. Jackson, 1992; Schubert, Lopez Schubert, Thomas, & Carroll, 2002).

What is curriculum?

Curriculum is Latin for a racing chariot; and the verb *currere* means to run. While the term "curriculum" means many different things to different people (Posner, 2004; Walker, 1982), Taba's (1962) broad definition of curriculum as a "plan for learning" is generally accepted. Curriculum deals with planning and guiding learning in an educational context. Planning for learning may focus on the learner level, the classroom level, the school level, the municipality level, or the level of state. Curriculum planning at one level is inextricably linked to curriculum planning on other levels. For example, national educational policies can influence how learning is planned and guided within a municipality, school, classroom, and/or even with individual learners; and teachers planning lessons consider how to attend to the needs of specific learners while also meeting goals set by their school or municipality.

When it comes to planning and guiding learning, curriculum debate has historically been focused on the aims and content of learning. As early as 1859, Herbert Spencer asked what, for many, has come to be known as the classic curriculum question, "What knowledge is of most worth?" Schubert (1986) pointed out how this philosophical question comes to life in curriculum, as personal beliefs on what is worthwhile are embodied in a plan for learning.

In addition to the aims and content of learning, curriculum theorists have addressed additional factors that are considered constituent elements of curriculum, and many of these component lists also include instructional strategies as well as learner assessment (cf. Eash, 1991; Klein, 1991; Marsh, 2004; Posner, 2004; Taba, 1962; Tyler, 1949). Klein's 1991 list of nine essential elements is among the most comprehensive. It consists of: goals, objectives and purposes; content; materials and resources; activities; teaching strategies; assessment; grouping; time; and space. Building on this work, van den Akker (2003) presented these elements as spokes in a spider web, with an additional component at the center of the web: the rationale. He used this metaphor to stress the fact that, while a focus on specific components may occur from time to time, any dramatic shift in balance will pull the entirety out of alignment. Though it may stretch for a while, prolonged imbalance will cause the system to break. Much educational design research focuses on limited elements of curriculum (often materials, resources, learning activities, or teaching strategies), though some are more comprehensive. This lens is particularly useful to educational design researchers – even those focusing on more narrow aspects, such as the design of formative assessments – for understanding the curricular context that influences enactment of their interventions.

Charters (1923) wrote that curriculum thought should emanate from a matching of ideals with activities. Goodlad, Klein, and Tye (1979) distinguished a range of curricular representations, which make transparent the matching of ideals with actual classroom activities and outcomes. This typology begins with initial intentions (ideal curriculum), then proceeds to their written form (formal curriculum), moves on to the interpretations made by its users (perceived curriculum) as well as the way it is enacted in the learning setting (operational curriculum) and concludes with the way it is experienced by the pupils (experiential curriculum) plus, ultimately, learner achievement (attained curriculum). Van den Akker (2003) condensed these to the intended, implemented, and attained curricula. Each of these are influenced by myriad aspects of the context, including; social, political, cultural, economic, organizational, and historical factors. Alternative representations of curriculum have also been described in the literature. For example, attention has been given to the norms and values of society, which may be explicit, implicit (Eisner, 1994) or hidden (Posner, 2004).

The field of curriculum, which historically emphasizes the aims and content of learning as well as the social, cultural, and political characteristics of the context in question, helps us position the interventions created through educational design research within larger, living systems. The intended, implemented, and attained curricula offer a very useful lens for viewing the interventions that are created though educational design research.

Curriculum theory

In their widely used curriculum text, now in its fourth edition, Marsh and Willis (2007) adopted the following three categories for classifying curriculum theorizers: prescriptive theorizers create models or frameworks that help improve school practices (e.g. Ralph Tyler, Hilda Taba); descriptive theorizers identify how curriculum development takes place in educational settings (e.g. Decker Walker, Joseph Schwab); and critical-explanatory theorizers particularly describe deficiencies and sometimes comment on best practices in curriculum development (e.g. Elliot Eisner, William Pinar). Three curriculum planning models which demonstrate the categories identified by Marsh and Willis and have also been influential on our thinking are: Tyler's rational–linear approach (1949); Walker's naturalistic deliberative approach (1971a, 1990); and Eisner's artistic approach (1979, 1994). Please refer to the original texts or to Marsh and Willis (2007) for a detailed overview. These orientations are presented in brief below, along with their implications for educational design research.

Tyler

Tyler (1949) proposed what has now become referred to as the "rational–linear approach" as one potential way to view and construct educational programs, encouraging others to develop alternatives, and stating clearly that his work was not a manual for constructing curriculum. However, in the years to follow, many readers have indeed treated it more as a recipe than part of a menu. The approach is founded on four basic concerns: defining appropriate learning objectives; establishing useful learning experiences; organizing learning experiences to have a maximum cumulative effect; and evaluating and revising the curriculum. Tyler's work ushered in an era of behavioral perspectives of curriculum by defining the purpose of instruction as changing behavior from "entry behavior" to the "terminal behavior" as specified in terminal objectives that were stated in observable and measurable forms. It is noteworthy that his work targeted curriculum developers, not teachers. Tyler's own work with teachers in the 1930s encouraged unconventional, alternative approaches to improving curriculum. Our view of educational design research has been influenced by Tyler's goal-oriented thinking: the need to seek understanding of the existing, "entry" situation and map the pathway to the desired, "terminal" situation, all the while acknowledging that there are likely multiple pathways to accomplish this and evaluating the effectiveness of the road taken.

Walker

Walker's (1971a, 1971b) deliberative approach is a formalization and extension of what people naturally do in developing curricula. His work focuses on making those processes transparent, especially through communication. His deliberative approach was derived from years of experience in national curriculum project groups as well as carefully documented participant observation across 3 years in the Kettering Art Project. His observations and reflections led him to identify three basic phases. During the platform of ideas phase, participants are encouraged to discuss, debate, and even argue, until a platform or consensus of clarity about conceptions, theories, aims, images, and procedures begins to emerge. The deliberation phase also involves discussion, but here the focus is less on where to go and more on how to get there. It involves: identifying facts; generating alternative actions; considering costs and consequences; and choosing the most defensible alternatives. The actual creation of the curriculum including subject instructions, teaching materials, and activities is referred to as design. Walker's work presents a useful and descriptive approach to what actually happens in large-scale, relatively well-funded design projects. While implementation considerations are clearly the focus of many deliberations, his model focuses on the design of curriculum. Our view of educational design research has been powerfully influenced by the emphasis on negotiating shared understanding, gradually progressing from chaos toward common clarity and direction, to define and pursue the design of educational interventions.

Eisner

Eisner (1979) argued forcibly for an alternative to behaviorist, objectives-driven approaches to education and stressed the multiple, subjective, constructed ways in which people make meaning and learning processes are enacted. Eisner mapped seven dimensions of curriculum in curriculum planning, and pointed out how context influences these: goals and their priorities; content; types of learning opportunities; organization of learning opportunities; organization of content areas; mode of presentation and mode of response; and types of evaluation procedures. He emphasized that his artistic approach was not comprehensive, and that the ideas he proposed were not tied to any particular sequence. More telling of his approach than these dimensions are their underlying ideas about important considerations within each dimension. Eisner's approach offers general guidelines only, leaving actual planning and decision making in the hands of the curricular "artist." From his perspective, the teacher is at the forefront of the process of curriculum development, and the interests of individual students should be emphasized. In a similar manner, we strive in this book to provide stimulation and considerations for a creative design research process, which is not tied to specific methods or a prescribed sequence.

Implications for educational design research

In addition to the influences of specific theorists mentioned above, the field of curriculum development brings to design research a sensitization to the fact that plans for guiding learning are inherently connected to multiple levels simultaneously (learner, classroom, school, municipality, and state), even though interventions may focus on only one. The historical perspective of this field encourages design researchers to question the relevance of specific projects, and the values purveyed through them. Work in the field of curriculum development also explains the need for designed interventions to strive for alignment (between goals, content, teaching strategies, assessment, materials, activities, grouping, time, and space). Finally, the focus on matching intentions and attainment importantly draws attention to understanding and steering the process that connects them: implementation. Our interest in conducting design research related to curriculum development prompted us to study existing models for conducting educational design research; the subsequent section shares key lessons they have taught us.

Lessons from existing design research models

In addition to descriptions of specific design research instantiations, including the seminal work of Brown (1992), several models and frameworks for design research are evident in the literature. Our views of educational design research have been heavily influenced by this literature, and this section shares several important observations and insights we have gleaned from studying it. It is not our aim to describe the models and frameworks in detail, as such discussions are best found in the source publications written by the authors themselves (see Table 3.2 for an overview and the Appendix for references). Rather, with the ultimate goal of explaining how this work has enriched our conceptualization and modeling of educational design research, the following discussion highlights dominant themes as well as specific features that are given unique treatment in different

Table 3.2 Design research models and frameworks

Title	Reference
Questions and methods for design research by integrative learning design framework phase	Bannan-Ritland and Baek, 2008
The osmotic model	Ejersbo et al., 2008
The design research process	Jonassen, Cernusca, and Ionas, 2007
Conceptual model of design research in the curriculum domain	McKenney, Nieveen, and van den Akker, 2006
Predictive and design research approaches in educational technology research	Reeves, 2006
Design research from a learning design perspective	Gravemeijer and Cobb, 2006
Defining characteristics and six key questions	Reinking and Bradley, 2008
Principles of design-based research	Wang and Hannafin, 2005

models. It begins by discussing the variety in model types, and main phases in the design research process. Thereafter, various ways of discussing and representing the dual theory and practice focus of design research are described. The section concludes with indications of how different models and frameworks are, indeed, use-inspired. The italicized text denotes concepts that are incorporated into the generic model presented in the subsequent section of this chapter.

Different types of educational design research models

Some authors have described educational design research through visual models (Bannan-Ritland & Baek, 2008; Ejersbo et al., 2008; Jonassen, Cernusca, & Ionas, 2007; McKenney, Nieveen, & van den Akker, 2006; Reeves, 2006), whereas others have described it through frameworks (Gravemeijer & Cobb, 2006; Reinking & Bradley, 2008; Wang & Hannafin, 2005). The *visual models* seem particularly useful for framing ideas of what the *overall enterprise* looks like. In contrast, the frameworks seem more useful for understanding specific elements or phases of educational design research. Some models and frameworks include attention to characterizing important aspects of educational design research (McKenney, Nieveen, & van den Akker, 2006; Reinking & Bradley, 2008; Wang & Hannafin, 2005); for example, Wang and Hannafin (2005) argued for nine principles of educational design research. Most models and frameworks also address the process of educational design research, though some offer general characterizations while others describe specific phases of the process. Of those describing specific phases, the level of detail given varies greatly. At one end of the spectrum is Reeves' (2006) minimalist model, which focuses on four main phases in an iterative process. In contrast, Bannan-Ritland and Baek (2008) provided a highly specified model featuring 14 steps across four main phases as well as guiding questions and applicable research methods for each phase. Models with *lower levels of specification* offer less detailed guidance, but by being more open in nature, they more easily *lend themselves to customization* than the elaborated models would imply. All of the models and frameworks we have seen depict the process *from the researcher perspective*.

The educational design research process

The educational design research process has been described as iterative (Kelly, 2006), as well as flexible (Reinking & Bradley, 2008). While *multiple (sub-)cycles* of activity are clearly present across most models and frameworks, *flexibility* is present in all models, but more obvious in some models than in others. For example, the model presented by Jonassen, Cernusca, and Ionas (2007) clearly shows several pathways that could be taken, whereas that of Reeves (2006) focuses on a specific iterative cycle: problem analysis; solution development; iterative refinement; and reflection to produce design principles. Of the phases addressed, most models give attention to an initial orientation; many describe a design or development phase; and all refer to some kind of evaluation or empirical testing. During these three main phases, different aspects receive greater or lesser attention across different models.

The initial phase includes investigating the problem at hand. The central orientation of starting from a problem may be explicitly stated (e.g. Ejersbo et al., 2008; Reeves, 2006) or implied (e.g. McKenney, Nieveen, & van den Akker, 2006; Reinking & Bradley, 2008). It involves *exploring and analyzing* the existing situation in terms of both current knowledge and current practice. For example, Bannan-Ritland and Baek (2008) described needs analysis, literature survey, theory development, and audience characterization as steps in this first phase of, in their terms, informed exploration. Similarly, Reinking and Bradley (2008, p. 74) recommended starting the investigation by asking the question: "What is the pedagogical goal to be investigated, why is that goal valued and important, and what theory and previous empirical work speak to accomplishing that goal instructionally?"

The design phase is often shown to involve *drafting* and *prototyping* to build solutions (Bannan-Ritland & Baek, 2008; McKenney, Nieveen, & van den Akker, 2006; Reeves, 2006). Reeves (2006) specified that design is informed by design principles derived from existing literature as well as existing products and interventions in practice. In other models, the role of literature in shaping design (as opposed to understanding the problem, described above) is often implied, but not directly visible. While present in most models, the design process seems to receive relatively less attention than the other two phases. This seems surprising, given the prominent role of *design* in educational design research. However, it could be that authors choose to emphasize the research aspects in publications intended for a research audience.

Evaluation through empirical testing is explicitly present in nearly all the models and frameworks, as is the notion that the results feed into subsequent design cycles. Several of these devote explicit attention to the need for *revisiting the evaluation* and its findings in order to yield outputs. Reeves (2006) prominently included a phase of reflection to produce design principles and enhance solution implementation. Gravemeijer and Cobb (2006) described in detail their process of *retrospective* analysis to produce theory. In a slightly different way, McKenney, van den Akker, and Nieveen (2006) indicated that trade-off decisions must be made between what is theoretically legitimate; viable in practice; and effective when implemented in authentic settings.

Dual focus on theory and practice

Nearly all the models and frameworks attend to the dual trajectories of design and research. For example, one of Wang and Hannafin's (2005) principles is to support design with research from the outset. It is interesting to note that the duality is, in some models, represented by parallel research and design processes and, in other models, by one integrated process. Demonstrating parallel processes, Ejersbo and colleagues (2008) presented an elegant model clearly showing two cycles (one for research, another for design), which strongly resemble the empirical and regulative cycles, respectively. The authors commented that both cycles would ideally run synchronously, but state that this ideal is often not the reality. It has caused us to wonder: might that be different if the processes were more tightly integrated? An example of tight integration may be seen in the work of Bannan-Ritland and Baek (2008). Here, elements of the *research and design activities are seamlessly integrated* into one coherent process.

The models and frameworks also evidence duality in the way they portray the products of educational design research. Most of them identify both *practical and theoretical results*. For some, it would seem as though theory building is the main goal and practical solutions are a fringe benefit (e.g. Jonassen, Cernusca, & Ionas, 2007). In other models, these two products appear to be given more equal weight (Ejersbo et al., 2008; Reeves, 2006). One model depicts not only two, but three products of educational design research. McKenney, Nieveen, and van den Akker (2006) argued that design research should not only yield useful products and design principles, but that the project should also be shaped in such a way as to contribute to the professional development of its participants.

Indications of being use-inspired

All models and frameworks show indications of being use-inspired, but in different ways. This perspective is abundantly clear in the models that devote explicit attention to *implementation and spread* of interventions, e.g. through deployment and dissemination (Ejersbo et al., 2008) or implementation and diffusion (Bannan-Ritland & Baek, 2008). This is also evident in models and frameworks that feature *interaction with practice* either explicitly (e.g. Reeves, 2006) or implicitly (McKenney, Nieveen, & van den Akker, 2006). For example, Ejersbo et al. (2008) emphasized that the problem should be explored in collaboration with the problem owners; similarly, Reinking and Bradley (2008) stressed the importance of focusing the inquiry on something that is valued by practitioners are well as researchers. The consideration of *actual use* is also apparent in models that devote explicit attention to contextual factors (McKenney, Nieveen, & van den Akker, 2006; Wang & Hannafin, 2005). This is facilitated by an approach and a mindset that is *contextually responsive* from the very start. The responsiveness is most often shown in models and frameworks by arrows from (field) testing toward refining either the practical or the theoretical work in progress and/or outputs (cf. Bannan-Ritland & Baek, 2008; Reeves, 2006; Reinking & Bradley, 2008).

Generic model for design research

The model as a whole

This section presents a generic model for design research in education. In creating this model, we sought compatibility with studies reported across the literature working at different scales, toward varying theoretical goals, in diverse settings. We did this by adhering to the defining characteristics of educational design research as described in Chapter 1. This meant that the model would portray a process that could easily lend itself to being: theoretically oriented, interventionist, collaborative, responsively grounded, and iterative. We also sought to devise a model that would allow, if not encourage, use of core ideas from the fields of instructional design and curriculum development, insofar as they are consistent with prevailing views and practices of educational design research. From the field of instructional design, this included a systematic problem-solving mentality; planned but flexible iterative approaches; and the need to anticipate implementation and understand context throughout the entire process. From the field of curriculum, this included explicitly encouraging both artistic and deliberative approaches; seeing how interventions at any scale are inherently connected to different levels within larger living systems; and a sensitivity to the role of enactment in aligning attainment with original intentions. In addition, we aimed to synthesize insights gained from reviewing existing models for educational design research.

Building on previous models and frameworks for educational design research, we aimed to devise a visual model portraying the overall process from the researcher perspective. To render it customizable across the rich variety of approaches, only the essential elements of educational design research would be included. In it, the following features were to be visible:

- Three core phases in a flexible, iterative structure: investigation/analysis; design/prototyping; evaluation/retrospection.
- Dual focus on theory and practice: integrated research and design processes; theoretical and practical outcomes.
- Indications of being use-inspired: planning for implementation and spread; interaction with practice; contextually responsive.

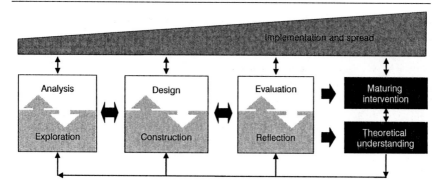

Figure 3.3 Generic model for conducting design research in education

The generic model shown in Figure 3.3 depicts these three features, each represented by different shapes. The squares represent the three core phases. The arrows between the different elements indicate that the process is iterative and flexible. It is iterative because results from some elements feed into others, over and over again. It is flexible because, while some general flow is indicated, many different pathways could be taken. The dual focus on theory and practice is made explicit through the rectangles, which represent the scientific and practical outputs, respectively. The model shows a single, integrated, research and design process. Finally, the model offers indications of being use-inspired. The trapezoid represents implementation and spread, showing that interaction with practice is present from the start, and that the scope increases over time. The bidirectional arrows indicate that what happens in practice influences both the ongoing core processes and ultimate outputs (thus being contextually responsive), and vice versa.

Three main phases in a flexible, iterative process

The generic model shows that educational design research progresses through three main phases, each of which involves interaction with practice and contributes, directly or indirectly, to the production of theoretical understanding and the development of an intervention, which matures over time. The overall cycle is an iterative, flexible process that integrates the empirical and regulative functions described previously. Building on the process description given in Chapter 1, we find it useful to think about an overall study and its sub-components in terms of different sized cycles, namely micro-, meso-, and macro-cycles.

Micro-, meso-, and macro-cycles

The overall process of educational design research reflects the previously named regulative cycle. Within that, three micro-cycles can be identified. Each time one of the three main phases is undertaken, one micro-cycle takes place. This is

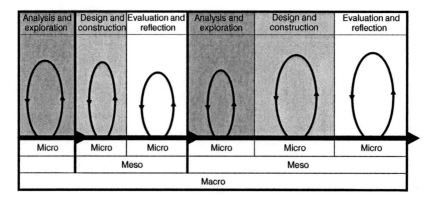

Analysis and exploration	Design and construction	Evaluation and reflection	Analysis and exploration	Design and construction	Evaluation and reflection
Micro	Micro	Micro	Micro	Micro	Micro
	Meso			Meso	
Macro					

Figure 3.4 Micro-, meso-, and macro-cycles in educational design research

because each main phase constitutes its own cycle of action, with its own logical chain of reasoning. Both the analysis and exploration phase, and the evaluation and reflection phase are empirical cycles, featuring data collection. The design and construction phase is different; it is a deliberative–generative cycle. While the design and construction phase is informed by the findings from the other phases as well as literature and interaction with practice, it does not – *by itself* – follow the empirical cycle. This micro-cycle does, however, follow a sound, coherent process to produce an intervention in draft, partial, or final form.

Figure 3.4 shows a sample design research process, consisting of six micro-cycles. Often, several micro-cycles of activity are combined, e.g. in reporting, or before major decisions are made, thus creating meso-cycles. Like those shown in Figure 3.4, meso-cycles contain more than one of the three core phases, but less than a complete process of educational design research. For example, during a meso-cycle, an initial prototype could be created (design and construction) and tested (evaluation and reflection). The entire design research process, as reflected in the generic model, constitutes a macro-cycle. While a macro-cycle could be comprised of three micro-cycles (e.g. one from each phase), most educational design research macro-cycles involve numerous meso-cycles over long periods of time.

Analysis and exploration

The analysis and exploration phase constitutes one (empirical) micro-cycle; in terms of the regulative cycle described by van Strien (1975, 1997), it includes problem identification and diagnosis. During *analysis*, in-house expertise is sought and a literature review is conducted to gain theoretical inputs that will shape understanding of the problem, context, and other relevant topics (e.g. subject matter content analysis or teacher professional development strategies). The literature review is also important for developing a scientifically relevant angle for the study, where the problem in question can be seen as a particular instance of a research-worthy phenomenon. In addition, collaboration with practitioners is sought to shape a better understanding of the educational problem to be addressed, the target context, and stakeholder needs. As the understanding of the problem and setting begins to solidify, a more open-ended *exploration* takes place, where similar problems and their solutions are explored. The main products resulting from this phase are both practical and theoretical. From the practical perspective, this phase generates a clear understanding of the problem and its origins as well as specification of long-range goals. In addition, partial design requirements are determined by exploring the opportunities and boundary conditions present; and initial design propositions are generated based on contextual insights. From the theoretical perspective, this phase produces a descriptive and analytical understanding of the given class of problems, as manifested in this case within a particular context.

Design and construction

During design and construction, a coherent process is followed and documented to arrive at a (tentative) solution to the problem. Unlike the other two main phases which follow empirical cycles based on a research chain of reasoning, the micro-cycle of design and construction resembles that of creating (not testing) a conceptual model. It involves rational, purposeful consideration of available knowledge, as well as puzzling over the relationships and arrangements of concepts that are both internally consistent and externally useful. To emphasize the interaction between conceptualization and creation, we describe this as a deliberative–generative cycle. During *design* (similar to planning, in van Strien's [1975, 1997] regulative cycle), potential solutions to the problem are generated, explored and considered, then mapped using a variety of techniques. In this stage, the core ideas underpinning the design – including their theoretical and/or practical grounding – are articulated, which enable the underlying design framework to be shared and critiqued. In addition, guidelines for actually building the solution are delineated. *Construction* refers to the process of taking design ideas and applying them to actually manufacture the solution. This generally takes place through a prototyping approach, where successive approximations of the desired solution are (re-)created. The results of this phase from the practical perspective are obvious: the intervention is conceived and assembled. From a theoretical perspective, the frameworks underpinning design as well as the justification for design decisions are articulated.

Evaluation and reflection

Like the analysis and exploration phase, the evaluation and reflection phase constitutes one (empirical) micro-cycle. The work conducted in this phase can be compared to evaluation in van Strien's (1975, 1997) regulative cycle. We use the term evaluation in a broad sense, to refer to the empirical testing that is done with a design (that is, the – not yet applied – frameworks that underpin the intervention) or a constructed intervention (that is, the embodiments of design in initial, partial or final form). As discussed in Chapter 1, *evaluation* may pertain to testing conducted on or through an intervention. Depending on various factors including long- or short-term goals, the type of intervention and a project's stage of development, evaluations may study: soundness, feasibility, local viability, broader institutionalization, immediate effectiveness, and/or long-term impact. *Reflection* involves active and thoughtful consideration of what has come together in both research and development (including theoretical inputs, empirical findings, and subjective reactions) with the aim of producing theoretical understanding. Reflection is benefitted most when approached through a combination of systematic and organic techniques. The results of empirical findings as well as critical reflection are then used to accept, refine, or refute the conjectures, frameworks, or principles that are portrayed in design documents (e.g. design frameworks) or embodied in actual (prototypes of) interventions. From a practical perspective, the activities in this phase lead to ideas for redesign and/ or conclusions about a particular intervention. From a theoretical perspective, the knowledge produced by the combined activities in this phase contributes to a broader theoretical understanding concerning either the type of intervention being studied (in research conducted on interventions) or phenomena directly related to the intervention (in research conducted through interventions).

Two main outputs

The generic model depicts two main outputs from educational design research: maturing interventions and theoretical understanding. Both outputs ripen over time and can be more locally relevant or more broadly applicable. The intervention itself contributes directly to practice (by addressing the problem at hand) and indirectly to theoretical understanding (as one example of how specific, articulated, design frameworks can be reified). The theoretical understanding is produced through (usually several) micro and/or meso-cycles of design research. The empirical findings and resulting conjectures provide important building blocks for theory, and can also contribute indirectly to practice as these ideas may be shared among professionals and used to build new interventions.

Interaction with practice: implementation and spread

As depicted in the generic model, each of the three main phases of research and development are approached from an implementation perspective; that is, from the mindset of working toward actual use. This is consistent with the action phase in van Strien's (1975, 1997) regulative cycle. From the very start, *implementation and spread* – including real contextual opportunities and constraints – are taken into consideration. The involvement of educational professionals begins early, and this involvement generally increases over time. This can include many kinds of professionals whose work relates to educational practice, such as: teachers, administrators, teacher educators, examination agencies, inspectorates, policy makers, and textbook publishers. During analysis and exploration, this involvement is geared primarily toward clarifying the problem and shaping understanding of constraints within which a design will have to operate. This includes anticipating how the design will align with the needs and wishes of practitioners and other stakeholders, as well as gaining a sense of important system factors related to the problem. During design and construction, practitioners can offer valuable ideas, serve as co-designers on a team, or even drive the endeavor. Even if practitioners are not involved directly in design and construction, this work is informed by an implementation perspective – that is, the choices made reflect anticipation of the messy, varied realities of educational contexts. While early design work may be evaluated outside the target setting, eventual testing in context is essential. Across the phases, implementation and spread are facilitated by refining understanding of determining factors, including: attributes of the intervention; strategies used for enabling implementation and spread; context and surrounding systems; and the actors involved.

Balancing analytical and creative mindsets

As is typical in the fields of instructional design and the learning sciences, the existing literature on educational design research places strong emphasis on the analytical processes involved in analysis, design, and evaluation. The roles of theory and empiricism are dominant, as are the values of transparency and discipline. We embrace these perspectives wholeheartedly. At the same time, we are inspired by work in the fields of curriculum as well as the engineering sciences that value and encourage creativity in design. This seems fitting, given that the interventions being designed here are innovations – new kinds of solutions to complex educational problems. The generic model therefore emphasizes the need to embrace and foster creativity in educational design research by drawing explicit attention to some parts of the process which have an observably creative orientation in the model presented above. While analysis, design, and evaluation also involve creativity, this orientation is particularly prominent in exploration, construction, and reflection. We also stress the role of creativity throughout Part II of this book. In the chapters on the core phases of analysis and exploration; design and construction; and evaluation and reflection, we offer strategies and perspectives that feed research and development work that is focused, rigorous, and critical and, at the same time, open-minded, imaginative, and resourceful.

From modeling educational design research to conducting it: toward Part II

The next section of this book provides guidance on actually conducting design research, and is structured by the generic model presented above. The first three chapters relate to the core processes of analysis and exploration; design and construction; and evaluation and reflection. Thereafter, attention is given to implementation and spread, also in relation to these three processes. As stressed in the first two chapters of this book, we reiterate here that design and development work in practice is not a linear process that lends itself easily to prescription (cf. Kirschner, Carr, van Merriënboer, & Sloep, 2002; Ross et al., 2008; Visscher-

Voerman, 1999) and the same is true of educational design research. The model presented in this chapter shows a flexible process, and the sequence of chapters in this book simply cannot represent the iterative, highly varied pathways that characterize design research projects.

Inspired by Lumsdaine, Lumsdaine and Shelnutt's (1999) "whole brain approach," to product engineering, the chapters in Part II use an analogy to describe the analytical and creative orientations across the three core phases of educational design research. We recommend that design researchers consciously pursue fulfillment of two roles: detective and inventor. The detective is highly rational, seeking knowledge that is grounded in evidence from the field and supported by scientific understanding. For example, literature's most famous detective, Sherlock Holmes, regularly cautioned the police against forming premature theories based on insufficient data. By contrast, the inventor is original, striving to innovate and embracing opportunity. This mindset is evident in the actions and words of Wilbur and Orville Wright, who invented the airplane; Orville Wright said, "If we all worked on the assumption that what is accepted as true is really true, there would be little hope of advance" (McFarland, 2000, p. 314). While the detective characteristics may seem more aligned with research and the inventor characteristics might be more obvious in development, our recommendations in Part II of this book integrate creative and analytical approaches in both research and development.

Part II

Core processes

Chapter 4

Analysis and exploration

John Dewey has been credited with saying that "A problem well stated is a problem half solved." The main goal of analysis during this phase of educational design research is problem definition. Through contextual analysis and needs assessment, as well as literature review, initial perceptions of the problem are refined and causes for the problem are explained. The main goal of exploration, which may be conducted alongside analysis activities, is to seek out and learn from how others have viewed and solved similar problems. Exploration is often conducted through site visits, professional meetings, and networking. This chapter describes the micro-cycle of analysis and exploration. It begins with an overview of the main activities and outputs in this phase. Then, the aforementioned perspectives of the detective and inventor are addressed, in light of analysis and exploration activities. Setting the stage for the remainder of the chapter, attention is given to what problems are, and examples are described of misconceived problems. Thereafter, the analysis process is discussed in detail, with attention to its objectives, and how to plan for, conduct, and make sense of the endeavor. Exploration is also addressed, followed by a description of the products generated during this phase.

Main activities and outputs

During the analysis and exploration phase, collaboration with practitioners is sought to shape a better understanding of the problem to be addressed. Literature review is carried out to assess if the problem is researchable and if educational design research can, indeed, make a needed contribution to both problem resolution and scientific understanding. If that is the case, then the results of the literature review are used to inform data collection efforts, and to build frameworks that help interpret the findings. Preliminary investigation of the environment in which the problem exists is conducted to define the problem, ascertain potential causes, explore the context and gain insight into the needs and wishes of stakeholders. As understanding of the problem begins to take shape, exploration into comparable contexts can shed new light on ways of viewing, clarifying, and solving problems. In addition, the process of reaching out to practitioners, experts, and researchers begins to create a network of "critical friends" who may be able to inform the

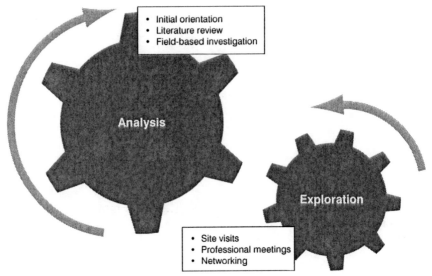

Figure 4.1 Main processes within the analysis and exploration phase

research. If these individuals and groups might eventually participate in the study, early involvement can help foster ownership in the solution. These activities are shown in Figure 4.1.

The primary result from this phase is a better understanding of the problem at hand, ideally in the form of clear problem definition and articulation of long-range goals. In addition, by clarifying contextual insights and exploring the boundaries of feasible changes that address the problem, partial design requirements as well as initial design propositions can be outlined. Design requirements are factors (often constraints) which should frame design choices (e.g. the project can modify learning activities, but the assessment system is fixed by external authorities and cannot be changed). Design requirements generated during this phase are tentative and partial, and relate to understanding needs and context (e.g. new learning activities must be aligned to the existing assessment system). During the phase of design and construction, additional design requirements are specified (e.g. relating to how the intervention will function).

Analytical and creative perspectives

As discussed at the close of the previous chapter, design research is served by both analytical and creative perspectives. While the analysis activities (literature review, problem definition, context analysis, and needs assessment) tend to be more analytical, and the exploration activities (site visits, professional meetings, networking with people) tend to be more open-ended, both are served by the detective and inventor roles. The detective is highly focused, systematic, and critical. This perspective particularly serves the analysis phase by helping identify and understand problems through evidence, warding off premature closure on

Table 4.1 Examples of analytical and creative perspectives during analysis and exploration

	The detective...	Tasks	The inventor...
Analysis	Reads for understanding	Literature review	Reads for inspiration
	Is assigned a problem	Problem definition	Uncovers an opportunity
	Studies what is	Context analysis	Questions why this is so
	Asks what is problematic	Needs assessment	Asks what is desirable
Exploration	Specifies pros and cons	Site visits Conferences and meetings	Seeks new paradigms
	Requests feedback	Networking with people	Asks for ideas

the causes of the problem and especially on promising solutions. By contrast, the inventor is open-minded, inquisitive, and resourceful. During the analysis phase, this mindset helps look for opportunity and un(der)tapped resources in the target setting that could be leveraged when designing solutions. Examples of how these perspectives inform each of the main tasks in the analysis and exploration phase are presented in Table 4.1. The analysis and exploration description given in this chapter strives to stimulate both the detective and the inventor orientations in design researchers.

Setting the stage for analysis and exploration

This first phase is often revisited

Bannan-Ritland and Baek (2008) refer to the different kinds of work conducted during this stage as "informed exploration." Edelson (2006) commented on the assumptions of design research, pointing out that:

> It begins with the basic assumption that existing practices are inadequate or can, at least, be improved upon, so that new practices are necessary. The underlying questions behind educational design research are the same as those that drive innovative design: What alternatives are there to current educational practices? How can these alternatives be established and sustained?
>
> (p. 103)

It is important to ask such questions at the start of an educational design research endeavor. But because new insights very often lead to new questions, we may also return to this phase, in search of new or deeper understanding. For example, if a design research team were testing an intervention, and discovered that it worked very well under Condition X, but poorly under Condition Y, this might cause the team to rethink some of their initial assumptions and ideas.

It might also cause them to ask, "How often do Condition X and Condition Y naturally present themselves? Why? Are there effective and sustainable ways to create Condition X?" Because most educational design research processes commence with this phase, the description given in this chapter is written from the perspective of exploring new problems. When this phase is revisited later in a design study, it may be shorter, but the same basic orientation still applies.

Legitimate problems versus solutions in search of problems

Throughout this book, we use the term "problem" as it is commonly used in instructional systems design – to describe the discrepancy between the existing and the desired situations. We use the term "solution" to describe the educational intervention (program, product, process, or policy) that is created in response to the problem at hand. Problems can relate to a wide range of areas. Some problems are identified more by practitioners, others are identified more by researchers; both are explored, confirmed, redefined, or cast off based on further investigation into both research perspectives (e.g. what does the literature say about this?) and practice perspectives (e.g. what do professionals say about this?). From the start, we begin to develop both theoretical perspectives (situating the problem among others in its class) and practical perspectives (addressing the immediate concerns of those involved) for viewing the same problem. Here are a few examples, on differing themes, showing theoretical and practical perspectives for each, respectively:

- Teacher turnover: The loss of high-quality teachers in underprivileged settings is in a downward spiral; less than half of the classes in this school have had a single teacher for the entire academic year; attrition during the academic year should be eliminated, or at least reduced to <10% to offer a more stable learning environment.
- Transfer: Students can accurately perform mathematical calculations for tests, but have difficulty determining which operations should be used in real life settings; too many graduates of our vocational educational and training program cannot get or keep jobs for which they should be qualified.
- Technology use: Teacher use of technology frequently constitutes mere replacement of existing (less complicated and expensive) materials, and sometimes even a decrease in the quality of learning interactions; only one of every eight middle school teachers in this district uses the tablet computers provided to them and their students in ways that are transformative with respect to how instruction is planned, implemented, and evaluated.

All of these examples constitute negative differences between the existing and the desired situations, and therefore they all can be legitimately viewed as problems. It is essential to separate legitimate problems from potential solutions. While this may sound obvious and easy to do, the temptation to start with a potential solution can be great, especially for new design projects. It is not uncommon to hear things like, "School leaders require training in intra-personal skills," "Mathematics learning should be more practical," or "Our teachers need to use more technology in the classrooms." These are not legitimate problems. Rather, they are proposed semi-solutions or, in some cases, solutions in search of problems.

Problems are verified in literature and practice

Educational design research begins with efforts to clarify the nature of the problem, its causes, and what would demonstrate resolution if the problem were to be solved. Even when a problem seems evident and potential solutions appear to be available already – in fact, especially when potential solutions are readily available – careful analysis and exploration are crucial to ensuring that a legitimate, research-worthy problem is being addressed. Not all useful research has its origins in problems defined by practice. For example, many researchers start from problems defined by existing (e.g. conflicting) data or gaps in literature. Adequately investigating how researchable a topic is, through literature, is necessary. The point here is not who offers up the problem to be examined, but rather, that the direct or indirect value of the research is seriously considered.

Setting a research agenda that is researchable and valuable to both practice and the development of theoretical understanding can be challenging. The goal is to unearth the most powerful overlap between researcher expertise/interests and practitioner needs/interests. It would be quite difficult to establish or build on a particular area of expertise if researchers simply went around asking practitioners willy-nilly about all the problems they would like to work on solving, and responded accordingly. At the same time, it is difficult for practitioners to appreciate the value that educational research has to bring if their only experience with it is being overwhelmed with requests to complete questionnaires, welcome observers into their schools, and skip lunches to give interviews, often for some vague project they don't really understand. During the initial process of analysis and exploration, we emphasize the need to respectfully and critically engage with practitioners in search of problems that: (a) they perceive and care enough about to bother solving; and (b) which also fall within the researcher(s) area of expertise. It is not uncommon for researchers to have identified a problem and tell practitioners that they probably suffer from it. Where feasible, we recommend a more open-ended approach: researchers specify theme areas related to their own expertise and interests, and ask practitioners if, within those areas, there are problems that they would like to seek to solve. This kind of conversation often takes place naturally when practitioners (or representatives thereof) participate in the research team or serve on an advisory board. We firmly believe that research partnerships which clearly start from a mutually beneficial stance set the stage for strong collaboration and yield the best results. At the same time, this approach can present considerable challenges, especially where external funding must be secured for work to commence. Please refer to Chapter 8 for more information on the value of "test-driving" core conceptions of the problem before a study is even formally proposed.

Analysis

About analysis

Blending reductionist and systems perspectives

Similar to why we advocate a balance between analytical and creative perspectives, we also encourage robust analysis to seek insights through a blend of reductionist and systems approaches. From the reductionist perspective, we seek to understand the problem, its direct and indirect causes, and to analyze each component. Here, understanding is sought by decomposing the problem situation into its constituent parts, and examining flaws in the components and/or their modes of interaction. This kind of approach can be very useful, especially for identifying the root causes of certain problems. It helps ensure that we will design solutions, and not merely treat symptoms. But to understand problems fully (and especially to design solutions to them), we also need a holistic understanding of the problem, and how components in its system interact. This usually requires immersing oneself in the phenomenon and its surrounding system, getting a good feel for it, and trying to make sense of why things are as such. Systems are composed of dynamic and complex sets of elements that, through interaction, function as a whole. Educational systems, like human bodies, are extremely complex; their inner-workings are far from being comprehensively understood. In addition, some aspects of the system are more subject to being influenced, or manipulated, whereas change can be difficult or impossible in other aspects of the system. The systems lens helps us to acknowledge changeable elements and those that seem unchangeable, and to seek out elements which are receptive for improvement.

Using both reductionist and systems perspectives during analysis, the aim is first to portray the situation as it is and provide explanations for this; second to assess what is desired; and third, to distinguish between potentially changeable and unchangeable elements in the target setting. The search for changeable and non-changeable elements can be referred to as exploring the jurisdiction of change. In legal terms, jurisdiction refers to the area within which a judge has the authority to make rulings. It can be a physical area (e.g. the fifth district court of appeals of California or the Supreme Court for Germany) or a legal area (e.g. civil litigation or criminal law). In designing interventions, the jurisdiction of change refers to the area(s) within which the design project is able (by own authority or through influence) to decide upon and implement change. Studying the jurisdiction of change entails looking at the context and asking things like, "Where, in the regular schedule of these busy teachers, can time for project work be created? Could existing department meetings be restructured? At what costs? How many extra hours would teachers be willing to donate? What if we pay for release time? How long would each option be sustainable?" It is important to ascertain which important factors can be changed, and which (within the scope of the project) cannot. For example, in light of Burkhardt's (1987) high stakes assessment maxim, What You Test Is What You Get (WYTIWYG), it might be reasonable to ask: "We can change the intended curriculum, but can we make commensurate changes in how learners are assessed?" Understanding the jurisdiction of change helps to design interventions suitable for actual use, beyond pilot testing.

Three main activities

Three main activities are undertaken to conduct analysis: initial orientation, literature review, and field-based investigation. Initial orientation, together with practitioners, begins to clarify the project in ways that are mutually beneficial to the parties involved. In contrast to a narrower, more focused literature review to inform the selected solution (see Chapter 5), a broad literature review is conducted toward the start of the analysis to gain theoretical inputs that will shape understanding of the problem, context, and relevant topics. Insights from literature are used to focus data collection during the field-based investigation, and to create frameworks for data analysis. During the field-based investigation, data are collected to portray the setting, its actors, mechanisms, and other relevant factors. It is also essential to explore the extent to which the problem is experienced by stakeholders as one worth fixing.

The three activities may be undertaken sequentially, but it is important to note that some of them may take place concurrently. In fact, these activities frequently develop in parallel and often even, in interaction with, one another. For example, it is quite common for literature review to begin early on and, while the review process informs field-based investigation, insights from literature may continue to be refined throughout the entire analysis and exploration phase.

The analysis concludes by synthesizing findings from all three tasks. Taken together, it is then possible to write a refined, complete problem statement which is both descriptive and explanatory. That is, it describes both the problem in detail and explains its root causes. In addition, several inputs for the design phase of design research are generated: long-range goals, partial design requirements, and initial design propositions.

Initial orientation

The analysis begins by writing a draft problem statement. These are usually descriptive, and incomplete in nature, like: "Current approaches to educating second language learners entering our postsecondary education institution are insufficient" and/or: "65% of all second graders in the district score below the national average on literacy exams, while the school district's target is no less than 30%." Initial orientation is largely informal, and conducted together with practitioners or professionals who experience the problem firsthand and ideally in their setting. In some cases, the initial orientation may have already started at the time of proposal writing. Depending on the problem that has been identified, various stakeholders from practice might be involved, such as teachers, students, administrators, or parents. Initial orientation can take place in various ways, though participation in (public) meetings about the problem and conversations with various stakeholders are probably the most common. Together, a draft problem statement is discussed, along with other factors that need to be understood in order to address the problem. The central question guiding the initial orientation is: "What do we want to know?" It can be useful to break this question down into the orientations previously discussed. These three questions can be used to set the meeting agenda:

- What do we want to know about the problem?
- What do we want to know about the context?
- What do we want to know about stakeholder needs and wishes?

About the problem

With regard to the problem, there are at least three issues that need to be probed during initial orientation: *What is the current situation?*; *What is the desired situation?*; and *What is already known or suspected about causes for this discrepancy?* Additionally, the problem needs to be portrayed in the system within which it resides. For this, questions are asked about the context.

About the context

The kinds of contextual factors that could be studied vary with the kinds of problems posed. The following six concerns can be useful in many educational design research projects:

- Stakeholders: Who is involved, directly and indirectly?
- Target group: What are their attitudes, abilities, knowledge, skills, and relevant demographic characteristics (e.g. uniformity of group; ages; experience, etc.)?
- Physical context: What facilities, infrastructure, software, and/or supplies are available? Which ones could feasibly be made available?
- Organizational/policy context: To what extent does the organization or sub-unit possess the autonomy and jurisdiction to make change? What policies and practices are relevant to the problem? What explicit and hidden power structures are present?
- Educational context: What does the current situation look like (e.g. content, pedagogy, exams, etc.)? What inter-curricular connections deserve particular attention when considering changes (e.g. other subjects, examinations, teacher development)?
- Viability: What are the strengths, weaknesses, opportunities, and threats (SWOTs) that would enable or hinder change in this setting?

During initial orientation, these contextual questions are not all answered. Rather, researchers and practitioners together examine these contextual questions and decide which ones are especially relevant to the problem at hand. A set of research questions is drafted, and ideas are exchanged on how to go about answering them. Greater understanding of the people involved (stakeholders) nearly always warrants further investigation, as described below.

About needs and wishes

Central to understanding stakeholder needs and wishes is determining the extent to which the parties involved view the problem as one worth addressing. Very rarely will this question yield a simple yes or no answer. Probing this question usually uncovers some explanations for the problem situation, and/or shapes understanding of the supports or hurdles that must be taken into consideration when designing a solution. During initial orientation, the task is to decide whose needs and wishes must be explored, and to discuss ideas about how that could be approached.

In many cases, the initial orientation marks the start of collaboration. As such, it also provides a vehicle through which researchers and practitioners begin to establish common ground and understand each other's perspectives (if they do not have these already). Researchers start to gain a sense of the day-to-day realities in which the practitioner problems are situated. At the same time, practitioners are exposed to the systematic, methodical approaches characteristic of the researchers. Expectations begin to be set for both parties, and this is also a time where initial ideas about roles begin to be exchanged. Example issues include: When might it be feasible for researchers to collect data? Could teachers also collect data? What degree of involvement is desired by the school or institution in designing a solution to this problem? While it is not yet the time for making any of these decisions, initial orientation should provide some inputs for thinking about these kinds of issues.

Literature review

The literature review serves two main purposes: it provides ideas which can help shape data collection and it can be used to identify frameworks (or important elements thereof) for data analysis. In conducting a literature review, it is often useful to assume that the problem which has been identified, or at least many of the themes associated with the problem, have been experienced elsewhere and actually studied. The literature review is best served by creating questions that are, in essence, posed "to" the literature. The literature review questions can be generated by thinking about this main question: "What can literature tell us about this kind of problem; this type of context; and given these, typical concerns of these kinds of stakeholders?" The goal of the literature review is not to find the answer to the question, "What should we do to solve this problem?" Rather the goal is to unpack and understand how others have experienced this or similar problems, and to examine how and why these problems were addressed, with what results.

Returning to the example where only one out of eight middle school teachers are using the tablet computers provided to them and their students in educationally transformative ways, literature review could explore such issues as: research on the use of tablet computers in schools; difficulties and successes in implementing tablet or laptop programs; learner attainment when tablets are used; or teacher and pupil attitudes toward the use of tablet computers. It could also explore barriers to technology use, as well as teaching, learning, and assessment practices involving tablet integration into middle school curricula. The insights gained from reviewing such literature could help clarify the nature of the problem and assist in the design of data collection instruments to be employed during the field-based investigation.

Many outstanding resources are available for guiding the literature review. Please refer to the Appendix for a list of sources giving detailed descriptions of this process. The following 10 steps are common to most literature review processes, including those conducted during early stages of analysis and exploration in a design research project.

1   Identify themes.
2   Draft research questions posed to literature.
3   Create a search plan.
4   Conduct the search.
5   Read abstracts to identify papers worth obtaining.
6   Obtain and scan full papers; snowball sample authors/journals/bookshelves.
7   Read and take notes from each source.
8   Group notes according to emerging themes.
9   Synthesize the groups of ideas.
10 Report the literature review.

Field-based investigation

Ideally, the field-based investigation affords researchers the opportunity to become somewhat immersed in the problem context and to begin to develop and refine ideas about why things are as such. In line with the initial orientation and the literature review, the field-based investigation is carried out toward three main goals: problem definition, context analysis, and needs assessment. The process follows an empirical cycle. Excellent resources are available for guiding the process of research planning, data collection, and data analysis, including those listed in the Appendix. The description in this section focuses primarily on specific concerns for educational design research.

Refining questions and selecting strategies to answer them

Draft analysis questions were formulated in the initial orientation. Based on insights from the literature review, it can be useful to revisit the draft analysis questions and consider revising them. Once the analysis questions are refined, attention must be given to determining the kinds of settings and actors that will be able to provide the information necessary to understand the problem, context, and stakeholder needs. Building on the work of McKenney (2001), four strategies are presented here: policy synthesis, field portrait, perception poll, and a SWOT analysis.

While not all strategies will be used in each instance, the first three strategies, policy synthesis, field portrait, and perception poll, are most powerful when conducted together. The rationale behind this stems from Goodlad, Klein, and Tye's (1979) curriculum representations, briefly discussed in Chapter 3. By studying the formal curriculum (policy synthesis), perceived curriculum (perception poll), and operational curriculum (field portrait) discrepancies between them can be identified, along with some of the causes for the discrepancies. Taken together, these strategies can also help shape understanding of factors that determine the implementation and spread of a potential solution.

The policy synthesis helps to understand the existing, formal mechanisms that steer teaching and learning in a particular context. It entails reading, discussing, and synthesizing policy documents and regulations related to the problem and its surrounding context. In a K-12 context, policy documents that may be studied include state standards, district action plans, or school protocols. In higher education, analogous policy documents can be obtained from governing bodies (e.g. Board of Regents) or professional associations (e.g. EDUCAUSE).

The perception poll strategy gathers information on stakeholder perceptions of the problem and their own context, as well as beliefs, attitudes, feelings, needs, and wishes. Relevant stakeholder perceptions could include those of teachers, children, parents, administrators, support staff, or other relevant groups. While stakeholder perceptions can be collected in written form, they are usually best obtained verbally, most often through interviews and focus group discussions.

The field portrait aims to gain a clear understanding of what is actually happening in the problem context. Depending on the problem, field portraits may portray organizations, schools, classrooms, teacher meetings, campuses, or other settings. Observations and often document analysis (e.g. of student work) are generally the most useful for obtaining an objective assessment of what is actually happening in the field.

The SWOT analysis brings another lens to seeing a problem, and can also provide inputs for considering solutions. A SWOT analysis examines the strengths, weaknesses, opportunities, and threats present within a particular context that (a) contribute to the problem; and/or (b) might help or hinder implementation of a solution to the problem. The four elements are defined here:

- Strengths: Attributes of the immediate target setting that mitigate the problem and/or could facilitate a solution, e.g. classroom teachers highly motivated to work on the problem.
- Weaknesses: Attributes of the immediate target setting that contribute to the problem and/or could hinder a solution, e.g. lack of supportive expertise to guide work on the problem.
- Opportunities: External conditions that mitigate the problem and/or could facilitate a solution, e.g. central management deems the problem worthy of addressing.
- Threats: External conditions that that contribute to the problem and/or could hinder a solution, e.g. budgets must be cut in the next year.

Strategies are usually selected based primarily on the research questions, and secondarily on the constraints of the study (e.g., time, personnel, costs, access to respondents). To decide which strategies to use, it can be useful to visualize how each one will relate to the analysis questions. A chart like the one offered in Table 4.2 may help. Generic analysis questions are given as examples, relating to the three main tasks of problem definition, context analysis, and needs assessment. Grey cells indicate potentially suitable strategies.

Determining methods

Once strategies for the field-based investigation have been selected, it makes sense to explore the most appropriate methods for obtaining the necessary

Table 4.2 Questions and strategies matrix

	Questions	Policy synthesis	Field portrait	Perception poll	SWOT analysis
Problem related	1. How is the problem related to discrepancies between policy, perceptions and/or practice?	▓	▓		
	2. How do stakeholders perceive the problem? Why do stakeholders think it exists?			▓	
	3. How does the problem manifest itself? What does it look like?		▓		
	4. What factors in this setting mitigate or contribute to the problem?				▓
Context related	5. What are the relevant organizational and curricular policies and regulations?	▓			
	6. What does current practice look like?		▓		
	7. What are stakeholder feelings, beliefs, attitudes, knowledge, skills, and relevant demographic characteristics?			▓	
	8. What factors would inhibit or enable a change in this setting?				▓
	9. Within what constraints would a solution have to function?				▓
Needs related	10. To what extent do stakeholders experience this as a problem worth fixing?			▓	
	11. What are stakeholder ideas pertaining to potential solutions?			▓	▓

information. Educational design research makes use of the same qualitative and quantitative methodological tools and strategies as other research genres. Given the nature of the leading questions at this stage, however, there is a tendency for qualitative methods to dominate in the analysis and exploration phase.

Choosing methods for a field-based investigation can be difficult. Obviously, the links between the affordances of particular methods and the questions being asked should be determinants in method selection. In addition, it is advisable to view the field-based investigation as a whole, and look for (combinations of) methods that make efficient use of available time and resources. In making choices, it is also preferable to employ several methods per question, as methods triangulation yields a more robust data set. Finally, it is important to ensure that various participant groups are heard. This helps (a) ensure a balanced portrayal of the situation; (b) achieve respondent triangulation; and (c) create broader ownership of the project.

Seven methods are among the most common for use during the analysis and exploration phase: interviews; focus groups; observations; questionnaires; tests; logbooks; and document analysis. The list below offers brief comments on using each of these methods during the analysis and exploration phase. Table 4.3 offers generic recommendations for methods suitable to the four strategies described above.

- Interviews: Can be used to deliberately target different kinds of stakeholders (e.g. experienced, novice; long-timers, newcomers) for their views of the problem and firsthand (emic) understandings.
- Focus groups: Can allow opportunities to gather insights about the problem, as participants bounce ideas off each other, and about the social interaction among the participants.
- (Non-)Participant observations: Can allow firsthand opportunities to see the problem or its context. The tools used may be more open, like a descriptive running summary (wherein the observer takes notes related to

Table 4.3 Strategies and methods matrix

Methods	Policy synthesis	Field portrait	Perception poll	SWOT analysis
Interviews	▓	▓	▓	▓
Focus groups			▓	▓
Observations		▓		
Questionnaires	▓	▓	▓	▓
(Pre-)tests		▓		
Logbook		▓		
Document analysis	▓	▓		

Legend: dark grey = highly recommended; light grey = may be useful in addition, depending on the circumstances.

observations, avoiding on the spot interpretations, e.g. "the teacher was interrupted by student misbehavior at least 10 times each hour" not "the teacher's class was unruly"); or more closed, like a checklist (wherein a list of possible observations, often drawn from the literature review, is used to record observations).

- Questionnaires: Can be helpful, if used sparingly – too much of these early on will not curry favor with most participants, who already have so many other demands on their time; online questionnaires, once a novelty, have become so commonplace that participants may ignore them. Shorter ones are more likely to be completed.
- (Pre-)Tests: Can be very helpful in establishing a baseline for later and understanding the current situation in the educational context.
- Logbooks: Can be also be perceived as labor-intensive, and are most useful with a few, easy to answer questions.
- Document analysis: Can be conducted using more open coding, or with the aid of a pre-formatted checklist, and can also include analysis of learning/performance assessments.

Planning

After the strategies and methods for the field-based investigation have been selected, it is necessary to plan for conducting the research activities. Especially since the research will be conducted in authentic settings, this usually entails a negotiation between the ideal research plan and that which is feasible within the project context. Thinking through such a negotiation therefore requires that consideration be given to the opportunities and constraints which could influence how activities are conducted. As planning for reality sets in, it could mean making additions or concessions with regard to the methods to be used. This often takes place through an iterative process as a plan for obtaining and analyzing the findings of the field-based investigation is written, discussed, and revised. Eventually, the plan should summarize decisions made thus far in the analysis, including the draft problem statement, research questions and main ideas from literature that will shape the field-based investigation. It should also map out the decisions made regarding strategies and methods.

Thereafter, the research plan should show how strategies and methods will actually be employed. It should demonstrate that careful, critical yet realistic attention has been given to the following considerations:

- Time: Given the strategies and methods selected, realistic allotments should be made for the time needed to create instruments, engage participants, collect data, analyze data, and report on the findings. Table 4.4 offers a sample timeline that, through grey shading, shows some typical parallel processes in a field-based investigation during this phase.
- Money: Although some costs may be covered through overhead budgets, a realistic budget should be made for the resources needed to create instruments (e.g. consultation with measurement specialists), engage

Table 4.4 Sample timeline for field-based investigation

Task	Sub-task/project week	1	2	3	4	5	6	7	8	9	10	11	12
Instrument drafting and revision	Interview scheme	■	■										
	Focus group agenda		■	■									
	Observation scheme		■	■									
	Document analysis checklist		■	■									
Participant engagement	Revisit participating institutions	■	■										
	Contact individual participants	■	■										
Data collection	Interviews			■	■								
	Focus group discussions				■	■	■						
	Observations					■	■						
	Document analysis						■	■					
Data analysis	Summaries						■	■	■				
	Syntheses								■	■			
Reporting	First draft									■	■		
	Feedback/revision/second draft											■	
	Feedback/revision/final report												■
Logistics	Purchase/reserve equipment	■											
	Arrange student assistants	■	■										
	Follow-up/thanks to participants											■	■

participants (e.g. communications costs), collect data (e.g. audio-video equipment, participant remuneration), analyze data (e.g. research assistants), and report on the findings (e.g. printing costs).

- Policies: The plan should also delineate how the research approach will accommodate important policies set by the research organization and/or the research setting (e.g. confidentiality, ethics, and participant welfare). Most research organizations offer guidelines on this through an Institutional Review Board (IRB) or Institutional Ethics Committee (IEC). Any data collected in schools will need to be approved by the local and perhaps district administration, a process that can take weeks rather than days.

When the plan is complete, it can be useful to obtain critical feedback from peers and/or external experts. But before asking others, it can be useful to consider the following:

- Take a look at the main analysis questions. Do they ask all that they should? Wander off-topic? Are there other questions that could or should be asked? Is the wording of the questions appropriate?

- Examine the actual strategies to be used (policy synthesis, field portrait, perception poll, SWOT analysis) as well as the methods planned (interviews, focus groups, observations, questionnaires, [pre-]tests, logbooks, document analysis). Are they logically the best strategies for answering the questions? Are these choices feasible, given the time, expertise, and resources available to the project?
- Who will do these things? Especially if working in a team, a field-based investigation plan should specify who will do which activities when.

Creating instruments

In order to collect data, it is necessary to design the instruments to be used in the study, or to obtain and possibly fine-tune existing instruments that have already been created and validated. In both cases, the core constructs addressed in each particular instrument should be clearly related to the research questions. This means that they will be aligned with specific aspects of the problem, the context, and/or participant needs and wishes.

Engaging participants

Depending on the questions being asked, different types of respondent groups can be useful in the field-based investigation during this phase. Populations commonly represented include people from the target group (e.g. teachers, learners); stakeholders (e.g. administrators, parents); and/or experts (e.g. pedagogy/subject area specialists, experienced policy makers). Selection of respondent types is driven primarily by the research questions being asked (e.g. whose perspectives will be useful in answering this question?) and secondarily by what is feasible (e.g. which people are accessible within the scope of this project?). At this stage, the sampling is often purposive or based on convenience, though random or stratified sampling can also be useful, depending on the questions being asked. If practitioners are in the design research team, they may have especially practical recommendations for how to gather information.

Collecting data

Specific procedures for data collection vary with the questions being asked and the instruments being used. However, data collection during this phase of educational design research frequently tends to demonstrate characteristics of naturalistic inquiry. Careful observation of an educational setting and the people in it, functioning under normal circumstances, is often necessary to begin to fully understand the problem and its underlying causes. In addition to the formally planned data sources, a field journal and (video) camera can be extremely useful. These tools can help document unplanned observations directly; indirectly, using them may prompt reflection and the generation of emerging insights.

Data analysis

The data analyzed in this phase tend to be more qualitative, though questionnaires and assessments might involve quantitative data. The books listed in the Appendix also provide guidance on the analysis of both quantitative and qualitative data. In addition to generic software such as Excel, some packages are particularly suited to and heavily used in social sciences research, such as SPSS for quantitative data analysis and N/Vivo or Atlas/ti for qualitative data analysis. The concerns that crop up while conducting data analysis during this phase of educational design research are not dissimilar from those that can crop up in other kinds of studies. Two important concerns are representativeness and trustworthiness of data. Representativeness refers to how well the data actually represent the problem, the context, and/or participant voices. Trustworthiness pertains to how valid and reliable each source of data is. Some data sources may be more representative and/or trustworthy than others. During data analysis, the quality of the data must be assessed and weighted. In addition to reducing and summarizing the data, emerging insights might point to the need for new questions to be "posed" to the data to gain a better understanding of the problem, context, and personal perspectives. For example, after observing that the problem manifests itself in differing levels of intensity, the data might be probed to explore: What does the problem look like in its most extreme form? How often does this occur? What seems to trigger this form of the problem? Is there consensus among stakeholders on the severity of the problem? Answers to the main research questions are generated and, after weighing the evidence (possibly together with participants through a member-check), conclusions are drawn.

Reporting

Field-based investigations conclude with reports that document the inception, process, and conclusions. While report formats can vary widely, two are distinguished here: project reports and journal articles. Project reports are often written from the practical perspective. They are intended for an internal audience (e.g. project team members, funding organizations) and focus almost primarily on the field-based investigation, often – though not always – with limited attention to related literature (assuming that the literature review has already been produced separately). Project reports often include more attention to how the findings that emerge from the field-based investigation will inform the next phase of the project (especially design goals and criteria). Very often, project reports, once they have served to inform stakeholders or stimulate project team deliberation, can be used as the basis for journal articles. But journal articles do differ. The main distinction is that journal articles are written to a broader scientific community, from a more theoretical perspective. This type of writing usually portrays the field-based investigation as a manifestation of a particular phenomenon (e.g. para-teacher learning needs in NGOs, or university instructor knowledge, skills, and attitudes regarding conducting assessment online). Serving as an example for a broader audience concerned with similar issues, more attention is usually given to related literature and instances of that phenomenon, understanding the problem and describing its origins, with comparatively less emphasis on implications for design. Although it may be difficult to replicate design studies, the reports should provide sufficient detail so that others can use the same methods and compare/contrast the results from other settings. Readers should also be able to analyze the findings independently to see if they draw the same conclusions. Both types of reports follow the same basic format, roughly: introduction and problem statement; theoretical framework; study design and methods; findings; discussion and conclusion.

Exploration

Objectives of exploration

As the conceptualization of the problem, and the context in which it is situated, begins to take shape, a more open-ended exploration is set into motion. The term "exploration" is used to denote the nature of this work, which entails finding new ways to look at problems and their solutions, as well as seeking out "the 'invented wheels'" others have developed to address (elements of) the problem, and discovering how they went about it. Investigating how others have viewed and solved related problems is useful for several reasons. First, this helps to refine understanding of the problem at hand as a manifestation of a certain phenomenon. A richer understanding can be constructed by exploring the work of others and becoming familiar with other instantiations of that phenomenon. Second, exploration of how similar problems have been tackled can allow design researchers to stand on the shoulders of others, and thereby get further, faster than they could on their own. Third, this process inevitably serves to motivate and inspire, usually by example (e.g. "Wow – I would love to be a part of something as rich and meaningful as this"), but sometimes through counter-example (e.g. "Our team can really do something that no one else has successfully tackled in a substantial way"). Finally, establishing networks with like-minded designers and researchers can serve the development work for years to come. Although not without focus, exploration is open-ended and flexible.

Strategies for conducting exploration

Much of the exploration in design research is informal. It is also generally an ongoing process, which takes place in the background while the more formal research activities (e.g. literature review, field-based investigation) remain at the forefront. For these reasons, it is often at threat of being poorly documented and snowed under when deadlines or more visible tasks require attention. This is part of why it is prominently included in the generic model. For the reasons given above, we consider exploration to be extremely useful, and argue that robust design and insightful design research are virtually impossible without it. The informal nature of exploration should not be confused with unplanned. On the contrary, it is highly recommended to plan activities that will allow exploration to take place, especially during the initial phases of a design study. Here, attention is given to three common activities: site visits (e.g. to schools, programs, training centers); professional meetings (e.g. professional and practitioner conferences first, research conferences second); and networking.

Site visits

In this face-paced day and age where we are both aided and challenged by the affordances of technology (e.g. video conferencing can save time and money; it can also be problematic, technically and socially), we feel compelled to emphasize that there is no substitute for paying visits to the physical places where solutions to educational problems come to life. Site visits usually take 1–2 days, and are often facilitated by a loose agenda that includes some time to get to know key players, discuss how design (research) is happening, and see the solutions and products being developed, ideally as they are used in the target setting. Plan to keep personal notes during site visits, and possibly take photographs. It can be wise to bring along a flash drive also, so that hosts can share information on the spot. Formal reports of site visits are rarely efficient, but it can be very practical to use email to thank hosts, recapitulate discussions/agreements, and to inform colleagues, while simultaneously transforming field notes and other salient data into easily retrievable archives.

Professional meetings

Though more formal than site visits, conferences and meetings are natural venues for conducting exploration, as attendees generally come to these with a "show-n-tell" mindset. That is, conferences are places where people come to present the work they have been doing and learn about that of others. To see the inner workings of designed solutions to educational problems, meetings of practitioners and other education professionals are especially useful, such as those of the relevant professional associations, trade shows, or special interest groups. Research conferences can also be useful, but these generally focus less on presenting designed solutions. While design researchers tend to have little difficulty getting to know fellow researchers, many encounter powerful "eye-opening" experiences when attending professional meetings, especially the first time.

Networking

Obviously, the site visits and conferences provide outstanding opportunities for networking. Networking is not a separate activity, but rather an essential component of any professional life. However, it is mentioned specifically here for newer researchers who are just beginning to establish professional contacts. It is rare to know ahead of time how a particular personal connection will play out (or not) at the time that it is made. When it comes to design research networks, external contacts can evolve into various formal or informal roles, including advisory boards, critical friends, expert evaluators, guest members of the team, etc. Having and showing curiosity about the work of another is the best way to naturally build a true network. Though it may sound obvious, it is especially important to take the time to become familiar with the work of an individual or team. When possible, be well-prepared – read about the work ahead of time and be ready to ask questions that are of genuine interest and also let that interest be seen. Doctoral students who have met leading researchers in person for the first time often express surprise at how approachable and helpful the scholar is. This positive interaction is greatly enhanced when a proper amount of "homework" has been done.

Products resulting from this phase

Findings from the literature review, problem definition, and field-based investigation are synthesized to produce four main products resulting from this phase: revised problem definition; long-range goals; partial design requirements; and initial design propositions. All of these products will feed into the next phase of design and construction. While each of the products is distinct, they are all based on the results from the main activities in this phase. Developing each product may best be done interactively, rather than in isolation. For example, thinking through and generating a refined problem statement may fine-tune ideas for the design requirements; design requirements (often constraints, which frame design choices) may influence long-range goals; and so on. As these outputs are finalized, it is important to ensure that they are well aligned before commencing to design and construction.

Problem definition

The problem definition describes the discrepancy between the existing and desired situations; and offers empirically grounded explanations for why the state of affairs is as such. Based on the findings of the field-based investigation, a refined, complete problem statement which is both descriptive and explanatory is created. Though it should be clear where additional detailed information can be found in a report, the problem definition should be succinct, and understandable to outsiders. Some examples of descriptive and explanatory problem statements are given below, including findings from both literature review and field-based investigation:

- Teacher turnover: The loss of high-quality teachers in underprivileged settings is in a downward spiral; less than half of the classes in this school have had a single teacher for the entire academic year; attrition during the academic year should be eliminated, or at least reduced to <10% to offer a more stable learning environment. Explanations include:
  - Teacher mentoring is perceived as weak or non-existent.
  - Classroom management challenges are a major reason for teacher attrition.

- Administrators are not perceived as helpful with respect to supporting new teachers.
- Based on school climate monitoring, the organizational conditions present are not conducive to stability.

• Transfer: Students can accurately perform mathematical calculations for tests but have difficulty determining which operations should be used in real life settings; too many graduates of our vocational educational and training program cannot get or keep jobs for which they should be qualified. Explanations include:
- The current curriculum offers contextualized practice (e.g. word problems) but very little authentic opportunities to practice choosing and using mathematical operations in real world contexts.
- Literature and resources for embedding authentic tasks in vocational curricula have expanded greatly in the last decade, but this trend is slower to permeate educational institutions.
- Given the current economic climate and remuneration in these industries, many graduates end up working two jobs and are often tired and distracted.
- Advice for first year students is poorly structured and not widely used. Students choose major fields of study through trial and error rather than through career and academic counseling.

• Technology use: Teacher use of technology frequently constitutes mere replacement of existing (less complicated and expensive) materials, and sometimes even a decrease in the quality of learning interactions; only one of every eight middle school teachers in this district uses the tablet computers provided to them and their students in ways that are transformative with respect to how instruction is planned, implemented, and evaluated. Explanations include:
- It is well documented that teachers struggle to align technology use in general and tablet use in particular with other dimensions of their lesson planning (e.g. objectives, instructional activities, and assessment).
- Several teachers are disinclined to learn how to integrate the tablets because colleagues at another school in the district have reported unfavorable experiences.
- Half of the teachers are concerned that the time needed to integrate the tablets will distract from instructional preparation for high-stakes tests; and they worry that their students would not perform well on these assessments.
- Technical issues such as recharging the tablets and breakage are a major concern for teachers.

Long-range goal

Long-range goals specify the overall aim of the intervention, based on the analysis and exploration which have shaped an understanding of both the problem at hand, and participant needs and wishes. In some cases, the ultimate design goal may relate closely to the original problem statement (e.g. related to the third example above, "the goal of the project is to have all of the district's teachers sufficiently knowledgeable, comfortable and confident in using tablet computers in ways that move instruction from a teacher-centered model to a learner-centered model"). In other cases, the analysis could have revealed such substantial underlying concerns, that one or more of these becomes the main focus (e.g. related to the teacher attrition example above, the goal of the project will be to address classroom management challenges). Very often, multiple goals will need to be weighed and prioritized. The final result should be one rationally chosen, clear, realistic, and measurable statement. While it is likely that sub-goals will be integrated, a single ultimate goal should be named. Refining the long-range goal to best describe a single ultimate goal helps weigh priorities and sharpen the project focus.

Partial design requirements

Based primarily on the SWOT analysis and literature review, design requirements are given for the solution being designed. The term "design requirements" comes from engineering design and is used to refer to criteria that frame a design task. Design requirements can relate to the function of an intervention, or how it must be tailored for those involved; these aspects are delineated in the next phase of educational design research, design and construction (hence, we speak of *partial* design requirements, here). But design requirements can also relate to specific information about the problem, setting, or stakeholders that must be taken into consideration when developing solutions. Design requirements translate such information into operational criteria that must be met. They often focus on factors that determine implementation. Design requirements are important because they give a design and construction team understanding of the freedoms and constraints within which they can operate. The more the team understands these boundaries, the better they will be able to think productively about realistic design alternatives. In addition, explicit attention to these boundaries can help to mitigate the risk of premature closure on solutions.

Often, the design requirements fall into the categories of freedoms, opportunities, and constraints, all of which help to clarify the project's jurisdiction of change. Understanding the jurisdiction of change is essential to designing for actual, and especially sustained, use. It means assessing what, in the long run, a given project can realistically aim to accomplish and what challenges are beyond its scope. For example, high degrees of freedom are often associated with teaching and learning resources and pedagogical strategies, since teachers generally have some level of curricular autonomy to experiment with these. Opportunities are frequently found by studying intrinsic motivators, organizational priorities, and stakeholder sense of moral purpose. Typical constraints in design research projects include not being able to change standards or assessments; and limited participant time. Mapping out the jurisdiction of change by studying constraints and freedoms helps to tailor interventions accordingly, and to mitigate use of temporary scaffolds that (a) cannot be sustained in the long run and therefore (b) render the findings of intervention testing less usable.

For example, thanks to Stenhouse (1975), it is well known that "there can be no curriculum development without teacher development," and in view of the professional development literature, it is well known that short-term teacher workshops have little impact and virtually no sustainability. If, through analysis, it has been determined that the funds and time for professional development in a given setting are extremely limited, then intervention designers targeting a new science curriculum will have to be extremely creative in finding ways to facilitate the kinds of teacher learning that will enable not just initial implementation but also sustained use. The analysis should also identify which, if any, elements of the existing science curriculum must be kept intact, which may be augmented, and which may be discarded. Through SWOT analysis and/or exploration, creative ideas are sought for working within the jurisdiction of change. This could include studying what drives professional development in a given setting and finding opportunities to capitalize on, like intrinsic motivators (e.g. aligning curriculum implementation with a certified course that gives professional development credit) or current priorities within the setting (e.g. connecting the science curriculum reform to a more privileged curricular focus such as mathematics). Additional considerations regarding planning for actual use are given in Chapter 7. Here are some questions that can help to tease out freedoms and constraints:

- What strengths and opportunities are present in the target setting which we can put to productive use?
- What weaknesses and threats are present in the target setting which we should try to mitigate?
- Related to the problem at hand, which factors do we consider, within the scope of this project, to be changeable and which are unchangeable?
- If we tinker with elements in this part of the system, what could be the results in another part of the system? How desirable would that be?
- What lessons can be learned from the work of others tackling similar problems in similar settings?

Initial design propositions

In this book, we borrow the term "design propositions" from organization science (cf. Romme, 2003) to refer to the core ideas that underpin, and are used as inputs for, design. These have also been referred to as design hypotheses (cf. Cross, 1990) or more recently, design conjectures (cf. Sandoval, 2004). We refer to *initial* design propositions here, because the design propositions that are actually used in design work are almost always revised after a more focused literature review during the design stage. Initial design propositions are based on the empirical data and refined understanding of the problem, context, and relevant participant perspectives. They may take the form of heuristic statements indicating stances taken toward salient issues. For example, an initial design proposition used in writing this book was "for people to be able to use design research in a meaningful way, they have to understand not just what it is and how to do it, but also why." Indirectly, design propositions are tested when interventions based on them are studied.

From products of this phase to design and construction

Documenting the problem statement, long-range goal, partial design requirements, and initial design propositions is important. Since arriving at these outputs is usually an iterative process fed by discussion of drafts, the documentation process is valuable for developing a shared understanding among design team members. It also captures team thinking at a specific moment in time, and can be very useful to refer back to, even some time after actual design work commences. Finally, revisiting these documents can be useful later on, when communicating design decisions to audiences outside the project team.

Done well, the outputs of analysis and exploration can be worthy in their own right, from both practical and scientific perspectives. In addition, they lay the foundations for the next major phase of educational design research. As discussed in Chapter 5, the problem definition, long-range goals, partial design requirements, and initial design propositions are all taken as starting points during the phase of design and construction. Here, too, the dual perspectives of detective and inventor can be useful.

Chapter 5

Design and construction

There are no one-size-fits-all steps for tackling different design challenges within the context of educational design research. There are, however, processes and activities which are often useful. Developing a repertoire so that design researchers can select and use the most fruitful and fitting approaches for a specific educational design study is the focus of this chapter.

As described in Chapter 3, the micro-cycle of design and construction may take place repeatedly, and inputs for this work can come from either of its flanking phases: analysis and exploration, or evaluation and reflection, as well as interaction with practice through implementation and spread. The micro-cycle of design and construction involves, and makes transparent, a deliberative–generative process that yields a well-considered intervention which is grounded in both theory and reality. This phase does not – on its own – involve empirical data collection, though it is often described in literature as a meso-cycle (that is, in combination with another phase, such as evaluation and reflection). After discussing the main activities and outputs during this phase, attention is given to how the analytical and creative perspectives are valuable during design and construction. Thereafter, the stage is set for the rest of the chapter by introducing several useful terms and concepts. Then, this chapter presents different activities that can be undertaken to serve design (exploring and mapping solutions) and construction (actually building the solutions). Ideas are presented in linear fashion, which loosely approximates the order in which these activities might logically be carried out. However, as stressed earlier, each design project is different. Not all activities described here are useful in all projects, others are likely to be added, and, several activities described in this chapter often take place simultaneously.

Main activities and outputs

The processes of design and construction are systematic and intentional, but they also include inventive creativity, application of emerging insights, and openness to serendipity. Throughout this phase, ideas about how to address the problem tend to start off rather large and vague; and gradually they become refined, pruned, and operationalized. The work is guided by theory, as well as

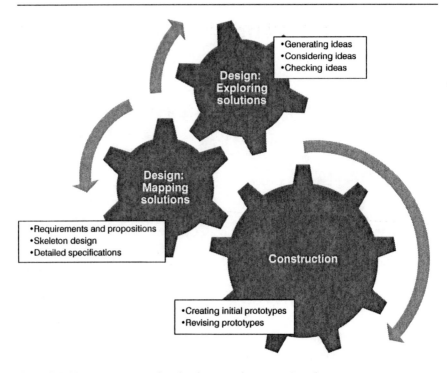

Figure 5.1 Main processes within the design and construction phase

local expertise and inspiring examples. During design, potential solutions are explored by generating ideas, considering each, and checking the feasibility of ones that seem the most promising. Once a limited number of options have been identified, potential solutions are gradually mapped from a skeleton design to detailed specifications. Once (partially) mapped, the solution is constructed, usually through a process of prototyping. Early prototype versions of the intervention tend to be incomplete; sometimes several are tested. Later versions are usually more detailed and functional. Often, the design and/or construction processes lead to new insights, prompting new cycles (e.g. featuring context analysis or new solution mapping). Figure 5.1 shows the main processes within this phase.

The design and construction process can lead to several outputs. Exploring and mapping potential solutions can yield documents that describe potential designs to be created. These can range from broader descriptions of the skeleton design, to more detailed design specifications. The construction process yields the solution itself, which may lend itself to actual representation in a physical form (e.g. a teacher guide, educative software) or indirect representation (e.g. process guidelines for a particular approach to teaching). Any of these outputs can be the subject of evaluation and reflection.

Table 5.1 Examples of analytical and creative perspectives during design and construction

	The detective...	Tasks	The inventor...
Design	Weighs the quality of ideas	Exploring solutions	Welcomes weird and wild ideas
	Seeks ways to make ideas more practical	Mapping solutions	Pushes commonly accepted boundaries
Construction	Maintains focus	Building solutions	Tinkers with possibilities
	Is steered by the data	Revising solutions	Is guided by intuition and inspiration

Analytical and creative perspectives

As discussed in previous chapters, both analytical and creative perspectives serve design research. Taken together, the design activities (exploring and mapping solutions) and construction activities (building and revising solutions) presented in this chapter might aptly be described as what Walt Disney called "Imagineering." Disney visionaries use this patented term to describe the master planning, design, engineering, production, project management, and research and development undertaken in their creative organization. We find the blend of the words *imagination* and *engineering* useful to emphasize the need for both creative and analytical viewpoints throughout the design and construction phases of educational design research initiatives. Examples of how the detective and inventor perspectives inform each of the main tasks in the design and exploration phase are presented in Table 5.1.

Setting the stage for design and construction

About the process

The importance of documenting design

While some researchers and inventors have "eureka" moments which seem to erupt all by themselves, scholars of innovation say that the majority of new ideas which actually get taken up are the products of collaborative thinking over extended periods of time. Johnson (2010) and Kelly (2010) both suggest that seemingly original ideas be viewed as connections, in our brains and among people. If we want them to grow, we must cultivate them not separately, but more like ecologies and networks – by creating environments where ideas can connect. Ironically, this means we also need to *plan for the unexpected*. Knowing this, it is important to build into design research trajectories, the time and the mechanisms that will allow new insights to be generated, (re-)connected, and subsequently integrated into design. Documenting the evolution of ideas so that others can understand the process is central to the enterprise of educational design research. Sharing clear, honest documentation to make the evolution and its underlying rationale as transparent as possible to others is an essential aspect of what distinguishes educational design research from educational design, which does not have the goal of informing the broader scientific community.

The evolution of design requirements and design propositions

Briefly mentioned in the previous chapter, design requirements and design propositions are both instrumental in steering design and construction, but in differing ways. Design requirements specify criteria the intervention should meet, and/or conditions under which it must function. Design requirements are closely tied to the long-range goal and they essentially describe either what the intervention will address in a particular context, or what will powerfully shape it. In contrast, design propositions provide guidance on how to achieve the long-range goal. Based on theoretical understanding, empirical findings, and local expertise, design propositions may further specify what a design should look like, but especially delineate how and why it should have certain characteristics. While both may change over time, design requirements (tied closely to a project's goals) tend to evolve less throughout the course of a design study; whereas design propositions (about how to meet those goals) are validated, refuted, or refined when interventions are tested, during the phase of evaluation and reflection. Table 5.2 shows examples of how design requirements and design propositions differ.

General competencies for design and construction

Designing solutions to educational problems fundamentally involves change. Obviously, change is evident when it comes to implementing an intervention. But it is also evident when we change how we view a setting, the needs of those in it, or what might be prioritized to address a problem, which was central to the previous chapter on analysis and exploration. To design and construct robust solutions to educational problems, we must be open to change. We must be willing to explore solutions in ways that might challenge the status quo. In some cases, we even need to adopt new paradigms to help us identify and create solutions. Many factors influence how change is viewed or tasks are tackled in the design and construction phase, but three are particularly noteworthy: teamwork, communication, and creativity. We therefore briefly discuss each of these before describing ways to generate ideas, map solutions, and arrive at interventions.

Teamwork

Design and construction is a largely social phase, informed by analysis of data from the flanking phases and insights from literature, but also largely driven by interactions among the people doing the creating. Educational design research often cycles between individual and team activities. While actual construction is often done by individuals, teams frequently collaborate to generate, connect, and refine design ideas. Working together stimulates convergent development

Table 5.2 Design requirements and design propositions distinguished

	Design requirements	Design propositions
Origin	Primarily determined by context; secondarily determined by theory and expertise	Primarily determined by theory and expertise; secondarily determined by context
Informed most by	Analysis and exploration	Literature review and craft wisdom (initially); and empirical testing (later)
Product focus (example)	Address priority issue: in the current curriculum, learners consider ratio and percent extremely boring and irrelevant topics	The new curriculum should help teachers present examples of how percentages are used in real life (e.g. interest rates) to motivate learners and actively engage them in the topic
Product shape (example)	Heed constraint: teachers are willing to spend 1–3 hours per month on their professional development related to inquiry, preferably during school time	Teacher workshops should be tailored to take place during one of the two regularly scheduled monthly team meetings
Process focus (example)	Use opportunity: schools want to implement computer supported collaborative learning (CSCL) during the coming school year	Formative testing of the CSCL environment should be completed in time for teachers to have a preview of the system (no later than 3 weeks before summer vacation)
Process shape (example)	Take weakness into account: One school leader and three of the seven department heads expressed skepticism about using tools for school self-assessment, primarily because they saw little need for change	Before emphasizing the benefits of tools for self-assessment, time and activities must be structured to allow key personnel the opportunity to see and own the problems associated with having no regularized self-assessment system in place

of team member ideas, intentions, and understanding about the task at hand. Shared understanding among team members mitigates the chances for internal miscommunication when tasks are distributed. However, even when working in a team, it is often challenging for diverse people such as workshop facilitators, researchers, instructional designers, assessment writers, software developers, and/ or publishers to share a common understanding of where a project is headed. Although team collaboration can sometimes be tedious, even contentious, design researchers have stressed repeatedly that both the design and the research tasks require teamwork (cf. Burkhardt, 2009; Burkhardt & Schoenfeld, 2003; Collins, Joseph, & Bielaczyc, 2004; Könings, Brand-Gruwel & van Merriënboer, 2005).

Studies have been conducted and tools have even been developed to facilitate teams in identifying and reaching common ground for productive collaboration (e.g. Kirschner, Beers, Boshuizen, & Gijselaers, 2008).

Teamwork differs from culture to culture. Complementing the more western "divide and conquer" tradition, Japanese approaches to teamwork are often quite different and increasingly admired. In their book, *The Knowledge-Creating Company: How Japanese Companies Create the Dynamic of Innovation*, Nonaka and Takeuchi (1995) stress the importance of multi-disciplinary teams. In educational design research, it can be extremely important to include diverse: levels of expertise; personality types; life experiences; and views of the world. Such variety in team members brings different lenses for viewing the design challenge. Sir Isaac Newton famously claimed that his creative work stood "on the shoulders of giants." As ideas from one person (or lens) trigger ideas from another, teamwork makes it possible to stand on the shoulders of peers as well as giants. Teams are not composed randomly. Rather, our quest for "hybrid vigor" is served by a team of carefully selected individuals, whose interactions are likely to yield the kinds of vibrant ideas that can meet the design challenge. This often calls for at least researchers, content experts, designers, and practitioners to be involved (see also discussions of the linkage system and program champion in Chapter 7).

Effective teams often exhibit certain characteristics, such as strong group cohesion. While personal "chemistry" can play a role, other factors can positively influence group cohesion. For example, frequent, required interaction balanced by independent work is generally found among cohesive teams. (It should be noted that the most productive ratio of teamwork to individual work often differs for each member, so it can take some time to establish the best overall balance.) Another trait that is usually visible in cohesive teams is a shared goal orientation and vision. Similarly, teams appear to be more cohesive when their members share similar attitudes and values toward their work. Limiting external distractions is also important for teams to "gel" as a group, as is developing sufficient trust, particularly in each other's abilities to resolve differences. Another characteristic of effective teams is that the different members are aware of, understand, and accept their different roles within the group. One important role to have in the group is that of a clear leader. The leader, who may change from one project to the next (or after one micro-cycle within a project), is responsible for nurturing the coherence of the group, prodding it along when it is mired, and exercising authority to finalize decisions.

Communication

In many endeavors, and certainly throughout educational design research, it is extremely important to know how to listen and interact productively. Strong written and verbal communication skills are needed throughout most activities described in this book. Something that facilitates communication in any specialization is a common language, and design teams are no different. Even for an educational scholar in a closely related area, the vernacular among educational design teams can be nearly incomprehensible to outsiders. Equivalent to linguistic shorthand, a shared language provides designers with tools to communicate specific and/ or complex ideas in single words or phrases. A shared language signifies shared concepts, and allows designers to talk about them more clearly and concisely than would be the case if they could only discuss ideas in "plain language." For example, the University of California at Berkeley curriculum development team at the Lawrence Hall of Science holds regular "fencepost meetings." The design team knows that fencepost meetings are large meetings where the whole group provides input to the major organizing components – the "fenceposts" – of a unit (after which a pair of developers works to flesh out the details, the "boards between the fenceposts"). Based on the name alone, staff members know largely what to expect from these meetings and how to prepare for them.

Good communication is fostered by individual traits as well as design team traits. For effective communication, it is important for design team members to have faith in fellow colleagues and most importantly to respect one another. Team members must feel confident that open communication will yield the best results. Team members must be able to give and take constructive criticism, not implying or inferring personal judgment. In addition, team members must feel that genuine concerns – while they may not be resolved – are heard, and not simply diverted, downplayed, or brushed off. Competent communicators consider how ready a fellow team member may be to productively receive certain feedback and adjust their communications accordingly.

Designers use models, mock-ups, sketches, and stories as their vocabulary (Neumeier, 2008). Design documents, which are used to explore and map solutions, as well as to develop prototypes, are a main tool for communication among team members. They range from simple/rough, to complex/detailed, and generally evolve over time. Especially in multi-disciplinary design teams, design documents are often created more in parallel than in series. Time and space must be allocated in a design process to allow the people drafting different documents to share their work in progress and interact with one another. Creating and fine-tuning design documents certainly serves to communicate with members of a team, but is also essential for sharpening one's own ideas. The exceptional design genius may be able to "see" a full design, rich with detail and consequence, from the very start. But most designers bring ideas more gradually into focus. The process of explicating ideas in the form of design documents thus also promulgates their refinement.

Creativity

Alongside disciplined inquiry, educational design research is served by an environment which encourages creative thinking. According to Lumsdaine, Lumsdaine and Shelnutt (1999, p. 153), "What we believe about creativity has a major impact on how much creative thinking we do and how we encourage others to express their creativity." Of course, creative thinking is not always equally valued by all individuals, organizations, and cultures. Intentional and unintentional barriers to creative thinking often need to be acknowledged and removed before creative ideas can really flow. Common barriers to creative thinking include: false assumptions (e.g. assuming something is impossible or assuming something is not important); habits (e.g. looking at a problem in isolation or following the rules); or attitudes (e.g. negativity or uneasiness about risk, failure, or the unknown).

It is important, especially in heterogeneous teams, to ensure that efforts are made to engage all participants in ways that make use of their unique expertise or affinity with the design challenge. Eccentric ideas can be wonderful, perhaps not so much for their exact content, but for the stimulation they provide for other ideas. Some wild and crazy ideas may be unproductive if they are too far "off-the-wall," but if they spur original paths to more creative solutions, they are worth entertaining for a while. For example, someone working on an educational design project focused on enhancing girls' career interests in science, technology, engineering, and mathematics might suggest that young girls forego piano lessons for programming courses. Another participant might be tempted to squash the idea prematurely by stating, "We already tried that with Logo and BASIC, and it didn't work." An open, creative listener thinking without the barriers of false assumptions, old habits, and conservative attitudes, might see a powerful connection – an unexpected way to put the seemingly old idea to imaginative use. For example, perhaps girls could be intrigued by exposure to an old-fashioned player piano and subsequently become interested in studying the "program" that runs it.

Creativity must be encouraged actively. People need time, space, and (though the opposite is true for a small few) no pressure. Has anyone ever come up with their best idea in a crowded office meeting, crammed between two other appointments on the calendar? Maybe, but this is not likely. One thing that can be done to free up the time and space to allow people to "play" with ideas is to go on a retreat. This could range anywhere from several hours to several days, taking place at a restaurant, resort, state park – pretty much anywhere but the office. During such an event, external facilitators can be very useful, as their presence allows all participants to fully engage in creative brainstorming. Facilitators can play different roles, e.g. ensuring that everyone is heard; providing an external view; and/or producing a session summary. Creative facilitators can lead groups through various idea generation and consideration techniques, like the ones listed below. Other types of facilitators may be able to prod the group to take risks or hold up a conceptual mirror to reflect the ideas as they are flowing. Creative thinking is not only important during initial stages of design. It also comes into play during construction and revision of prototype solutions. (In fact, whether engaged in design or not, researchers often need to draw upon their creativity, e.g. to devise appropriate measures for data collection; or to render data collection less invasive, time-consuming or obtrusive.)

Design

Exploring solutions: what shall we design?

The analysis and exploration phase yields several products that provide starting points for design. The long-range goal and problem definition describe the design challenge and its origins. The partial design requirements and initial design propositions give early ideas about tackling that challenge. These early ideas are further elaborated and refined throughout the design and construction phase, starting with the exploration of potential solutions. Here, ideas are generated, considered, and checked.

Idea generation

Smith (1998) identified 50 strategies, tactics, and enablers for generating creative ideas. The most common approach to generating ideas is brainstorming. In brainstorming, ideas are spawned with the intense burst of a storm, the wilder the better. Building on ideas is encouraged, and judgment is to be reserved for later. It is often useful to start off with a brief warm-up, maybe involving a humorous element, to set the mood. For example, free association can stimulate the imagination. In free association, symbols or words are either written or spoken. Starting with one word/symbol either written for all to see or spoken aloud, each person draws/writes/speaks the first thing that comes to mind. Below are some useful techniques for enhancing brainstorming.

- Synectics: Rooted in the Greek word *synectikos* which means "bringing forth together," this technique stimulates new and surprising ideas through (sometimes outrageous) analogies, prompted by a question like, "If your course on statistics were a television show, which one would it be and what would it be like?"
- SCAMPER: Asks questions to generate additional ideas from an existing list, prompted by each word in the acronym: Substitute (e.g. Different ingredient?); Combine (Combine functions?); Adapt (e.g. Can this be like a previous idea?); Magnify/modify (e.g. Grow? Add? Change?); Put to other uses (e.g. Repurpose?); Eliminate (e.g. Simplify?); Rearrange/reverse (e.g. Shuffle? Transpose?)
- Slip writing: People write ideas on slips of paper and pass them around; ideas are changed or augmented along the way; contributors may be named or anonymous; the same or a different group sorts and evaluates the ideas.
- Picture taking: Using (cell phones with) digital cameras, participants leave the meeting area to take pictures of novel or familiar objects from creative angles, the more unusual the better; projected images are then shared with the group, who engages in free association and then uses the associations as starting points for new ideas.

Other techniques for idea generation tackle the process in a more analytical and systematic manner. For example, based on clearly specified design goals and requirements for the solution, a morphological chart can be employed to list solution functions and solution components. It can be used in either direction, but is most often helpful when taking big ideas and operationalizing them into specifics. The usefulness of this technique hinges on the quality of the design propositions. But these are rarely well defined at the start of a project, unless the project builds on substantial previous work. This technique is thus usually more

Table 5.3 Sample morphological chart

Broad propositions	Mid-level propositions	Specific propositions (multiple options)		
Clarify real world relevance	See career opportunities	Invite guest speakers	Use real cases	Show job postings
	Increase motivation	Concrete tasks	Fun tasks	High-yield projects
Develop improved planning skills	Address study and time management	Offer reading and note-taking tips	Explain about time budgeting	Teach backwards mapping
	Make pace adjustable	Reading	Guided self-study	Individual work
	Offer practice opportunities	Mini thinking exercises to apply study skills	Exercises during classes to address study skills	Map week, month, and semester planning
Foster student relationships	Encourage interaction	Buddy system	Poster fair, online forum	Team prepared presentations
Clarify personal growth	Feedback	Expert coaching	Peer review	External review
	Reflection	Journal	Presentation	Videotape

useful once broad design propositions have been well established (e.g. through a focused literature review). Table 5.3 shows a sample morphological chart. The chart was developed in response to the question, "Given your understanding of the failure/drop-out problem in this master's program, what are potential solutions?" Similar to design principle distinctions given elsewhere in educational design research literature (cf. Linn, Davis & Bell, 2004; McKenney & van den Akker, 2005), it shows propositions of three grain sizes: broad (dark grey), mid-level (medium grey) and specific (light grey). A classic morphological charting process would start with broad propositions, then delineate mid-level propositions, before generating specific propositions.

Idea consideration

"A man may die, nations may rise and fall, but an idea lives on," said John F. Kennedy. This section is about sifting through, considering, and judging ideas to find the one (set) that has the power to live on. Critical consideration of ideas is not something that happens only during the initial design of a solution. Ideas are generated, deliberated, and selected throughout many phases in the educational design research process. During idea consideration, critical thinking is essential. Critical thinking is greatly enhanced when a robust set of design requirements can frame the consideration. For example, the constraints identified during the SWOT analysis form such requirements. Ideas that cannot work within those will be discarded, and feasible approaches will be compared in terms of their risks and benefits.

There are many ways to compare potential solutions to problems. Four techniques that are often useful to stimulate critical thinking are:

- De Bono's hats: Participants take turns considering ideas from one of six roles, each of which focuses on different aspects: White hat – facts and information; red hat – feelings and emotions; black hat – being cautious; yellow hat – being positive and optimistic; green hat – new ideas; blue hat – the big picture. Considerations are captured aloud or on paper.
- Courtroom challenge: The two best ideas are represented in a mock courtroom. Their "cases" are made by opposing teams, who try to convince the judge that one is superior (or guilty/not guilty of a particular design flaw).
- Strengths/weaknesses matrix: Design requirements are listed vertically, and design options are listed horizontally. As the matrix is completed, each design option is ranked in terms of its perceived ability to meet each criterion. Rankings can be +/–; +++/– – –, numerals, happy/sad faces, etc. When numerical rankings are used and tallied, this is called the Pugh method.
- Weighted ranking: This is an extension of the strengths/weaknesses matrix, in which each of the criteria is given a weight of importance. A design that scores equally well on "cost" and "reliability" will have a higher score for "reliability," if the feature of reliability has been weighted as more important (e.g. multiplied by a factor of 3).

While decision making is fed by rational, analytical perspectives, such as those generated using the methods above, these perspectives do not drive the endeavor alone. As stated before, a limitation of some of the more systematic approaches (e.g. weighted ranking) is the quality of the design requirements being used. If decisions are made based only on what is known, there is a risk of overlooking the fact that educational design researchers cannot know everything. There should be a voice of instinct, intuition, and positive thinking. Also, decision making (in initial design or later) will rarely involve consideration of one factor at a time. More often, trade-off decisions will have to be made (e.g. the most effective option is not very feasible; the ideal scenario is insufficiently practical; the practical option might not be effective enough, and so on). Both practical and theoretical perspectives, derived from the field and from literature, are urgently needed to help weigh potential options.

Idea checking

Once a limited number of ideas have been deemed worthy of pursuit, it can be useful to check their inner logic and potential viability in the target setting. Comparing new ideas with initial design propositions can be a way to check the alignment of potential solutions with what is already known from literature. Comparing new ideas with the partial design requirements can help to check the alignment with what is known about the context (and the system in which is resides) as well as the people involved. To facilitate the comparison process, it can be helpful to map out how a particular intervention is intended to work, by explicating its underlying assumptions. One powerful way to do this is through the creation of a logic model. Logic models describe inputs, processes, outputs, and outcomes of an intervention. While logic models can be developed at various stages in the design process, they are often most useful after a potential solution has been decided upon and before it has been mapped or constructed.

Logic models depict the solution and its outcomes, showing the assumed "if-then" relationships that yield the desired outcomes. As such, they represent the theory of change underlying an intervention. Logic models portray inputs (including, but not limited to, the designed intervention), processes (implementation of the designed intervention), outputs (evidence of implementation) and outcomes (benefit or change that results). Logic models can be basic, showing the four elements described above, or elaborate, depicting great detail or additional influences on the intervention, such as contextual factors. There are many formats and templates for logic models, showing relationships and feedback loops, with varying levels of detail and even nested layers of concepts. Table 5.4 shows an example of a logic model for an intervention that aims to develop teacher sensitivity and ability to meaningfully engage with children in multi-cultural classrooms, with the overall goal of improving pupil learning gains during collaborative projects. Additional resources and information about the logic modeling process are available online and in print (e.g. Kellogg Foundation, 2004; Mayeske & Lambur, 2001).

Mapping solutions: when fundamental understanding is applied

Refining design requirements and design propositions

Taken together, the design requirements and the design propositions constitute much of the fundamental understanding that is put to applied use when interventions are designed and constructed. As mentioned previously, the design requirements give more guidance on what is to be accomplished in a specific setting, whereas the design propositions inform how that can be done and why. After potential solutions have been explored and selected for mapping, it is often useful to revisit, elaborate, and refine the design requirements and design propositions. As noted earlier, this remains an ongoing process throughout the design research trajectory, although the design requirements (related to the goals of the intervention) should stabilize earlier.

Design requirements pertaining to freedoms, opportunities, and constraints were identified through the analysis and exploration phase. Now that a solution has been determined, functionality requirements may also be set. These may be inferred from what is already known about the target setting, from literature, or it may be necessary to revisit the analysis and exploration phase to gather additional inputs. For example, if the solution chosen is technology-based, but no data on

Table 5.4 Logic modeling template and example

Inputs	Processes	Outputs	Outcomes	Impact
What is needed	Activities	Immediate results	Effects	Measurable change
• Lesson materials • Teacher awareness • Pupil motivation • External expertise • Financial support • Cultural expertise	• Hire facilitators • Develop materials • Professional development • Awareness campaign • Secure grant • Create instruments	Number and description of: • materials made • facilitators hired • workshops held • teachers trained • children reached	• Increased educator sensitivity to cultural differences • Improved climate of multi-cultural classrooms • Higher learning results on collaborative projects	Substantial differences reflected in pre- and post-intervention data from: • teacher interviews and questionnaires • classroom observations • pupil assessments

technology infrastructure, attitudes toward technology use, or technological expertise and support were initially collected, literature may give some guidance, but it would probably make sense to revisit the field to learn more about such aspects in the context in question.

Once the solution is known, design propositions must also be elaborated and refined. This is initially accomplished through literature review. Whereas the previously discussed literature review (conducted during analysis and exploration) primarily informed understanding the *problem* (e.g. What causes insufficient learner engagement?) the focus of this literature review is specifically to inform design of the *solution* (e.g. How can learner engagement be increased?). Often, the literature review continues throughout development, informing and refining the design propositions and thereby also the intervention, until the intervention becomes reasonably stable. As understanding begins to take shape, design propositions are frequently integrated. In educational design research literature, many terms have been used to describe the integrated, theoretical underpinnings for design, such as conjectures (Sandoval, 2004), principles (Linn, Davis, & Bell, 2004), and frameworks (Edelson, 2002).

Design propositions serve the practical goals of educational design research, by helping to sharpen the focus of an intervention and provide solid grounds upon which design choices can be made. They serve the theoretical goals of design research by providing starting points for the theoretical framework that is used to focus empirical testing conducted on or through the intervention. They also help to document and track the evolution of design insights. Earlier design propositions tend to be more sketchy and written for internal audiences. Careful establishment, articulation, and refinement of (integrated) design propositions, with the goal of developing and sharing theoretical understanding, are critical aspects of educational design research that set it apart from other design work. Empirically tested and validated design propositions often form the basis of the prescriptive/normative theoretical understanding produced by educational design research. For example, building from ideas about teacher pedagogical content knowledge, Davis and Krajcik (2005) presented a set of design propositions (they use the term "heuristics"), to further the principled design of materials intended to promote both teacher learning and student learning. As another example, Edelson (2001) presents an integrated set of design propositions (he uses the term, framework) for designing technology-supported inquiry activities.

Skeleton design

As described above, theoretical and practical understanding that informs design is expressed through design requirements and design propositions. These ideas are put to use when potential solutions are mapped. This is generally a gradual process, which starts off identifying the main lines, or skeleton of a solution, and increasingly fleshes out details. Constructing a skeleton design is important because it helps designers identify core design features and distinguish these from supporting ones. As the design and construction process ensues and the temptation for "feature creep" increases (i.e. adding features to the design that were not originally planned), the skeleton design, along with design requirements and design propositions, can help weigh the costs and benefits of proposed additions.

There is no set format for a skeleton design but, generally, attention is warranted to at least: materials/resources; activities/processes; and participation/ implementation. Materials/resources include the physical artifacts that will be part of the intervention. Activities/processes describe the main events through which the intervention will be carried out. Participation/implementation gives additional detail on how actors will engage during those events. Through the skeleton design, it should be clear which components are new, and which components, if any, already exist within the target setting. For example, the skeleton design may mention that teacher meetings will be held. It should also specify if those meetings are separate from, or integrated into, regularly scheduled ones. Table 5.5 gives examples of the kinds of content areas addressed in the skeleton design.

The skeleton design may also indicate the scope of the project, defined primarily in terms of goals, people, time, and budget. Linking the long-range goal to specific components in the design can help establish and maintain focus.

Table 5.5 Five examples of content areas to be elaborated in a skeleton design

Design task	Materials/resources	Activities/processes	Participation/ implementation
In-service program	Worksheets Guidebook Workshop agenda Videos	Expert coaching Peer observation Workshops	Individuals (coaching) Pairs (observations) Groups (workshop)
After school science program	Science toolboxes Workbooks Facilitator guide	Children conduct semi-independent inquiry activities	Children (groups) Facilitators (individual)
University level course	Reading lists Online lectures Discussion threads Assignment descriptions Assignments Exam	Online lectures Face-to-face working group meetings In and out of class assignments Take exam	View lectures out of class Small group in class meetings Individual and pair assignments Individual exam
E-learning environment	Software User guide Informative website	Teacher meetings On-computer activities Off- computer activities	Meetings in teams Children do on- and off-computer activities during regular class time
Curriculum materials	Printed booklets Worksheet masters Digital tutorials	How-to courses	Individuals and teams of teachers Administrators

Often, writing and rewriting the project goals succinctly helps researchers/ designers to separate out long-range and interim goals. The people bearing mention in the skeleton design can include the target group, the researchers/ designers, experts, and additional stakeholders, who will, directly or indirectly, be involved in creating or implementing the design. Timelines should indicate the start and end of the project, as well as the anticipated flow of the project, indicated by milestones. A cautionary note: project timelines tend to be chronically overoptimistic, with the (re)design and construction phase usually being the most drastically underestimated. Finally, the budget indicates the anticipated project expenditures. It usually provides an estimate of people hours and material costs.

Skeleton designs are generally created for internal audiences only, although they may be described for external audiences in project proposals. They can be used as a kind of organizer for identifying components that require further specification. Before doing so, it may be useful to visit the phase of evaluation and reflection. Feedback (e.g. through expert appraisal) on a skeleton design could crush or affirm initial ideas or, more likely, refine them. Taking the time to refine skeleton designs can save valuable resources that might otherwise have gone into detailing ill-advised components. If not subjected to formal appraisal, the skeleton design should at least be checked for alignment with the design requirements and design propositions.

Detailed design specifications

Once the skeleton of a design has been set, it is necessary to further specify aspects of the entire intervention, and/or of specific components of the intervention. This may happen in one fell swoop, but it is usually a more gradual process, eventually resulting in detailed design specifications which provide the information needed to begin "manufacturing" the intervention. There are usually clusters of ideas about the substance of the intervention (the design itself), as well as the design procedures and processes (how it gets created). If design is compared to cooking, substantive specifications describe the finished cake in careful detail, so well that the reader ought to be able to imagine it quite clearly. Procedural specifications, on the other hand, are like the cooking steps in a recipe. For example, substantive specifications for educational software will likely describe the content, learning supports, and interface design. This might include screen mock-ups, with comments printed in the margins, highlighting certain aspects or describing certain functions. Procedural specifications for educational software will likely include developer team meetings, indication of how often and through which mechanisms feedback is collected, procedures for making revision decisions, and so on. As with the skeleton design, it is strongly recommended to evaluate detailed specifications before commencing with construction. Here too, even if not subjected to formal appraisal, the detailed design specifications should be assessed for alignment with the design requirements and design propositions.

Construction

After solutions are designed (above) specific components of the actual intervention are constructed. While it may be possible to "build" a complete intervention all at once, educational design research most often involves creating successive approximations of the desired intervention, each of which is informed by research. Returning to the culinary metaphor above, construction is akin to the act of cooking. During evaluation and reflection, the chef and selected customers test the food, and this phase is revisited to make adjustments, based on the feedback. We like this metaphor because cooking, like powerful educational design, is best served by a blend of systematically planned action (based on knowledge of ingredients – propositions – and how they can be blended for healthy interaction), and creative inspiration at the time of concoction.

Building initial solutions

Prototyping has traditionally been associated with engineering and is a well-established, systematic approach to solving real world problems in many fields, including education. For example, Newman (1990) described a process he calls formative experiments for exploring how computers can be integrated into classrooms. Reinking and Watkins (1996) describe how a series of experiments was conducted to both investigate the effects of, and to redesign, a unit to promote independent reading of elementary students. Nieveen (1999) describes a prototyping approach based on consecutive formative evaluations, along with the framework that was used to evaluate three different quality aspects of those prototypes. This section describes what is meant by prototypes in educational design research and the forms that they may take. Suggestions on how to orchestrate the prototyping process and prototype in teams are also provided.

Prototypes in educational design research

During construction, many detailed decisions must be made. These are largely steered by the design requirements and design propositions; and guided by the skeleton design and detailed design specifications. However, since it is virtually impossible to specify every single detail ahead of time, a substantial number of design decisions will be made during actual construction. Successive approximations, like those mentioned above, are commonly referred to as prototypes. While the design ideas mentioned above (requirements, propositions, skeleton design, detailed specifications) do go through iterative refinement, they are not considered prototypes, because they represent the planned solution. Rather, we use the term "prototype" specifically to describe various draft versions of the constructed solution.

Prototypes can encompass a wide range of artifacts, such as software, books, websites, and so on. While some parts of the solution cannot be created ahead of time (e.g. the interaction that occurs during classroom enactment), prototypes can be made directly for some components (e.g. products or written policies) and indirectly for others (e.g. tools that guide processes or programs). Examples of components that can be prototyped include:

- Product component (direct): Semi-functional learning software.
- Policy component (direct): Organizational documentation or memo.
- Process component (indirect): Guidebook for teachers to plan, enact, and reflect on their own lessons.
- Program component (indirect): Agenda and activity descriptions for school leadership development.

Forms of prototypes

Prototypes range from partial to complete components of the desired solution. They often contain samples of what the finished product might look like; and they may exhibit "functional" or "dummy" features. For example, a visual prototype of a software program can be created in PowerPoint, just to illustrate the interface design, and operationalize the "look and feel." It might be done for the entire program, or for several components. Different forms of prototypes have been identified in literature, including: throw-away; quick and dirty; detailed design; non-functional mock-ups; and evolutionary (cf. Connell & Shafer, 1989). For example, a paper prototype of a software program would constitute a non-functional mock-up.

There are several ways in which initial prototypes differ from more mature ones, and these are represented as a continuum in Table 5.6. First, the components that are elaborated in early prototypes generally do not represent all elements of a solution. This is often intentionally done (e.g. "we wanted to pilot the first module before developing the whole series/course/program"); but not always (e.g. "once we began prototyping, we realized we had to build in a whole new section with support for second language learners"). Second, prototype functionality tends to increase over time. This is particularly common for technology-based interventions. Third, prototype components gradually transition from temporary versions to more enduring ones. Earlier on, it can

Table 5.6 Maturing prototype features

| | As intervention matures, prototypes grow and stabilize | | |
	Initial	Partial	Complete
Parts elaborated	One or few components	Several components	All components
Functionality	Mock-up	Semi-working	Fully working
Permanence	Throw-away	Mix of throw-away and evolutionary elements	Evolutionary

be much more sensible to throw away (pieces of) the prototype (e.g. distracting features in an interactive learning environment; activities that did not function as anticipated); but as approximations of the desired solution become increasingly successful, more and more of the solution becomes stable. Rather than starting over or trying new alternatives, refinements are made to a solution (e.g. interface tweaks; re-sequencing learning tasks), the essence of which remains constant while detailed fine-tuning and embellishments continue over time.

An example of prototyping in educational design research is described by Williams (2004). She explored the effects of a multimedia case-based learning environment in pre-service science teacher education in Jamaica. Her dissertation provides a detailed account of both the design and formative evaluation of the prototype learning environment, and the effects of its use on pre-service teacher learning. Williams' design and development account clearly described how design propositions related to cooperative learning were initially conceived and integrated into three prototypes of the learning environment, before arriving at a final version. The description also addresses how empirical findings and other considerations prompted revisions in prototypes of the tool.

How to manage prototyping processes

Because this book discusses educational design research in general, the range of solution types that could be constructed is vast. It is therefore impossible to address them comprehensively here. Instead, attention is given to orchestrating the process. The moment of actually constructing prototypes is when design notions are instantiated. In this process, direct prototypes (e.g. materials/resources) as well as indirect prototypes (e.g. activity/process tools) are constructed. This may be accomplished by individuals, working with a sketch pad or a computer. But teams can also build prototypes, sometimes using computers but often using pens, posters, or large display boards to create mock-ups.

It is possible, though not so likely, that the design research endeavor will feature the development of one, single prototype component. But given the interventionist nature of design research, it is more likely that several components of a solution will be prototyped. For teams, but also for individuals working on design research, it is quite common for development of different components to be going on simultaneously. For example, in developing a technology-rich learning resource for a university level course on geometry proofs, prototype components could include lesson plans, an online proof tool, learner assessments, and a workshop with teachers. Overseeing all this requires masterful orchestration.

Being able to see the project like a jigsaw puzzle and plan for the construction of its constituent parts is extremely helpful. Many strategies and tactics that apply to generic project management can be useful during the prototype development in educational design research. For example, project management reminds us to pay careful attention to how our resources are allocated. An over-allocated resource is one that has more work demands than the time frame allows. Though it may be the culture of many work environments, we often find that researchers (especially graduate students) could be well described as over-allocated resources.

This should give pause, as overall project productivity is threatened when resources are over-allocated. Below, several tools are described to help with orchestrating design research prototyping:

- Critical path: Flow-chart style representation of main activities (elaborate ones include supporting activities), where bold lines indicate essential tasks and trajectories, and thin lines represent preferred, but not required, tasks and trajectories.
- Gantt chart: Convenient, straightforward, two-dimensional overview of project development and supporting activities, with components shown vertically and time shown horizontally.
- Milestone map: Target dates for completion of certain elements, which can be listed separately or integrated into a Gantt chart.
- RASCI matrix: Clarifies roles and responsibilities in projects as those who are: Responsible (who does the work, often the lead researcher); Accountable (who is ultimately accountable for thorough completion, often a principal investigator or graduate supervisor); Supporting (who helps the person responsible, like a research assistant); Consulted (with whom there is two-way communication); and Informed (who are kept up to date on progress through one-way communication, like funders).

Many books and electronic tools provide insightful and practical support for project management. Please refer to the Appendix for recommended sources.

Prototyping in teams

Very few projects are undertaken as a one-person show. Most successful design research projects involve varied expertise on a multi-disciplinary team. Yet even in the case of projects undertaken by a single graduate student, there will be moments when additional expertise is needed. In some cases, outside experts will actually construct elements of the design (e.g. a computer programmer builds software). In other cases, project collaborators will co-construct design components (e.g. teachers and design researchers collaboratively plan lessons). And still other elements will be created by the core project members themselves with critical input from outside experts (e.g. subject matter specialists give guidance or examples). In addition to the project management techniques listed above, it can also be useful to create a document that plans and tracks who is creating what, and the envisioned timeline from start to completion.

Each project demands its own range of specific expertise. In educational design research, it is common to seek out expertise related to the media being used, the content being addressed, the intended pedagogy, and those with a strong sensitivity to what may be accepted in the target setting. Media experts include those who put prototype components into publishable form, such as desktop publishers (some clerical staff members are wonderful at this), software developers (ranging from hobbyists to professionals), and website designers (many institutions have these people in-house). Content specialists include subject matter experts, who often work in research, practice, or both (e.g. faculty in a university department of mathematics education often conduct their own research and supervise teaching practice). Pedagogy specialists may also have more of a background in research (e.g. researching the use of serious games as a learning strategy) or practice (e.g. a corporate trainer with expertise in adult learning). Many experts will possess a combination of specialties (e.g. pedagogical content knowledge experts specializing in inquiry learning in science). It is extremely useful to have practitioners on the design team, with their sensitivities to the affective and practical aspects of the target context being high among the many contributions they can make. Practitioners often help "keep it real" by being able to voice interests and concerns that are likely to be shared by others, and determining what is (or is not) feasible, in the target setting. For educational design researchers working in or from a university, it may be possible to expand project resources at little or no cost by providing internships or learning opportunities to students from other types of programs. For example, students from graphics design courses might be able to produce artwork for e-learning environments and students in computer science courses might be able to do some initial programming.

Revising solutions

Design ideas and constructed prototypes can be evaluated through various strategies and methods, which are described in detail in Chapter 6. The evaluation of designs and constructed (prototype) interventions generally concludes with revision recommendations. This can include suggestions on what to add, what to remove, what to alter, or even what to repeat in a design. This section briefly discusses the use of such recommendations to revise design documents or prototypes. It starts by describing different kinds of findings and then discusses considerations in reaching revision decisions.

Different kinds of evaluation and reflection findings

The stage and focus of an evaluation will set the boundaries for how far-reaching revision recommendations may go. Both design ideas (e.g. design requirements, propositions, skeleton design, or detailed specifications) and constructed prototypes can be evaluated, although it is less common to conduct anything other than an informal critique of design requirements and propositions. But even if only a prototype is evaluated, the findings are quite likely to have implications for the design ideas, especially the design propositions. For example, the formative evaluation of a prototype learning environment may yield specific recommendations regarding the prototype itself, which could then be incorporated into new versions of the skeleton design and detailed design specifications. But those recommendations may be based on important concepts, which warrant integration into the design propositions and may prompt another cycle of literature review.

The empirical testing of prototype features may yield findings which are more prescriptive, showing how to move forward with design. But more often, evaluation activities will reveal descriptive findings, which clearly need to be considered when revising the intervention, without specifying how the design should be improved. For example, the observation and interview data from the evaluation could provide more nuanced insight into how large or small an innovative jump an intervention is, in comparison to current practices. Or it may reveal more about user characteristics (e.g. most of them have never seen this kind of tool before; teacher beliefs about this topic are highly varied; or children have some, but not all of the prerequisite skills). The evaluation could also reveal participant preferences (e.g. they are happy to do this, but mostly during evening hours), or contextual factors that were not examined in the initial phase of analysis and exploration. In fact, an evaluation may point to the need to revisit the analysis and exploration phase. For example, in testing a professional development program where teachers bring learner assessment data to meetings and learn how to plan lessons to meet specific needs, design researchers might come to question the quality of the assessments teachers bring with them. Before redesigning the program, it may be necessary to analyze currently available assessments and explore what other assessment options might be feasible.

Considering revisions

In considering how to proceed with the findings from evaluation and reflection, some design teams use established procedures for logging feedback, systematically reviewing it and creating a written trail of how it was addressed or why not. Often, it can be useful to sort problems on the basis of their complexity. Some evaluation findings will be rather straightforward and easy to use (e.g. correction of typographical errors). Some will not be easy, but the pathway to revision will be clear. Many will pose complex challenges. Complex challenges are those for which a solution is unclear or not readily available; for which numerous options for solutions exist; or for which the logical revision(s) would be beyond the scope of the project. Very often, complex challenges are prompted by tensions between differing design goals. For example, what is practical for users might make it easier to implement, but less effective; or what has been shown to be effective is not sustainable. In some cases, insufficient practicality is a barrier to even studying effectiveness. To illustrate, if an online learning environment has poor usability, it may have low effectiveness not because of the content, but because of the inadequate human–computer interface (Reeves & Carter, 2001). Revisiting design requirements and design propositions can sometimes help to weigh up options in such cases. Consulting experts (in person or through literature) may also help.

In dealing with complex redesign challenges brought into focus by evaluation, it is important to remain distanced and open-minded. It is also critical to stay in touch with the main goals to ensure that revisions reflect responsive evolution (e.g. redesign to better meet the stated goals) and not "mission creep" (e.g. redesign changes goals without realizing it). Especially those intensively involved in the project might do well to take a break after analyzing the results and before determining revision suggestions. In some teams, the agreements are made that design authority changes hands at this point. The idea behind this is that designers can become so attached to their work that they are unable to do what is sometimes necessary in prototyping: "kill your darlings." Occasionally, it can be productive to concentrate (partly) on other issues, while looking to see if a solution may be found indirectly, through working on the related problems.

It is wise to plan the revision process, just as it is wise to plan the initial development. A general rule of thumb for the timing of revisions is that it pays off to tackle simple issues that take relatively little time immediately, using the "touch it once" principle. That is, if it takes a relatively short amount of time to do, it is more efficient to do it immediately than to carry it around on the "to do" list. It is also important to initiate changes in a timely fashion, so that those which take a long time, even if they require little monitoring, do not hold up development. Complex problems should be sorted into those that will be tackled in the redesign; those that cannot or will not be solved prior to the next evaluation but will be addressed; and those that will be left unaddressed. Documenting each of these is extremely important to help reconstruct events when reporting on the process (cf. Chapter 9). Bulleted lists or tables of issues/actions work very well; these can be sent around to the design team for review and comment. It is also important to ascertain if the changes are more superficial (e.g. constituting improved actualization of the design propositions); or more substantial (e.g. altering the underlying design propositions). Planning the revision process may also include building in time to consult literature, especially when more substantial changes seem necessary.

Products resulting from this phase

Kurt Lewin famously said that "Nothing is as practical as a good theory" (Reason, 2001, p. 182). Throughout this phase, good theories are put to practical use in designing and constructing solutions to problems. Both design ideas and constructed prototypes evidence attention to fundamental understanding and applied use. This section briefly recapitulates the two main types of outputs from the micro-cycle of design and construction.

Products describing design ideas

Products resulting from design activities relate to exploring potential solutions (generating ideas; considering ideas; and checking ideas) as well as mapping potential solutions (refining design requirements and design propositions; establishing a skeleton design; and setting detailed design specifications). Design requirements and design propositions capture significant concepts and fundamental understanding that are used to steer the design process. Design requirements, based largely on the findings from analysis and exploration, delineate functions, criteria, opportunities, constraints, or conditions to be incorporated into the solution. Design propositions are based largely on literature, and constitute the postulated mechanisms that will enable designs to work. While the products of exploring solutions mostly serve the practical goals of educational design research, the products of mapping solutions contribute to both practical and theoretical goals. The skeleton design and the design specifications bring the solution closer to reality; and when design requirements and especially propositions are explicated and shared, contributions can be made to theoretical understanding.

Products embodying design ideas

Products resulting from construction activities embody the design ideas. These are often successive prototypes of the desired intervention. Prototypes serve the practical goals of design research by actually being (parts of) the solution to a practical problem. They can also serve the theoretical goals of design research, by providing manifestations of design propositions and case examples of interventions to be studied.

From products of this phase to other phases

Developing the products of this phase, which either describe or embody design ideas, may clarify to designers that additional analysis and exploration is needed before redesign and/or testing should take place. For example, in constructing an intervention that includes use of social media, designers may conclude that they require additional understanding about how and when the target group currently uses specific social media tools and functions. But more frequently, some form of evaluation and reflection takes place next. Even with early products describing or embodying design ideas, the process of evaluation takes the products of this phase as starting points. Subsequently, evaluation findings and conclusions are reflected upon, a process which can lead to new insights, conjectures, hypotheses and/or ideas for (re)design.

Chapter 6

Evaluation and reflection

In developing nearly any intervention, informal evaluation and reflection takes place throughout the development process. This chapter is concerned with the evaluation in design research that intends to inform an external scientific community as well as drive intervention development. This kind of evaluation is conscious, systematic, and formalized. Here, the term "evaluation," is used in a broad sense to refer to any kind of empirical testing of interventions that have been mapped out (designs) or constructed (prototypes). Reflection pertains to retrospective consideration of findings and observations (not to assessment of personal performance). This chapter begins by describing the main activities and outputs of the evaluation and reflection micro-cycle, which has its own logical chain of reasoning, before discussing how the detective and inventor mindsets can be of value. The stage is set for evaluation and reflection with a brief characterization of the process. Then, the evaluation process is described as a series of steps, starting with establishing a focus and concluding with reporting. Thereafter, the role of reflection and the processes that support it are addressed. The chapter concludes by recapitulating the main outputs from this phase, and briefly discussing what might come next.

Main activities and outputs

During the evaluation and reflection phase, design ideas and prototype solutions are empirically tested and the findings are reflected upon, with the aim of refining (theoretical) understanding about if, how, and why intervention features work. Evaluation follows an empirical cycle consisting of nine steps:

1 Establish the focus.
2 Frame guiding questions.
3 Select basic strategies.
4 Determine specific methods.
5 Draft and revise a planning document.
6 Create or seek instruments.
7 Collect the data.
8 Analyze the data.
9 Report the study.

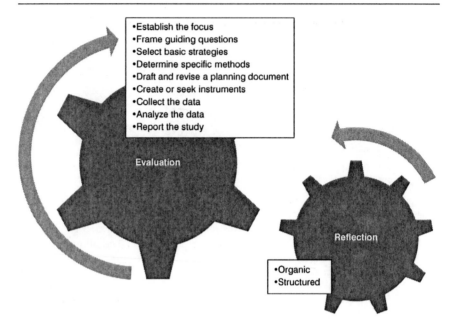

Figure 6.1 Main processes within the evaluation and reflection phase

Reflection can take place organically or through more structured techniques. These activities are shown in Figure 6.1, which illustrates the main processes within this phase.

Resulting from this phase is a better understanding of the intervention, the appropriateness of its intentions, what it looks like when implemented, and the effects it yields. In addition, by investigating the intervention, design propositions are indirectly tested. Reflection on the findings helps generate explanations for the results, and new or refined ideas concerning design (requirements or propositions; skeleton design; or detailed specifications) and/or prototype solutions. (Please refer to Chapter 5 for additional information on these distinctions.)

Analytical and creative perspectives

As stated in the introduction to this chapter, the term "evaluation" is used in a broad sense to refer to any kind of empirical testing of interventions that have been mapped out (designs) or constructed (prototypes). In this phase of design research, the term "reflection" is used to describe the retrospective consideration of findings and observations. (Note: this chapter does not address reflection on personal performance.) Reflection is integral to any serious inquiry, although it is less frequently discussed than evaluation. As with the other phases of design research, it can be worthwhile to explicitly stimulate both the analytical and the creative mindsets. Table 6.1 gives examples of what that can mean in this phase.

Table 6.1 Examples of analytical and creative perspectives during evaluation and reflection

	The detective...	Tasks	The inventor...
Evaluation	Builds tight lenses	Frames the inquiry	Is open to be surprised
	Executes a plan	Collects the data	Seizes unplanned opportunities
	Deduces and induces	Analyzes the findings	Questions why this is so
Reflection	Judges what was	Considers processes	Asks what if
	Ascertains meaning	Considers findings	Connects to other ideas

Setting the stage for evaluation and reflection

It has often been stated that design research is evolutionary in nature, and that it is open-ended. This does not mean that design researchers lack goals or a clear sense of direction. But it does take into account that, with humility and curiosity, design researchers undertake to navigate innovation and scientific inquiry amidst the multi-layered, complex systems that comprise educational realities. It is a basic assumption at the initiation of design research that disciplined and systematic inquiry, coupled with creative innovation, will uncover ways to achieve the intended goals. The evolutionary, open-ended characterization thus refers to the fact that this – largely pragmatic – group of researchers does not pretend to have more than strong hypotheses as to how certain goals can be met, and that these ideas are validated, refined or refuted along the way. In other words, design researchers know where they want to go and have faith that the research process will get them there, even though they do not always know how the journey will play out.

The evolution in design research is generally prompted by new insights, which usually lead to new questions. As such, shift in the emphasis of inquiry generally takes place between, not within, a micro-cycle. For example, formative evaluation may be conducted *on* a digital teacher guide to explore how teachers perceive and use this type of resource. The evaluation may show that teachers highly value the way the tool helps them structure formative assessments. In a subsequent study, the inquiry could employ teacher use of a digital teacher guide as a *means* to understand how teachers make sense of learner data, or the kind of knowledge teachers generate when they reflect on pupil assessment data. These findings could inform redesign, and prompt another study on the digital teacher guide. Intervention development is best served by early and frequent evaluation and reflection. Substantial improvements can be made to even global intervention designs, thus limiting unnecessary depletion of temporal, financial, emotional, and human resources.

Evaluation

Establish the focus

Role of the intervention

The first step is to establish the focus of the study. Simply put, we step back from the research and development work thus far and ask, "What do we need to know now?" Usually the questions that come up have to do with either testing a specific feature of the intervention or perhaps the intervention as a whole; exploring some phenomena that the intervention is known to, or might, engender; and/or gathering new inputs for design. Often new questions arise directly from findings in a previous micro-cycle. Establishing the focus is like setting an agenda, and thus benefits from being conducted through dialogue with fellow researchers and practitioners, while also being informed by the relevant literature.

In establishing the focus, it can be useful to determine the role of the intervention in the evaluation. In some cases, the intervention is *what* will be studied; in other cases, the intervention contributes to *how* a phenomenon will be studied. This is where distinguishing between the orientations of research on and research through interventions can be particularly useful:

- Research on interventions: If the aim is to generate knowledge about a particular type of intervention, the intervention in question constitutes one manifestation of that type. The theoretical framework presents how existing knowledge about that intervention type will be used to shape the investigation, and is closely aligned with the integrated design propositions. The study focuses on specific aspects of the intervention itself.
- Research through interventions: If the aim is to generate knowledge about something other than a particular type of intervention (e.g. the phenomenon induced or manipulated by the intervention), then we view the intervention at hand as the context or possibly the treatment in the study. The theoretical framework focuses on issues related to the particular phenomenon under investigation, and is only indirectly connected to the integrated design propositions. The primary focus of the study is on this phenomenon, and not on the intervention, although the findings will likely yield implications for the intervention.

Research on interventions and research through interventions may be conducted simultaneously, e.g. during one micro-cycle of evaluation. However, as described above, the frameworks and research questions guiding each type of investigation differ, and it is both important and difficult to untangle these. When attempting to explore both at the same time, it can be useful to establish coordinated, but separate, plans and activities for each strand within the micro-cycle. This may be accomplished, for example, by having two graduate students working on one design project, one focusing more on the intervention itself, and the other focusing more on the phenomena it engenders. For example, Oh, Liu, and Reeves (2009) conducted a multi-year design study *on* optimizing authentic tasks as learning activities in an online graduate course, which was informed by research conducted *through* three iterations of the course, studying group work and self-regulated learning.

Phase and focus of evaluation

An intervention's stage of development usually has implications for the kinds of questions that present themselves to be answered. As described above, intervention testing often involves studying several aspects at once. Evaluation may be conducted with more formative goals (identifying routes to improvement) or more summative goals (assessing overall value) – usually with the aim of facilitating some kind of decision. Many evaluations in design research pursue both kinds of goals simultaneously. For example, research on interventions may seek to understand how to improve a design (formative) while also assessing how well it is working to engender a desirable phenomenon (summative).

McKenney (2001) used the term "semi-summative" to describe a research phase of study that aimed to provide the basis for decision making but still evidenced many traits of formative evaluation. Building on this work, and also that of Reeves and Hedberg (2003) and Raval (2010), we distinguish six foci important in educational design research evaluation; these can be relevant to both research on and research through interventions. Not all design studies attend to each focus described below. However, these foci exhibit similarities with those mentioned elsewhere in literature (Burkhardt, 2006, 2009; Gorard, Roberts, & Taylor, 2004; McKenney, Nieveen, & van den Akker, 2006; Schoenfeld, 2009b).

The six foci can be clustered into three concerns: internal structures of an intervention; how it is used in practice; and effects. These three clusters are well aligned with three stages of testing adapted from software engineering and often seen in design research: alpha, beta, and gamma testing. In the description below, two foci are described for each stage of testing.

ALPHA TESTING

Alpha testing concerns early assessment of design ideas, initially using "white box" techniques. In software engineering, white box techniques test the internal structures of an application to make sure they work logically, but not its functionality per se. In educational design research, we could say that white box techniques are used to test underlying hypotheses, conjectures, and constructs, as embodied in preliminary design documents (e.g. design propositions, detailed design specifications). This type of testing relies primarily upon logical analysis by experts. This phase then moves to "black box" techniques, which test functionality of initial intervention prototypes. Here, too, the focus is on the internal structure of the design, but including concern for functionality as well. Alpha studies involve the collection of data to primarily ascertain:

- Soundness: The ideas underpinning a design and/or how those ideas are instantiated; testing can be done on the underlying constructs (e.g.

design requirements or design propositions), how they are applied in design (skeleton design, detailed design specifications), or embodied in prototypes.

- Feasibility: The potential temporal, financial, emotional, and human resource costs associated with creating the intervention.

BETA TESTING

Beta testing is conducted with working system components within a more or less functional system, and focuses on use in context. In educational design research, this is where the functionality of an intervention and how it interacts in context are studied in-depth. Beta studies mainly explore:

- Local viability: How an intervention survives in the immediate context (e.g. classroom) and why. This relates directly to how the intervention performs, in ways that were intended (e.g. fidelity), and not planned (e.g. adaptations, side effects). Indirectly, this relates to factors that influence its implementation (e.g. perceived value, clarity, compatibility with existing policies or practices, and tolerance to variation in enactment).
- Institutionalization: How an intervention becomes absorbed within the broader educational organization (e.g. school) or, if appropriate, system; this relates to the organizational conditions and support for the innovation (e.g. expertise, finances, policies, leadership attitudes).

GAMMA TESTING

In software engineering, gamma testing is performed before the final release (the software is believed to be complete and free of errors, but the manuals and packaging may not yet be in final form). However, we distinguish gamma testing in design research slightly differently: it takes place with a nearly final, or at least highly stable, version of the intervention. Gamma studies are mostly used to determine:

- Effectiveness: The extent to which the intervention meets its goals when implemented on its intended scale (which could still be small); this is studied with no scaffolds or temporary supports in place.
- Impact: The extent to which the intervention engenders a measurable change in the target setting; this tests if reaching the goals set actually yields the desired change and also examines unplanned effects. It may also explore wider appeal and spread of the intervention.

The foci described here (feasibility, soundness, viability, institutionalization, effectiveness, and impact) help clarify the main concerns in each of the three stages (alpha, beta, gamma). However, this is not to suggest that intervention testing progresses rigidly, mastering certain aspects before moving on to others. From the start, *consideration* is given to all focal areas; but it does not make sense to try to *empirically test* them all at once. One way of considering multiple aspects of the intervention while testing a few specific ones is to view the intervention in different forms; these are addressed below.

Intervention forms: intended, implemented, attained

As briefly described in Chapter 3, Goodlad, Klein, and Tye (1979), van den Akker (2003), and others distinguish different representations of curriculum: that which is intended; that which is implemented; and that which is attained. These distinctions are also useful in focusing the evaluation in a design study. Here, different forms of the intervention are distinguished. The intended form of the intervention refers to what it sets out to do. The implemented form of the intervention is that which is actually used in practice. The outputs and outcomes of an intervention constitute its attained form. For example, a primary school physical activity program could intend for children to experience three 1-hour periods of team sports per week, with the goals of improving children's attitudes toward cooperative work and lowering the school's average body mass index (BMI). Due to inclement weather and teacher illness, the implemented program might consist of two 1-hour periods of team sports per week. The attained intervention may then be an increase in children's attitudes toward cooperative work but no change in BMI.

Linking forms to phase and focus of evaluation: starting points

There are clear links between the phases of testing and forms being tested. Alpha testing primarily concerns initial intentions; beta testing primarily concerns implementation; and gamma testing primarily concerns attainment. However, many issues warrant consideration before they can be tested. For example, it does not make much sense to endeavor to ascertain the effectiveness of an intervention as a whole, when it has only been partially implemented under near-to-actual circumstances. But it makes a lot of sense, from early on, to gather indicators of effectiveness under certain conditions. Similarly, researchers may prioritize establishing the presence of effects, such as learning gain, before attending to how the ownership of an intervention may shift into the hands of practitioners. But if the results of the study are to be of practical use, ideas for doing so must be collected at some point, given that the findings obtained when interventions are implemented with non-sustainable amounts of support can be very different from what happens when extra funding resources are no longer available.

Table 6.2 illustrates the direct links between phases of testing and forms of interventions; these are indicated by the cells in grey. The plain cells demonstrate how indirect consideration can be given to the other four foci during each phase of testing. Table 6.2 does not provide a comprehensive representation of evaluation foci, but it does offer some useful starting points. Each design study is unique, thus requiring that the focus be tailored to the specific combination of theoretical and practical goals; target settings; and resources involved.

Table 6.2 Phase and focus of evaluation for different forms of intervention

Phases	Forms		
	Intended intervention	*Implemented intervention*	*Attained intervention*
Alpha testing (Internal structure)	Test design intentions: • soundness • feasibility	Test assumptions about implementation; what will render: • local viability • institutionalization	Test assumptions about success: • what will render effectiveness and impact • how will these be measured
Beta testing (Use in context)	Explore alignment and conflict between intervention attributes that boost viability and institutionalization, and those of: • soundness • feasibility	Explore: • local viability • institutionalization	Measure: • potential effectiveness and impact • (prevalence of) fostering and hindering conditions for success
Gamma testing (Effects)	Reflective assessment of intentions and ideals; were they: • sound and feasible • appropriate and sufficient	Study how factors contributing to: • local viability, and • institutionalization influence effectiveness and impact	Measure actual: • effectiveness • impact

Frame guiding questions

Shavelson, Phillips, Towne, and Feuer (2003) distinguished three generic questions often raised in design research and recommended methods that could suit each: What is happening? Is there a systematic effect? and Why or how is it happening? From the practical perspective, the primary concern is with how and to what extent the problem is being addressed by the intervention. From a theoretical perspective, the main concern is understanding how an intervention does or does not work and, especially, why. Studying if, how, and why interventions work, requires attending to their goals, the ways those goals are pursued, and if or to what extent they are achieved. This section discusses the kinds of questions that frequently guide evaluation, structured by the three stages of the testing described above: alpha, beta, and gamma.

Questions during alpha testing

Questions about the intentions of an intervention are typically the main focus in alpha testing. Here, the feasibility and soundness of the design ideas are studied. Questions asked about the intended intervention may help evaluate design propositions, or the way in which those ideas have been put to use in a specific prototype. It can also be useful to pose questions about the alignment of design intentions with: stakeholder needs and wishes; opportunities and constraints; or other boundary conditions set by the context in question (relating to viability and institutionalization). Finally, questions can be posed to test assumptions about how the intended intervention will solve the problem. Sample guiding questions during alpha testing include:

- How robust and complete is the theoretical and pragmatic justification for these design ideas?
- How well are the core design propositions embodied in the design?
- What changes must be made to the underlying ideas or the design itself to increase the plausibility and probability that it could meet the intended goals?

Questions during beta testing

Many factors affect how interventions are implemented in practice, including how well they are aligned with core elements of the context, such as the curriculum; assessment frameworks; practitioner expertise; prevailing attitudes and beliefs; local culture; and the textbooks, programs, and materials that have already been adopted. Questions about the implemented intervention especially focus on if and how it engenders intended processes when used in the intended setting, and how sustainable they are likely to be (viability and institutionalization). Studying implemented interventions can also afford opportunities to check and possibly refine design requirements and design propositions. This process can also allow for the testing of potential effectiveness and impact, as well as an intervention's tolerance, described below.

In engineering, tolerance usually refers to how precisely design specifications must be met during production. In the design of educational interventions, tolerance refers to how precisely design intentions must be enacted for the intervention to be true to its goals. For example, in developing a technology-rich learning environment for early literacy, it can be assumed that different teachers will use it in varying ways; investigation is needed to explore the variation in use and its differing effects. Returning to the same example, when teachers find ways to alter the learning environment or how it is used, and the result does not meet the intervention goals well or at all, the intervention tolerance is low. If the learning environment is enacted as planned or differently, and the intervention goals are met, then the intervention tolerance is high. "Lethal mutations" (cf. Brown & Campione, 1996) can be the result of intolerant interventions, whereas highly tolerant interventions "degrade gracefully" (cf. Walker, 2006).

The notion of tolerance is especially important when it comes to generating theoretical understanding that serves prescriptive/normative purposes. Exploring intervention tolerance requires observing multiple enactments of an intervention, sometimes across different settings. During investigation, the focus is on how specific designed elements of an intervention are enacted, in order to understand what levels of precision and variance will still enable them to serve their intended purpose. For designs to weather the often myriad and changing climates of classroom settings, and theoretical understandings to be transferrable, it is necessary to identify which design ideas (e.g. propositions) are more and less tolerant to the variation in enactment which inevitably comes along with differing contexts, resources, expertise, acceptance levels, etc. in educational settings (see also Chapter 7). Sample guiding questions during beta testing include:

- How relevant and usable do practitioners perceive and experience the intervention?
- What intended and unintended processes are engendered by the intervention?
- What makes embodiments of certain mechanisms more resilient than others?

Questions during gamma testing

Questions about the attained intervention guide investigation of effectiveness and impact. As is common in other fields (e.g. health care), it can be useful to distinguish between studying effectiveness as opposed to efficacy. Effective interventions meet their goals under regular "real world" conditions, with no external support (this excludes any supports that have been institutionalized, or absorbed into the system). Effectiveness studies involve actors (e.g. teachers and learners) representative of the ultimate target participants in the intervention. In contrast, efficacious interventions are those that provide positive results under controlled, often highly favorable, conditions, such as when researchers themselves conduct teaching experiments in classrooms not usually their own. Translating efficacious practices to "regular" practice settings to produce the desired results constitutes an extremely challenging aspect of many educational design research projects. Thus, studying what is attained in design research is more than ascertaining if and to what extent something works. To move from efficacious to effective designs, we need to know things like: What fosters and hampers success under ideal circumstances? To what extent is it possible to create the fostering conditions in representative classrooms? How can hindering conditions be mitigated? Sample guiding questions during gamma testing include:

- How effectively does the intervention solve the problem? Under which conditions?
- What is the long-term impact of the intervention?
- In representative classrooms, how prevalent are the conditions that foster and inhibit success?

Select basic strategies

There are many ways to examine the intended, implemented, and attained intervention. This can include subjective responses of experts and participants'

Table 6.3 Functions and strategies matrix

		Developer screening	Expert appraisal	Pilot	Tryout
Alpha	Feasibility	▓	▓		
Alpha	Soundness	▓	▓	░	░
Beta	Local viability	░	▓	▓	
Beta	Institutionalization	░	▓	░	
Gamma	Effectiveness			▓	▓
Gamma	Impact				▓

Legend: dark grey = frequently useful; light grey = maybe useful, depending on the circumstances.

perceptions of the intervention (e.g. captured through think aloud protocols or interviews); actual behaviors (e.g. documented in classroom observations or computer users' click streams); or reconstruction of "critical incidents" that occur during implementation (e.g. as collected through participant logs or in retrospective focus groups) to name a few. But before selecting specific methods, four basic strategies frequently used in design research are described. The strategies are inspired by Nieveen's (1997, 1999) approaches to formative evaluation: developer screening, expert appraisal, pilots, and tryouts. Often these strategies are used in combination with one another, and different strategies are generally used at different stages in the life cycle of a project. Strategies for evaluation are selected based primarily on the research questions, and secondarily on the constraints of the study (time, personnel, costs, access to respondents, etc.). To decide which strategies to use, it can be useful to visualize how each one will relate to the evaluation functions. A chart like the one offered in Table 6.3 may help. Here, recommendations are given for strategies that serve particular evaluation functions, related to the alpha, beta, and gamma testing phases. The remainder of this section offers information about each strategy.

Developer screening

Developer screening is especially useful for studying the internal structure of a design or constructed prototype. It can also provide assessments about how it will likely work in the target setting. While informal evaluation is nearly constant in design projects, the developer screening described here is a formalized process of critically assessing the design work. In developer screening, initial design ideas are evaluated, and those considerations are documented and analyzed. Data are usually collected through focus groups, questionnaires, or checklists; interviews may also be used. The instruments can be closed or open in nature; they can be quantitative, qualitative, or both. For example, a quantitative method that might be used is a variation of the Lawshe (1975) process for establishing the content validity of research instruments. Lawshe's process involved asking experts to judge if research instrument items measure the knowledge or skill in question with the expectation that at least 50% of the experts had to agree about the validity of any given item to keep it in the instrument. In developer screening, developers can be asked to rate how well specific elements of the design reify the design propositions. Quantitative ratings may help validate a design, and qualitative techniques may especially useful to flush out new perspectives. For example, a focus group might be asked to consider questions like: Are important constructs missing? How plausible is this hypothetical learning trajectory? Or, how can the design capitalize on what teachers already know about this issue?

From some research perspectives, internal evaluation of this nature could be criticized, because of the biases involved. But articulating and critiquing the design rationale is critical to this kind of research. To advance understanding of what constitutes good design and how to achieve it, the decision making underpinning design work must be transparent. The lack of transparency in design research decision making, especially when based on qualitative data, has, in fact, been criticized in recent literature (Torrance, 2008). It can be extremely useful to bring someone from outside into the team to facilitate the developer screening process. Not only does this enable the whole team to participate, it can: lend more credibility to the screening; encourage developers to engage more critically; and bring increased objectivity and balance to the process. In addition, if the facilitator is a researcher from a similar project, it offers that person a nice look at "someone else's kitchen" and can be a mutually beneficial experience.

Findings from developer screening can contribute to scientific understanding as well as to intervention development. Another important contribution that can be made by developer screening is in fostering communication, especially in larger design teams. First, developer screening invites critical reflection, which may not otherwise be given by members of the design team who do not perceive it as their place or their responsibility to call into question a process that has been set in motion. Second, this process can help elicit tacit knowledge about how to tackle the design challenge. Often, such knowledge is not explicated because people (perhaps mistakenly) assume that they have a shared knowledge base. Finally, during developer screening, it may become clear that outside expertise is needed to advance a design. As discussed in Chapter 5, the need for clear and frequent communication using the expertise of the team as a whole (and sometimes seeking outside help) is substantial. Systematically planned and conducted developer screenings can help address this concern. In developing their augmented reality platform for environmental simulations, Klopfer and Squire (2008, p. 212) conducted developer screening by reviewing user scenarios, which helped to "get inside the head of the user" to understand potential needs and desired functionalities.

Expert appraisal

External expert appraisal involves subjecting the design work from early on to critical external review (e.g. Have you considered X? What about Y?). It can also provide different perspectives for looking at phenomena, helping design teams see things that may have been overlooked or misunderstood. Expert appraisal is also used to collect ideas for improvements. Finally, this process may be used to verify or validate the intervention, when framed to answer questions like: Are we doing the right things? Are we doing them right? Expert appraisal refers to a process whereby external experts in a particular area are brought in to review (elements of) the intervention. Different types of experts can provide guidance for the systematic improvement of interventions. Expert appraisal can be conducted with design documents, although it is more commonly conducted with prototypes. Data are often collected through interviews, questionnaires, or checklists, though other methods may be used. Depending on the stage of development and the questions guiding the investigation, experts may be asked to validate, judge, critique, or contribute to the intervention.

Expert appraisal often involves having experts "walk through" salient components of the intervention, and then give feedback. For example, if an intervention features a teaching or learning resource, experts may "walk through" the resource, much like a regular user would, being asked to share impressions and reactions along the way verbally (e.g. think aloud protocols); by tinkering with the resource itself (e.g. making notes in margins, or drawing over what is on paper or on screen); or in a formalized instrument to be used concurrently or immediately following the walkthrough (e.g. checklist). Advisory board meetings can provide wonderful opportunities for expert appraisal. Alternatively, if the heart of the intervention relates to some kind of process or procedure, site visits with (non-)participant observation and interviews could be more appropriate. Expert appraisal of documents generated when the intervention is tested can also be valuable. Vesper, Herrington, Kartoglu, and Reeves (2011) reported on the expert appraisal of an innovative e-learning course whereby experts provided feedback on interface and usability design after being presented with an extensive storyboard for the program.

Pilot

Pilots can help researchers and practitioners begin to get a sense of how the intervention will perform in various contexts and what kind of real world realities need to be addressed for the design to have a chance of success under representative conditions. The term "pilot" refers to any field testing of the intervention in settings that approximate, but do not completely represent, the target context. These are "live" tests of the intervention, where one or more contextual factors are non-natural. Examples of non-natural contextual factors could include: working with small groups of learners and not whole classes; trying the intervention out in a different location (e.g. in the school, but not in the regular classroom); trying the intervention out after regularly scheduled classes; researchers – not teachers – teach lessons; bringing in temporary computers instead of using the school's computers, or using only one lesson out of a series. Often, though not always, the non-natural conditions under which pilot testing is conducted render more stability or certainty than would be present if the intervention was deployed under completely natural conditions.

Pilot testing usually takes place in earlier stages of intervention development, and tends to be small scale. Some common methods of data collection during pilots include: video review, discourse analysis, structured (non-)participant observation, interviews, questionnaires, assessments, participant logbooks, focus groups, document analysis, and computer logs. Sometimes, the pilot testing of an intervention is also used as an opportunity to test and revise research instruments that will be used later (e.g. in the tryout). The research design in pilots varies greatly. Some pilots employ the use of experimental design, with systematic variation of intervention features working like different treatments. Here, pre/post-test measures seek evidence of an effect. This is often complemented with other (usually more qualitative) measures that portray the intervention in action with the aim of explaining how and why the effect is found (or not). In the words of Cobb, Confrey, diSessa, Lehrer, and Schauble (2003, p. 9), the design "is subject to test and revision, and the successive iterations that result play a role similar to that of systematic variation in experiment." Linn and Hsi (2000) provide a detailed account of such an approach in exploring fruitful pathways to science learning involving computers, teachers, and peer learners. Lehrer and Schauble (2004) offer a rich description of what a pilot study can look like and explain how their active instructional involvement shaped not only data collection, but their own understanding. During their pilot testing of an intervention intended to help students understand variability through data modeling, student interactions were captured on video and supplemented with researcher observational notes. In addition, students were interviewed immediately after lessons ended.

Tryout

Tryouts are used to study how interventions work, what participants think or feel about them, and the results they yield. Tryouts take place when (a prototype of) the intervention is field tested in a natural setting. It is socially responsible to undertake a tryout once an intervention is mature enough that it won't inordinately disturb the normal functioning of schools, classrooms, or other learning contexts. As with pilots, many data collection methods can be used; the choice depends most on the questions being asked and what is feasible given the context. Creativity is frequently needed to structure the research design of tryouts to fit into live educational settings (e.g. scheduling of courses or topics; or changing cohorts of students).

As with the other strategies, multiple types of questions can be addressed within the scope of one tryout. For example, de Vries, van der Meij, Boersma, and Pieters (2005) describe two successive design experiments, and the data-driven refinements in-between, in which a child-friendly email tool was used in primary schools to support collective reflection. Two prototypes of the tool were tested in five primary classrooms, with the research focusing on: how well the design propositions were embodied in the intervention during enactment (soundness); how practical it was to use in those classrooms (local viability); and how well it supported collaborative reflection through writing (effectiveness).

Determine specific methods

Once basic strategies have been selected, the methods that will be used for the investigation must be determined. As has been stated repeatedly throughout this book, design researchers draw from both quantitative and qualitative methods, often using a combination of the two. The methods are selected based on the most accurate and productive way to answer the research questions. Accurate methods are able to collect the specific kind of information that is needed to answer the research question(s) well. Productive methods make sense within the constraints of the project. Some highly accurate methods will be too costly, time-consuming, or too invasive to be productive in light of the overall intervention. Gorard, Roberts, and Taylor (2004) refer to this stance as "methodological fit for purpose" (p. 581) and stress its importance in general and in design research in particular, as have others (Shavelson, Phillips, Towne, & Feuer, 2003). They note that design studies often require mixed methods, as do others (cf. Bell, 2004). Many books are available to offer in-depth information about various research methods. Please see the Appendix for specific methodological suggestions.

Seven methods are among the most common for use during the evaluation and reflection phase: interviews; focus groups; observations; questionnaires/checklists; (pre/post) tests; logs/journals; and document analysis. The list below offers brief comments on using each of these methods during this phase. Table 6.4 offers generic recommendations for methods suitable to the four strategies described above.

- Interviews: Often used to probe more deeply into issues uncovered through another method (e.g. questionnaire). Since they are not anonymous, there can be a risk of respondents giving socially desirable feedback concerning the intervention.
- Focus groups: Can be used to articulate, understand, and refine a shared platform of design ideas among developers and/or experts. They can also provide a slightly more distanced opportunity (than interviews) for participants to discuss their perceptions and experiences of the intervention.

Table 6.4 Strategies and methods matrix

Methods	Developer screening	Expert appraisal	Pilot	Tryout
Interviews	dark grey	dark grey	dark grey	dark grey
Focus groups	dark grey	dark grey	light grey	light grey
Observations		light grey	light grey	light grey
Questionnaires/checklists	dark grey	dark grey	light grey	light grey
(Pre/post)tests			light grey	light grey
Logs/journals			light grey	light grey
Document analysis	dark grey	dark grey	light grey	light grey

Legend: dark grey = frequently useful; light grey = may be useful, depending on the intervention type.

- (Non-)Participant observations: Allow precious, firsthand opportunities to witness and, if appropriate, participate in, the intervention; these are virtually essential for understanding pilots and tryouts. These are not always used as formal data sources, since they can be time-consuming and difficult to analyze.
- Questionnaires/checklists: Can be efficient for researchers but generally time-consuming for respondents. Questionnaires are often used in before/after measures (e.g. of attitudes) or to rate experiences. Checklists are often used to identify presence of certain (un)desirable characteristics of an intervention.
- (Pre/post)tests: Can be used to document current status or measure change from previous status, often in combination with other methods. Even with high-quality assessments, these can provide indications, but rarely hard evidence of intervention effects.
- Logs/journals: Can be generated by computer (e.g. mouse clicks or eye-tracking) or by participants (e.g. daily reflection booklets); the human-generated ones are often kept during, and sometimes after, interventions are implemented.
- Document analysis: Can be used to appraise components of the intervention (e.g. design specifications or a working prototype) or to gain insight into its results (e.g. learner work).

Draft and revise a planning document

As methods are selected and methodological ideas begin to solidify, it is important to document and check the emerging research plans. A planning document provides an overview of the activities and timelines for a study, and is useful for assessing how well the study is likely to meet its goals. A planning document can be checked for its methodological soundness (e.g. triangulation of data sources and data collection times) and feasibility (e.g. levels of invasiveness, costs, or time needed). It can also help to plan and keep track of the many different tasks involved (e.g. meeting with stakeholders, creating resources, hiring facilitators, obtaining IRB approval, creating instruments, coaching assistants). The project management resources recommended in the Appendix may also help in this regard.

Create or seek instruments

In order to collect data, it is necessary to create the instruments to be used in the study, or to review, obtain, and fine-tune existing instruments that have already been designed and validated. Because design research is often conducted to create new solutions to problems, it can be difficult to find suitable instruments. But searching can be worthwhile, as the time and effort involved in creating new ones that are reliable and valid can be substantial. Many resources are available to help guide this process; recommendations are given in the Appendix.

Select participants

Different participant populations may be sampled for different purposes. Common participants in intervention evaluation include developers, practitioners, experts, and learners. Developers can range from members of the design team who have been engaged with the design task from early on, to individuals constructing sub-components of the intervention with minimal involvement in its conception. Practitioner involvement in evaluation may take place through many roles, including that of developer, expert, facilitator, or implementer. Teachers are most frequently involved in evaluation. Other practitioner groups include educational specialists (e.g. library and media specialists, gifted consultants, remedial instructors, or school psychologists) and educational leaders (e.g. principals, instructional coaches, or department heads). Different kinds of experts can provide useful input during evaluation of educational interventions in design research. Content or subject matter experts can help improve, for example, the scope, sequence, and accuracy of learning content in an intervention. Instructional experts can assist by critiquing the appropriateness of the pedagogical dimensions of an intervention. If technology is involved, programmers and graphic designers can suggest how to enhance the functionality, usability, or aesthetics of a learning resource. Professional development experts can help anticipate conceptual, practical, or emotional requirements for an intervention's success. And the insights of textbook writers, curriculum developers, and testing experts can be extremely useful, especially for assessing how the intervention aligns with existing resources and frameworks. Learners can be involved in design research; most often, they are tested and/or observed during implementation of an intervention. In interventions targeting the education and care of young children, it is not unusual to ask parents to serve as respondents. It can be important to think creatively about ways to collect data that may simultaneously offer something to the participants, if this does not risk too much disturbance to the integrity of the data. For example, is it possible to conduct a focus group discussion with teachers as part of a professional development session that features collaborative reflection? Can a meaningful, on-task learning activity be designed around the use of pupil logbooks/journals?

Collect the data

General recommendations concerning data collection are available in the Appendix. This section discusses an issue that tends to crop up often during data collection in educational design research: specifically the conflicting roles of advocate and critic (cf. Design-Based Research Collective, 2003). In educational design research, the same individuals are often simultaneously researchers, developers, facilitators, and/or evaluators of the intervention.

For the advocate role, firsthand, detailed understanding of research findings is very beneficial. When designers participate in the implementation and testing of interventions, they are afforded the sometimes humbling opportunity to gain deeper and often sharper insights into not only the aspects of the design that succeed or fail, but underlying assumptions (e.g. about what motivates learners or what details teachers will care about). This provides rich opportunity for critical reflection and generating new ideas, as inputs for redesign are immediate and, coming from live observation, often more powerful than secondhand findings. An open-minded designer is quite likely to "see" implications for redesign during (or inspired by) pilot or tryout activities. For the critic role, the designer mindset also has benefits, as the intentions of the design are clearly understood. The critical researcher can see, for example, how well instruments are measuring the phenomenon they were intended to measure. The need and opportunities for making methodological adjustments may be more apparent to someone who deeply understands both the design intentions and the research goals.

But this comes at a cost, for the advocate and especially the critic. The methodological concerns, particularly bias, are substantial. Despite efforts to stimulate criticism, the potential for evaluator effect (Patton, 2001) and socially desirable responses stand to increase when participants know that the researcher is also the developer. Participants may react differently due to the designer's presence, and the designers may be, unintentionally or not, less receptive to critique. And even if the researcher collecting the data is not a developer, this kind of research in context can be fraught with challenges, such as these threats described by Krathwohl (1993): the Hawthorne effect (involvement in the study influences participant behavior); hypothesis guessing (participants try to guess what the researcher seeks and react accordingly); and diffusion (knowledge of the treatment influences other participants). In addition to triangulation, some of these threats can be mitigated by using unobtrusive data collection methods. Alternatively, design researchers may choose to embrace their role as a "nuisance variable," and compensate for this by clearly describing their presence in the research setting and discussing their real or potential influence on the data.

Analyze the data

The reading and resources in the Appendix provide guidance on processing, analyzing, and interpreting both quantitative and qualitative data. In the evaluation of interventions, the data analysis is often framed, directly or indirectly, by design propositions, if they have been woven into the research questions. That is, when the intervention is being evaluated, it is common to look for evidence of a certain construct in the intervention, its enactment, or its results. Data analysis culminates in drawing conclusions – answers to the main research questions. Very often, the next step for researchers is to decide how to address concerns in redesign (revising solutions is discussed at the end of Chapter 5). However, it is strongly recommended to take time for reflection before redesigning, as described later in this chapter.

Report the study

Studies documenting the inception, process, and findings from intervention testing are almost always reported internally, in the form of reports or memos.

They may also be reported externally, in the form of: conference presentations; articles in refereed journals or other periodicals; books; or publically accessible reports. Both internal and external reports attend to both practical and theoretical goals. That is, they attend to how the investigation will inform the next phase of intervention development as well as the contribution to theoretical understanding. Very often internal project reports, once they have served to inform stakeholders or stimulate project team deliberation, can be used as the basis for external publications. Both types of reports follow the same basic format, roughly: introduction and problem statement; theoretical framework; study design and methods; findings; conclusion and discussion. Please refer to Chapter 9 for additional information.

Reflection

> Concepts without experiences are empty, experiences without concepts are blind.
>
> Emmanuel Kant (1781, p. 129)

The value and functions of reflection

In the field of education, there is not only a great appreciation for reflection, but also some consternation about the fact that it has come to mean many different things to many different people. Sometimes these different interpretations are even at odds with one another. One of the most common uses pertains to considering one's own performance (e.g. as teacher or learner) and/or professionalism (as an educator). The goal is usually highly personal, and relates to the development of self. While reflection of a more personal nature can serve many purposes for researchers, this is not the kind of reflection discussed here. The kind of reflection described in this section is undertaken to develop the integrated research and development agenda.

In educational design research, reflection involves active and thoughtful consideration of what has come together in both research and development (including theoretical inputs, empirical findings, and subjective reactions) with the aim of producing new (theoretical) understanding. This is part and parcel of all long-term, thoughtful research. However, this process is often neglected in graduate programs, which is notable, given that these are the primary means through which we educate researchers. Yet, if we look at the scientific journals and books in our fields, it is clear that only some kinds of new knowledge grow forth directly from empirical testing. New theories, for example, do not present themselves in the form of research findings. Rather, they grow out of reflection. In scholarly publications, we typically share the products of reflection, and indeed some of the process, under the heading of "Discussion".

Much of the literature on reflection has close ties to philosophy, as Procee (2006) points out: Decartes, who declared self-inspection as the basis of his epistemology; Kant, who postulated the autonomous and enlightened subject; Dewey, who insisted on reflective experience; Horkheiner and Adorno, who criticized instrumental rationality; and Habermas, who embraced a broad concept of rationality. Donald Schön, a master of musical improvisation and conceptual structure who was also trained as a philosopher, called for professionals to better understand their actions by reflecting on them in his highly acclaimed work, *The Reflective Practitioner: How Professionals Think in Action* (1983). It can be useful for design researchers to view themselves as reflective practitioners. Schön (1983, p. 68) claimed that in so doing, each of us:

> … allows himself to experience surprise, puzzlement, or confusion in a situation which he finds uncertain or unique. He reflects on the phenomenon before him, and on the prior understandings which have been implicit in his [designing] behavior. He carries out an experiment which serves to generate both a new understanding of the phenomenon and a change in the situation.

Fostering reflection

Reflection can be driven by reasoning. Through this fairly transparent, rational process, connections between existing ideas can lead to new ones. Reasoning is used, for example, to determine cause and effect, to verify assumptions or to refute predictions. Because of their role in theory development, three forms of reasoning, deduction, induction, and abduction, were described in Chapter 2. Reasoning is essential for both research and design, but so are creative thoughts and feelings. Hammer and Reymen (2002) point out the need for inspiration and emotion to play a role in engineering design reflection, alongside rationality. New, useful insights may also be born out of less transparent, less planned processes, whereby insights and novel ideas seem to present themselves, sometimes quite suddenly. This moment is sometimes referred to using the Japanese word, *satori*. Literally, *satori* means understanding, but in the Zen Buddhist tradition, it refers to a flash of sudden insight or awareness. Creativity researchers do not yet fully understand the processes through which these, seemingly spontaneous, connections are made. But more is known about conditions under which they tend to occur. In the remainder of this section, recommendations are given on what design researchers can do to nurture the more spontaneous connections (referred to as organic reflection) and to encourage the reasoned connections (referred to as structured reflection).

Organic reflection

The term "organic reflection" refers to a kind of intended contemplation. For many people, this kind of reflection takes place under the shower, or during a commute to/from work. Sometimes it is the process of dialogue. It takes place during times when there is very little agenda, and the mind is relatively free to wander and make its own connections between ideas. This phenomenon is likely already quite familiar to the readers of this book. But it is mentioned here because, while organic reflection is not typically associated with professional work, it can certainly serve the work of design research. Three techniques that may fertilize organic reflection include:

- Well-timed breaks, with input: Look for a moment in the day where the work flow is naturally paused so as not to be overly disruptive (e.g. between articles, if the task is literature review), that can also afford a break away from the work place (take a shower, go for a walk, drive a car). Use that break time, in silence or in dialogue, for reflection.
- Seek *un*like-minded sparring partners: Find people with ideas that are not just new, but foreign. In print, in dialogue, or in silence, explore the ways of knowing and lenses for viewing that are concomitant with those ideas.
- Engage in "background" projects: Johnson (2010) discussed the value of maintaining background projects that can springboard new ideas. For example, innovative design projects, intriguing inquiry or literature study in new areas can trigger ideas, often by presenting new ways of looking at the world.

Structured reflection

The ideas about structured reflection presented here rest heavily on the work of Reymen et al. (2006), who derived a domain-independent engineering design model and studied its application in structured reflection. These ideas shape an understanding of *what* should be reflected upon, and *when* design reflection should take place. We are also charmed by the work of Procee and Visscher-Voerman (2004), who developed specific reflection techniques inspired by a Kantian epistemology. Here, this work is adapted to the context of educational design research and, in so doing, suggestions are offered for *how* reflection can be structured.

Reymen et al. (2006) assert that design reflection should focus on two areas. Applied to the context of educational design research, these are: the design challenge (e.g. difference between existing and desired situations and/or important factors in the design context); and aspects of the integrated research and development process. Based on the steps in a basic design cycle and mechanisms of reflective practice, they define reflection as a process that consists of three main phases: *preparation, image forming,* and *conclusion drawing.* Preparation and image forming mainly look into the past. Preparation consists of collecting the relevant facts or observations to be considered. Image forming involves selection and synthesis of those facts and observations. Conclusion drawing looks ahead, using the results from the first two steps to determine next activities. Reymen et al. (2006) point out the importance of setting aside certain moments for reflection. In the case of educational design research, an obvious moment for reflection is between one micro-cycle of evaluation and reflection and another of design and construction. But, especially if those cycles are long, interim moments may need to be identified for reflection. Interim moments should both start and end with reflection on the design challenge and the design process, and they should also give attention to when the next reflection will be, and what that means for structuring the work in the meantime. An important point Reymen et al. (2006) make is that the reflection should occur on a regular basis. While their work is focused on individual designers, they also emphasize that design teams (with all their variation in personality, intuition, creativity, and other skills) should reflect together regularly, and that support for this would be desirable.

The work of Procee and Visscher-Voerman (2004) is helpful for ideas on how the preparation, image forming, and conclusion phases can be structured. To understand their techniques, it is necessary to understand their roots, most elaborately described in Procee's (2006) Kantian epistemology of reflection in education. Central to this work is Kant's distinction between the realm of understanding and the realm of judgment, both of which are different from experience. Here, understanding refers to the mental ability to grasp concepts, theories, and laws; whereas judgment is the power to determine which ones are relevant in a particular situation. In essence, judgment mediates the interactions between understanding and experience.

Procee's approach to reflection focuses on judgment, and uses Kant's "four moments" in judgment to shape reflection: quantity (determining the "object of perception" in the "free play of the imagination"); quality (a special disinterested satisfaction in which feeling and understanding go hand in hand); relation (experiencing different connections in and around the "object"); and modality (the logical status of judgment). In relation to reflection, Procee (2006, p. 252) explains them like this:

> Each moment generates a different type of reflection. For instance, quantity – an indiscriminate concept (or image, or narrative) placed outside the experience – creates a reflective space that stimulates learning discoveries. It generates new and unexpected views on experience. Many practical proposals for reflection in education (for example, keeping a diary, or working together in a Socratic seminar) can be understood as realizations of this moment of thought. The moment of quality is about points of view that may be helpful to estimate (elements of) experiences and choices (that have been made). This aspect is more than a mere assessment of experiences because the standards for evaluation will provide the substance for reflection, too, as well as giving rise to feelings of harmony and disharmony. The moment of relation brings about dynamic elements by introducing points of view that are related to different visions from a professional as well as a social context. In the case of modality, reflection reflects on the reflection process itself and on aspects of (professional) identity.

Procee developed four techniques for reflection, based on Kant's moments in judgment; and introduced geometrical names for the different types of reflection: point reflection (quantity), line reflection (quality), triangle reflection (relation), and circle reflection (modality). Each of these techniques involves a partnership between the person doing the reflection and an assistant, whose only goal is to support the process of the person doing the reflecting (Procee & Visscher-Voerman, 2004). We add here that group reflection within a design research team can help reveal that some people view particular issues as irrelevant, while others may see these same issues as pivotal.

In this section, the focus and regularity of reflection, as considered by Reymen et al. (2006) is brought together with the four techniques for reflection as devised by Procee and Visscher-Voerman (2004). The amalgamation is applied to reflecting on the findings and experiences of educational design research. These strategies are presented in Table 6.5. The strategy column describes the geometrical name, its Kantian origin, and the main mechanism in focus for each strategy. For each cell in the table, examples are given in italics.

Both the theoretical and practical goals of educational design research are furthered through reflection. Through organic and structured reflection, theoretical understanding is developed through consideration of the findings (e.g. "What do these results tell us?") in light of how they were obtained (e.g. the soundness of the measurements, or how appropriate the choice of setting). In addition, consideration is given to what might have been happening, but was not measured; or what could have occurred if the research had been structured differently. These, and other reflective insights, often have immediate implications for refining the intervention. For example, reflecting on how teachers altered a learning environment may generate new ideas about features to include or needs to be met. Often, reflection also generates new questions to be explored.

Products resulting from this phase

Many interim products are generated during this phase, ranging from written theoretical frameworks, to research instruments and plans, to reports on intervention implementation and testing. Reflective musings may even be shared in written form. But toward furthering fundamental understanding and applied use, the main outputs from this phase are answers to research questions (and new ones for further investigation); implications for integrated design propositions; and issues/recommendations for redesign.

Theoretical understanding

Although fantastic tales to the contrary are known, most theoretical understanding is not advanced by singular brilliant insights coming in the flash of a moment, with the implications of certain findings sinking in all at once. Most of the time, assembling and puzzling over evidence is a slow, methodical process. Asking and answering research questions gradually leads to new insights, and often quickly leads to new questions. The theoretical understanding that is constructed through evaluation and reflection may hold local, middle-range, or high level applicability; this depends on the focus and methods of the study. A single cycle of evaluation and reflection can especially contribute empirical findings, hypotheses, or conjectures that constitute the building blocks of theory. This understanding can be used to shape descriptions, explanations, or predictions concerning certain phenomena. When integrated, such understanding can serve prescriptive purposes. This can take the form of design principles, which may be used to structure similar interventions, and/or refine the specific one being tested.

Table 6.5 Four strategies for structured reflection on educational design research

Strategy	Preparation	Image forming	Conclusion drawing
Point (Quantity) Induction	Identify one or more data points from which unplanned insight may be gleaned and ask a question. *Were there unanticipated processes through which the learners were highly engaged?*	Consider/discuss not the potential lesson to be learned, but think about the experience. Ask not only why questions, but also how and what. *Why did the learners seem so engaged? What were they doing? When? How did they interact?*	Use the results to formulate new hypotheses, questions for investigation, or revised design ideas. *How might this reflection be put to use? Do design requirements need to be revised? Or design propositions?*
Line (Quality) Norms	Take an observed instance in time and choose a role; distinguish between actor, process, and product in that instance. Consider norms that can relate to each one, and choose one or more norms that are suspected to hold importance. *During a lesson, the teacher (actor) listens well, appears motivated; (enacts a lesson (process) that is calm, hands-on, adaptive; resulting in learner (product) motivation, and attentiveness.*	Consider/discuss the norm(s) in light of the actual instance in time. Given the intended intervention, how appropriate and useful is it to be governed by these norms? *Did adhering to these norms interfere with the intervention? Did they enable it? Why might the teacher have behaved this way during this particular instance? What can be learned from this?*	Decide if norms need to be investigated further, or if changes to the intervention are necessary to reflect better alignment with, for example, pedagogical, cultural, or social interaction norms. *To what extent are the norms (which were inferred from observation) compatible with more broadly existing practices? Does the intervention encourage more (or, if they are not favorable, less) action governed by these norms? Should it?*
Triangle (Relation) Perspectives	Select a finding or instance to focus on, and list the different (groups of) people whose perspectives are relevant to the finding or instance; then eliminate the least relevant. *One group of learners became so strident about genetic testing that they revolted: boycotted class and held demonstrations instead.*	Hypothesize, on the basis of experience and/or data, how these people frame meaning and justify these with examples; then compare them. *Why did this group of learners care so deeply? Why did they express dissatisfaction with the teacher/school instead of with the scientists involved?*	What can be learned from "trying on" these other perspectives? *Are there outlooks/mindsets that are salient, but have been overlooked? Should something be done to minimize or encourage certain perspectives? In light of the study goals, do these perspectives warrant further investigation?*

Strategy	Preparation	Image forming	Conclusion drawing
Circle (Modality) Process	Identify the methods that have been used. *The study used interviews, video observations, pre/post test data, and analysis of learner assignments to explore pupil and teacher experiences with the new learning environment.*	Describe issues, questions, or problems that have been ignored or insufficiently addressed by those methods; which ones were addressed well? What made that method work? *Observation of inter-learner interactions proved less useful than hoped to understand individual reasoning pathways; this also yielded insufficient insight into learner processes to fully understand implications from learner assignments.*	What can be done differently? What (more) do we need to investigate in order to make improvements? What can be learned from what did yield "eye-opening" or powerful findings? *Instead of studying inter-learner interactions, conduct the video observations of learners while they are completing the assignments to try and understand the reasoning pathways.*

Recommendations for applied use

For many researchers, part of the appeal of educational design research is that insights from one study can be applied in the subsequent phase of design, a process which can be particularly gratifying. The application may be made directly to an intervention, or indirectly to its integrated design propositions. Consideration of potential refinements to design ideas or constructed prototypes is given in light of the original intentions, and should take into account potential risks of pulling internal aspects of the design out of alignment. As noted by Wang and Hannafin (2005, p.10), "In addition to improving the ongoing design, researchers also consider the influence of en route changes on the integrity of the design ... any changes to one aspect of the design need to be compatible with other aspects of the design." This process is not always clear-cut or smooth. It can involve distancing oneself from religious-like convictions, or design features that are regarded as offspring. Taking the issues identified through evaluation and reflection and deciding how to address them (or not) in the intervention design are issues of redesign, which is addressed in the "Revising solutions" section of Chapter 5.

From products of this phase to other phases

In earlier stages of educational design research, theoretical understanding and practical implications that result from evaluation and reflection generally prompt new cycles of analysis and exploration and/or design and construction. In later stages, the results of this phase may prompt another (e.g. large scale) cycle of evaluation and reflection or conclusion of the project. Very long term (e.g. 10 years or greater) design research projects may come to a close because the problem was satisfactorily solved and sufficient theoretical understanding was generated. More often though, projects end through natural selection, cessation of funding, or departure of (e.g. graduate) researchers. But when done well, the interventions created through educational design research can outlive the design research projects that created them. This can be the case when attention is given to implementation and spread throughout the entire trajectory, the topic of Chapter 7.

Chapter 7

Implementation and spread

The generic model for design research presented in Chapter 3 shows all three core processes (analysis and exploration; design and construction; and evaluation and reflection) interacting with practice through the (anticipation of) implementation and spread of interventions. It also suggests that the interaction generally increases as the project matures. Even though actual implementation and spread cannot take place until an intervention has been constructed, researchers and practitioners jointly anticipate and plan for it from the very first stage of analysis and exploration, e.g. by tempering idealist goals with realistic assessments of what is possible; by taking practitioner concerns seriously; and by studying what intrinsic motives and natural opportunities are already present in the target setting. This chapter starts off describing the basic mindset underlying implementation and spread in educational design research on any scale: planning for actual use. Thereafter, implementation is described in terms of adopting, enacting, and sustaining interventions; spread is described in terms of dissemination and diffusion. Next, determinants of implementation and spread are addressed. These are clustered into four kinds of factors: attributes of the intervention; strategies for change; the context, including its surrounding system; and the actors involved. Based on the issues raised throughout the chapter, specific considerations for interacting with practice during educational design research are given for each of the three main phases in the generic model.

Planning for actual use

The question becomes, what are the absolutely essential features that must be in place to cause change under conditions that one can reasonably hope to exist in normal school settings? In order to effect this ... I again need additional expertise, more methods if you like, that were not part of my training. I need to know a great deal more about school restructuring, teacher training and support, and teachers as researchers. I need to use ethnographic methodologies to study which aspects of the program are readily adopted and which are resisted. I need to know the conditions favorable for adoption. I need to study the sociology of dissemination. I need to know about public policy issues, and so forth. Again changes in theory and practice demand concomitant advances in methodology for the conduct, documentation and dissemination of research.

Ann Brown (1992, p. 173)

This chapter cannot sufficiently speak to all the needs for additional expertise expressed by Ann Brown in her seminal article on design experiments, but it does raise some important considerations. The considerations discussed here stem from the commitment to seeking theoretical understanding through the development and testing of interventions that solve real problems. This commitment entails a basic mindset of planning and designing interventions for actual use. Planning for actual use does not necessarily mean intending to bring about fundamental, large-scale change. In fact, planning for actual use may: reflect modest scope (e.g. few participants, short duration); be poorly defined (which is often the case at the start of design projects); or intentionally be temporary (e.g. limited to pilot testing). However, planning for actual use does mean assuming that designed interventions *could* take off, and striving to develop both theoretical understanding and practical solutions that *can* actually be used by others. Educational design research is conducted *in situ* to increase both ecological validity and the relevance of the research. Both of these are served by a mindset of planning for actual use.

Planning for actual use entails anticipating how interventions will be implemented and how they may (potentially) spread beyond initial testing sites. It also involves taking into account factors that influence the processes of implementation and spread. This chapter offers some considerations for designing interventions for actual use within educational design research projects. The related reading list in the Appendix contains both classic and contemporary literature concerning the design, implementation, and spread of educational innovations.

Implementation

If an intervention came in the form of a medicinal pill, then implementation would refer to issues such as whether it: is chewed; swallowed with water; taken after a meal; ground into applesauce; causes side effects; possibly over/under dosed; taken at will or under duress; and so forth. Implementation is what happens when the intervention is set in motion. Using the terminology in the logic model example in Chapter 5, implementation relates to the processes through which outputs are generated (e.g. lessons are taught; materials are used; workshops are held, etc.). It is common, but not at all necessary, for educational design research interventions to be implemented on smaller scales initially (depending on the grain size of the study that is being conducted: few children, few teachers, few classes, few schools, few municipalities) and increase over time, especially if the intervention matures and testing moves from pilot settings to actual tryouts (cf. Chapter 6). Regardless of scale, three main stages of implementation can be distinguished: adoption, enactment, and sustained maintenance.

Adoption

In the social sciences research literature, there are many different uses of the terms adoption, so it seems necessary to clarify how the term is used here. In this book, as in others (cf. Bartholomew, Parcel, Kok, & Gottleib, 2006), adoption is used to describe a decision to, even if only on a trial basis, use an intervention. In educational design research, the adoption process may begin as early as analysis and exploration, as practitioners and researchers collaboratively consider what problems are worth solving and become committed to testing potential solutions. Adoption may take place as a precursor to evaluation and reflection, when practitioners decide if they will (tentatively) use an intervention for testing purposes. Dix (2007) provided a theoretical framework specifically for studying the adoption of educational technologies in educational design research projects.

Enactment

Interventions are played out during enactment (e.g. learners use online learning environments; teachers try out new lesson ideas). Enactment is shaped by the intervention; those using it; the context in which it is situated; and the manner in which it is introduced. Planned and unplanned processes take place during enactment. Planned processes are often portrayed in terms of fidelity. Fidelity describes the degree to which the intervention is enacted with its intentions, methods, and strategies intact. Processes that were enacted, but unplanned by designers, include side effects – the unintentional fringe benefits and/or negative consequences brought about by an intervention. Other unplanned processes are those created by practitioners who (intentionally or not) alter interventions (e.g. to fit their own value systems, expertise, or contexts), and enact them accordingly. When done consciously, this process is referred to as adaptation, or reinvention (cf. Rogers, 1962, 2003). Many adaptations can be counter-productive (cf. Cuban, 1986); these have been referred to as "lethal mutations" (cf. Brown & Campione, 1996). But often adaptations are valuable. Clarke and Dede (2009) describe how design researchers can learn from practitioner adaptations that meet the goals of the intervention in ways different, or even more apt, than those conceived of by designers. This is an example of mutual adaptation (cf. Snyder, Bolin, & Zumwalt, 1992), a process that can be expected, if not explicitly sought, in educational design research.

Design researchers have increasingly called for greater attention to be given to enactment (e.g. van den Akker, 1998a). For example, Hoadley (2004) emphasized the need to study the interaction between interventions, the people involved, and the setting in which they take place. Tabak (2004) described the intervention as the "exogenous design" and calls for researchers to recognize, embrace, and study its interaction and tensions with the "endogenous design" – the materials and processes that are in place before any intervention is introduced, as well as those that are the result of enactment. Bielaczyc (2006) presents a "social infrastructure framework" that identifies critical elements of classroom social structures that should be taken into account when developing technology-rich learning environments. These include: cultural beliefs; learning and teaching practices; socio-techno-spatial relations; and interaction with the "outside world."

Sustained maintenance

Sustained maintenance refers to efforts required to continue, or at least attempt to sustain, an intervention with little to no external support. This often entails some degree of institutionalization, and is extraordinarily difficult (cf. Hargreaves & Fink, 2006). In educational design research, the considerations for sustained maintenance may be gathered as early as analysis and exploration, as practitioners and researchers collaboratively consider the strengths, weaknesses, opportunities, and threats present in a given context that might allow or prevent an intervention from thriving over the long term. The level of maintenance required to sustain an intervention is also a factor that is considered during design and construction, and related assumptions are often tested during evaluation and reflection. Not all design research projects require planning for sustained maintenance, but doing so stands to boost both the ecological validity and the relevance of the study. Fishman and Krajcik (2003) discuss usability as a guiding principle in the design of sustainable science curricula, and present a framework for examining this construct (which they relate to: the innovation's ability to adapt to the organization's context; the organization's ability to successfully enact the innovation; and the organization's ability to sustain the innovation).

Spread

Many design research projects do not aspire to achieve large-scale implementation, but most do strive to develop either (a) interventions that could, ostensibly, be implemented across schools, provinces, or states; or (b) design propositions or theories that can inform the development of such interventions by others. In educational design research, the term "spread" refers to the propagation of designed interventions (or their underlying ideas) to settings outside the initial field testing context. Spread entails more than increasing the number of sites for testing, participants, or schools; it is also more than superficially replicating processes, increasing instances of certain behaviors, or using particular materials. Fundamentally, the complex process of implementing and sustaining educational interventions involves the spread of underlying beliefs, norms and principles, professional judgment, and even moral purpose (Coburn, 2003; Fullan, 1982, 2003).

Different theories can be used to describe, explain, and predict the spread of interventions, but few are as well regarded as those of innovation theorist, Everett Rogers (1962, 2003), and educational change expert, Michael Fullan (1982, 1991). The relevance of these works for educational design research has been pointed out previously (Larson & Dearing, 2008). Rooted in sociology, Rogers (1962, 2003) described spread in terms of a decision-making process that features the seeking and processing of information, during which individuals strive to reduce uncertainty about the advantages and disadvantages of an innovation. This decision-making process centers around five steps: (1) knowledge (awareness that the intervention exists); (2) persuasion (interest in the innovation); (3) decision (adopt or reject); (4) implementation (trial); and (5) confirmation (continuing and or extending use).

While Rogers' work emphasizes characteristics of the innovation and the adopters, Fullan's work (1982, 1991) stresses the roles of various educational actors in social change. Notably, Fullan emphasizes the importance of understanding how micro and macro levels interact. This includes seeing change from the perspectives of learners, teachers, and administrators as well as the organizations and institutions that influence change, such as teacher associations, school districts, and government. The influences of both Rogers and Fullan are evident throughout this chapter, especially in the subsequent section on determinants of implementation and spread.

Engendering spread may not be an explicit concern of many design researchers, who may be so embroiled in just trying to get an innovation to work in one setting that broader use cannot be a priority. But developing theoretical understanding and interventions that are *worthy* of spread is something that concerns all design researchers. The problems tackled in educational design research are not idiosyncratic; rather, they are sufficiently prevalent and substantial to warrant scientific investigation. As such, the solutions designed to address them should be of value to others. Here, attention is given to two main processes through which interventions and their underlying ideas spread: dissemination and diffusion. Two sides of the same coin, dissemination has more to do with push, whereas diffusion has more to do with pull.

Dissemination

Dissemination is a one-way process, in which information is offered, or broadcast. In educational design research, information about interventions is shared, e.g. through conference presentations, workshops, journal publications, or other media. While effective dissemination often entails creating opportunities for interaction (e.g. workshops), the impetus is more like that of sowing seeds: putting information or ideas out in the hope that they may take root. Dissemination is kind of a counterpart to diffusion, and, in some cases, may be seen as a prerequisite, for example if information about an intervention is spread widely to raise awareness. Many design research projects use interactive websites to share information about their projects and sometimes showcase or allow open access to (elements of) designed interventions.

Diffusion

In educational design research, diffusion is the process through which interventions are pulled into practice from within. For example, practitioners exchange information, arrange demonstrations, or coach each other. It is not necessarily the scope of diffusion that measures an intervention's success, but its presence is one important indicator. Coburn (2003) refers to this as "spread within," and notes that it can be seen, for example, when reform principles or norms of social interaction become embedded in school policies and routines, or when teachers draw on those ideas and put them to use in other aspects of their practice, which were not explicitly addressed by the intervention. Diffusion tends to be less common than dissemination; and design researchers can sometimes be both delighted and overwhelmed when it starts to take place. While it can be rewarding to see an intervention take on a life of its own, it can be difficult to adequately respond to practitioner requests (e.g. for intervention support or additional materials), unless projects have budgeted accordingly – which is extremely difficult.

Implementation and spread are complex processes. Even with powerful resources and substantial effort, success is not guaranteed. But careful planning informed by understanding of the factors that influence these processes can increase the chances for success, as addressed in the subsequent section.

Determinants of implementation and spread

As discussed above, educational design research is undertaken to address important problems, with the ultimate goal of being useful to others (as well as to the research participants). While interventions are developed and tested in specific contexts, the interventions themselves and/or their underlying ideas will ideally hold wider value. For this reason, giving attention to factors that determine implementation and spread is important, even for short-term, small-scale studies. This section discusses factors that influence if, to what extent, and how an educational design research intervention is: adopted, enacted, sustainably maintained, disseminated, and/or diffused. This section is informed by literature on the spread of innovations in general (e.g. Rogers, 1962, 2003), in the field of education (e.g. Fullan & Pomfret, 1977), and specifically involving educational technology (e.g. Tondeur, Valke, & van Braak, 2008). The discussion is organized around four sets of factors: intervention attributes; strategies used for enabling implementation and spread; context and surrounding systems; and the actors involved.

Intervention attributes

Interventions that are prone to successful implementation and spread exhibit certain characteristics. During the inception, creation, and testing of interventions, educational design researchers may view these characteristics as criteria to be met. Further described below, interventions are more likely to undergo successful implementation and spread when they are: value-added, clear, compatible, and tolerant.

Value-added

Value-added interventions offer something better than what is already in place. The potential benefits – which are preferably highly observable (Rogers, 1962,

2003) – outweigh what must be invested in terms of time, effort, and financial resources. The cost/benefit analysis favors the intervention in both perception (people believe it will be worthwhile) and experience (people experience it as worthwhile). Value-added interventions offer a relative advantage (Rogers, 2003) at an acceptable cost (Doyle & Ponder, 1978). While some educational design research yields interventions primarily featuring tools or resources, much of it (also) focuses on deep, consequential change, e.g. touching teacher beliefs and norms of social interaction. Coburn (2003) refers to this as depth. It is difficult to achieve depth without certain levels of complexity (cf. Fullan & Pomfret, 1977; Rogers, 1962, 2003). Generally speaking, implementation and spread are slower and more difficult with more substantial, complex interventions. Value-added interventions do not necessarily exhibit depth or complexity, per se, but it is difficult to achieve lasting effects without them.

Cviko, McKenney and Voogt (2011) describe why teachers perceive added value in a technology-rich learning environment for early literacy. One of the main reasons was because it addressed a gap in the curriculum. Specifically, it helped kindergarten children learn about the functions and communicative purposes of written language: an area that is specified in the national targets for early literacy, but given very limited treatment in most textbooks and teacher materials.

Clear

Clear interventions enable participants to easily envision their involvement. Some educational design research interventions may be innately clear and easy to grasp. Alternatively, they may become clear through high levels of explicitness (cf. Fullan & Pomfret, 1977), a priori specifications of procedures (cf. Doyle and Ponder, 1978) and/or interactive mechanisms whereby developers and users co-define (elements of) the innovation. Especially during early stages of implementation and spread (e.g. adoption), interventions can become clear by being trialed on a limited basis before committing to use them (Rogers, 1962, 2003).

In the last 20 years, the role of exemplary materials in supporting curriculum change has been researched across the globe. In general, exemplary materials have been found to be especially useful during the initial phases of curriculum implementation, because they clarify implications for teachers. Based on several design studies, van den Akker (1998b) summarizes three main advantages offered by exemplary materials: clearer understanding of how to translate curriculum ideas into classroom practice; concrete foothold for execution of lessons that resemble the original intentions of the designers; and stimulation of reflection on one's own role with the eventual possibility of adjusting one's own attitude toward the innovation.

Compatible

Compatible interventions are congruent with existing values, cultures, practices, and beliefs (cf. Doyle & Ponder, 1978; Fullan & Pomfret, 1977; Rogers, 1962, 2003; Zhao, Pugh, Sheldon, & Byers, 2002). They may still be innovative, but the interventions and/or their underlying assumptions must not violate or reject fundamental concerns and principles of those involved. Compatible interventions are also aligned with aspects of the system that are, given the scope of the project, non-changeable (cf. McKenney, Nieveen, & van den Akker, 2006). This must be the case in objective reality (e.g. the intervention content is consistent with that addressed in fixed, external assessments) and subjectively. Participants can be quick to resist if they perceive the intervention might not fit their needs and context (e.g. it was previously tested in a school with very different characteristics).

Thijs and van den Berg (2002) described the field testing of an intervention which facilitated peer coaching of science teachers in Botswana. Part of the admittedly modest success of this program can be attributed to its compatibility with both the social system (culturally, it was more suitable to engage peer coaches than expert coaches) and the formal system (integrated with an ongoing in-service program). Its compatibility was largely dependent on the insights gained from a detailed needs and context analysis (Thijs & van den Akker, 1997; Thijs, 1999).

Tolerant

The notion of tolerance was briefly discussed in Chapter 6. Tolerant interventions are those that "degrade gracefully" (cf. Walker, 2006) during the natural variation in enactment that inevitably comes along with differing contexts, resources, expertise, acceptance levels, and so on. Tolerance refers to how precisely core components must be enacted for the intervention to be true to its goals. Using the terms introduced earlier in this chapter, tolerant interventions withstand (mutual) adaptation; they do not necessitate high degrees of fidelity. Clarke and Dede (2009) speak of "ruggedizing" interventions; this makes them tolerant to variation across different kinds of schools and populations. Specifically, they talk about rugged designs as those that are still effective under challenging circumstances, where some conditions for success may not be (sufficiently) present. Interventions that exhibit low levels of dependence on people and resources outside of the innovator's authority tend to be more tolerant (cf. Zhao, Pugh, Sheldon, & Byers 2002). In addition, interventions with a low loss function may also be more tolerant. The loss function is low when the detriment (or cost, in terms of effectiveness, good will, time, money, etc.) associated with enactment of the intervention that is, in some way, not true to certain underlying principles, is minimal.

Based on many years of intervention design, implementation, and testing, Thompson and Wiliam (2008) described their approach to tolerance (although their terminology is different). They recommended a "tight but loose" framework for scaling up teacher professional development, featuring "tight" adherence to central design principles with "loose" accommodations to the needs, resources, constraints, and particularities that occur in any school or district, but only insofar as these do not conflict with the intervention's underlying theory of action. Much of their work, and that of colleagues who have been directly or indirectly affiliated with the *Keeping Learning on Track* program (see also Wylie, 2008), has yielded lessons about intervention tolerance, gathered from empirical investigation and critical reflection on the tensions between the desire to maintain fidelity to a theory of action and the need to demonstrate flexibility in order to accommodate local situations.

Strategies for implementation and spread

The strategies used for facilitating implementation and spread can be powerful in shaping the uptake and use of interventions. Common strategies include awareness building, professional development, technical support, and participation. The choice for certain strategies is driven, to a large extent, by the theory of change underlying an intervention. As discussed in Chapter 5, interventions are planned to yield some kind of transformation, and it can be helpful to explicate the inner workings of that process (e.g. by creating and refining a logic model). Strategies employed to enable implementation and spread are, ideally, well aligned with an intervention's theory of change. In addition to an intervention's theory of change, strategies for implementation and spread are, often implicitly, shaped by perceptions of the way research outputs are used, and the researcher role(s) in the process.

Informed by the work of Rogers, and review of over 2600 research studies, Havelock (1969, 1971) published landmark work on the dissemination and use of scientific outputs. Havelock identified seven general factors that could account for how scientific outputs are taken up and used: linkage, structure, openness, capacity, reward, proximity, and synergy. He identified three existing modes in which those factors can be seen: social interaction; research, development, and diffusion; and problem solving. Based on the strengths of each approach, he proposed a fourth: a linkage model in which the resource system interacts collaboratively with the user system to stimulate each other's problem-solving behavior. Each of these models denotes different assumptions and expectations regarding the roles of research evidence and researchers in the applied use of theoretical understanding. Each model is briefly presented here, with the purpose of helping to clarify potential mindsets at work when educational design researchers (implicitly) opt for certain approaches to implementation and spread in their projects. Consistent with other literature on communication, Havelock used the terms "sender" and "resource system" to describe the origin of the information/intervention being shared (in this case, the design research team). The terms "receiver" and "user system" pertain to the target audience for the information/intervention.

Social interaction

Studies operating from this perspective rely greatly on the social interaction among the receiver group to transmit information about the innovation. The receiver and the receiver's needs are determined exclusively by the sender, who develops an intervention that is then brought to the attention of the potential receiver population. Receivers react to the intervention and share those reactions through social interaction, which influences decisions to try, accept, or reject an intervention. This model does not aptly describe the creation and initial implementation of most interventions developed through educational design research. However, it may portray the ways in which interventions spread.

Research, development, and diffusion

The research, development, and diffusion (RDD) perspective is similar to the social interaction model, in that the initiative is taken by the developer, based on a perceived receiver need. The main difference lies in the temporal focus of this model, as it centers on development. The research feeding development, as well as the diffusion taking place afterward, are often carried out by separate parties. Educational design research exhibits some characteristics of the RDD perspective, since it does build on existing knowledge and theories and focuses on the development of an innovation; and, sometimes, the interventions developed are handed off to other parties for further implementation and spread. However, the development process in educational design research features bilateral communication (between sender and receiver, or resource and user systems) whereas RDD is typically characterized as unilateral.

Problem solving

In contrast to the social interaction and RDD models, in the problem-solving model, the receiver identifies a need and initiates the process of change. The receiver (group) may undertake to solve the problem internally, or recruit outside assistance. The problem-solving receiver is generally not concerned with if, or to what extent, the solution developed serves the needs of other receivers. Many of the practitioners participating in educational design research exhibit characteristics consistent with this model.

Linkage

Combining some of the more powerful elements of the other three models, the linkage model starts with a focus on a felt need, and explicitly brings users (e.g. practitioners) and resources (e.g. researchers) together in a reciprocal relationship to stimulate each other's problem-solving behavior. It frequently involves intermediaries as well (e.g. professional development facilitators). This linkage not only improves problem-solving processes, it also creates an important social network. Given its focus on collaborative problem solving, educational design research clearly has elements of this model.

Since Havelock proposed the linkage model, much work has been done to unpack this basic notion and examine how it could be put to use, notably by Hall, Wallace and Dossett (1973) and more recently by Bartholomew, Parcel, Kok, and Gottleib (2006). This section discusses some of the benefits of considering the linkage model in shaping educational design research. Thereafter, the strengths and limitations of a common linkage strategy are briefly discussed: the program champion.

Bringing the planning and the using parties together through a linkage system serves several purposes in educational design research. For productive dialogue, both parties must seek to identify common ground (e.g. intervention goals, conviction about effective ways to meet them), and also acknowledge concerns that are not mutual (e.g. for researchers this might include methodological rigor; for practitioners, this might include time constraints). Researchers bring their own views pertaining to developing interventions, often related to: a passion for the project focus (e.g. interest and expertise in the topic at hand); some (un)structured notion of the development process (e.g. an articulated or implicit expectation of roles and tasks); and personal preferences for how good design (research) is conducted (cf. Visscher-Voerman and Gustafson's [2004] educational designer paradigms). Practitioners bring their own concerns to the discussion table, and their involvement stands to improve the overall quality of the intervention and its implementation. This is because: practitioners are able to help keep intentions and plans realistic (e.g. representing the voices of colleagues, students, or policy makers); their ownership and commitment can facilitate implementation (e.g. these people may become program champions); and their involvement can increase the face validity of the project (e.g. demonstrating that the intervention was born out of a real collaboration). Among other functions, the linkage system will anticipate and shape the intervention to play out favorably during the decision-making process that occurs when individuals and/or organizations consider adopting the intervention, how they tackle enactment, and what will affect sustained maintenance.

A valuable strategy for linkage used extensively in the public and mental health fields is that of a program champion (cf. Bartholomew, Parcel, Kok, and Gottleib, 2006; Riley, 2003). Knowledgeable and respected, a program champion is someone who is strategically connected to the implementation site, often (but not always) formally part of that organization. This person is often highly analytical, and can both anticipate and troubleshoot implementation concerns during design. Program champions can also facilitate implementation and spread. However, since charismatic leadership is rarely sustainable (cf. Fullan, 2003), the role of a program champion is better viewed as catalytic, rather than as a durable solution. Program champions can also help prevent discontinuation of an intervention. Program champions understand and bridge the context of research and the context of practice. Discussed in the following section, the context of practice plays a determining role in shaping the implementation and spread of interventions.

Context and surrounding systems

The processes of adoption, enactment, sustained maintenance, dissemination, and diffusion are strongly influenced by the immediate context in which interventions are used, as well as their broader, macro sociopolitical units (Fullan & Pomfret, 1977) or social systems (Rogers, 1962, 2003). In educational design research, intervention development is informed by multiple inputs, not the least of which includes (variation in) contextual factors. Sometimes these factors are temporarily adjusted for the purposes of study. This section briefly discusses the relationship between contextual factors and intervention design, before discussing the importance of understanding the broader surrounding system.

Contextual factors and intervention design

As described in Chapter 1 and throughout this book, the design of interventions in educational design research responds to needs in literature and in context. In so doing, characteristics of the context(s) in question steer development. Different goals, different researchers, and different types of interventions influence the ways in which contextual considerations are factored into design. Because educational design researchers strive to create solutions that will actually be used to solve real problems, interventions are designed to weather varying degrees of natural variation across differing contexts. Some designs intentionally work within a limited range of settings, while others are suited to a wider range but, inevitably, contextual realities determine substantial elements of the design.

Despite the importance of adjusting interventions to be compatible with the context, it is not uncommon in design research to reduce some of the implementation challenges by altering contextual factors. This is done, for example, when researchers teach lessons instead of teachers; when only exceptional teachers comprise the sample; when teacher release time is paid for by research funds; or when externally funded coaches temporarily are made available to schools. These kinds of tactics can be essential to getting a handle on how to fine-tune the core mechanisms of an intervention. But these can only function as temporary scaffolds – not permanent supports – that enable a portion of investigation for a limited time. Designing for actual use takes into consideration the fact that any such scaffolds will fade over time. When that fading is anticipated and the transition has been planned for, the results can be quite positive. But there are too many examples of powerful interventions ceasing to support high-quality teaching and learning because of insufficient planning for the user system to take on the responsibility of sustained maintenance. This kind of shift in ownership is notoriously problematic (cf. Coburn, 2003), but when successful, it can be self-generative (McLaughlin & Mitra, 2001). One of the reasons for emphasizing the need to seek practitioner collaboration early and set the goals collaboratively is to help minimize this challenging shift.

Reducing implementation challenges by altering contextual factors not only creates a larger shift hurdle, this also sacrifices some of the ecological validity of the findings. In the field of medicine, the quality of interventions and treatments is assessed by two related, but distinctly different criteria: efficacy and effectiveness. Efficacy measures how well something works under controlled circumstances (e.g. the extent to which a substance is capable of producing a certain effect). Effectiveness, in contrast, relates to how well a treatment works in practice (e.g. do people comply with the dosage, do the side effects render it unusable, and so forth). Efficacy is usually measured through randomized controlled trials, whereas effectiveness is usually measured through pragmatic trials. Even when conducted in authentic settings, educational design research that alters contextual factors to ease implementation yields results of efficacy, not effectiveness. Though this may be necessary in early stages of educational design research, actual use can only be achieved when intervention testing moves beyond efficacy to deep understanding of effectiveness.

Systems surrounding the immediate context

To understand how, why, and under what conditions interventions work, educational design researchers study not only the immediate context, but the surrounding systems. A systems lens views the educational setting as a dynamic, complex whole, whose constituent parts interact as a functional unit. Ideas, activities, and resources move throughout the system; and at times, they also move in and out of the (semi-permeable) system boundaries. Systems generally seek some kind of equilibrium or balance; and problems frequently arise when an extreme level of imbalance is present. Educational systems can be described in many different ways, including: levels, such as micro, meso, macro (e.g. classroom, school, nation); inputs (e.g. professional expertise, curriculum, exams, policies); and actors (students, teachers, school leaders, consultants). Educational systems are organic. While some patterns can be observed, they do not have a mechanistic nature that would allow great predictability. In part, this is due to the fact that, while some contexts may evidence higher degrees of stability than others, the educational systems are dynamic. The constant, sometimes dizzying, pace of change in primary, secondary, and tertiary education is far reaching. It concerns: learners, teachers, leaders; texts, curricula, exams; policies, funding, resources; expertise, priorities, accountability structures; and much, much more. This is both a blessing and a curse for the design researcher who wishes to make a change (the field of education is at least accustomed to constant change) but also study how it works and why (realizing at the same time that the factors at play can never be comprehensively taken into account). It can help to remember that change is a process and not an event.

Van den Akker's (2003) spider web metaphor (discussed in Chapter 3) demonstrates a systems lens from the perspective of curriculum at the micro level. Together with Thijs (Thijs & van den Akker, 2009), van den Akker also maintained that sustainable curriculum development attends to interconnected elements of a system at the macro level, such as curriculum developers; researchers; educational publishers; institutes for testing and assessment; inspectorates; teacher educators; policy makers; support agencies; schools and networks; and interest groups. The systems perspective is particularly notable in the work of Burkhardt (2006). In his article on strategic design, Burkhardt (2009) discussed common failures in design efforts and recommended ways forward, many of which have largely to do with understanding and accepting the harsh realities of the systems in which educational interventions are to operate. The absence of a systems view can yield unexpected consequences when interventions are implemented (Joseph & Reigeluth, 2010); the failure to acknowledge the "hidden curriculum" inherent in many school practices and the resultant resistance to change could be one such consequence.

Educational design research from a systems view does not necessarily mean that the intervention focuses on changing an entire system. Rather, it means that the intervention design takes into account how manipulations in one area of the system will relate to other areas of the system (e.g. how interventions may have unexpected effects, engender resistance, etc.). For interventions focused at the lesson level, this could mean: seeing how the topics in a lesson (series) fit into the existing curriculum; are addressed in current textbooks; are understood by practicing teachers; and are addressed on high stakes assessments. For interventions focused at the school level, this could mean: how the focus of the intervention resonates with teachers; the incentives or rewards that are (not) in place; and the expertise, leadership, time, bureaucratic requirements, and resources needed for the intervention to thrive, in addition to how it aligns with policies at the district or state level. For interventions concerning multiple schools, the vertical alignment (not just across schools but also with broader system levels, such as regions and states) of goals and notions about reaching them is of paramount importance (cf. Fullan, 2003). Contexts and surrounding systems are not static, and the people in them are largely responsible for making them dynamic.

Actors

The processes of implementation and spread are largely determined by the adopting unit (cf. Fullan & Pomfret, 1977) or the receiver (Havelock, 1969; Rogers, 1962, 2003), and how these people respond to change. Real change is difficult, deep (Coburn, 2003) and personal (Hall & Loucks, 1978). It is difficult, in part, because it is deeply personal. Coburn (2003) argued that interventions must concern deep and consequential change that go beyond surface structures or procedures. To achieve lasting effects, she suggested that interventions must ultimately address teacher beliefs (e.g. assumptions about how students learn, subject matter, etc), norms of social interaction (teacher student roles, patterns of dialogue, etc.) and underlying pedagogical principles (embodied in the enacted curriculum). Hall and Loucks (1978) emphasized the personal nature of change, advocating: the individual must be the primary target of interventions designed to facilitate change in the classroom; we cannot ignore the perceptions and feelings of the people experiencing the intervention process; individuals go through stages of perceptions and feelings, as well as stages of skill and sophistication using the innovation. There is a long history of literature that shows deep, personal change is most powerful (Fullan, 2003). There is also growing evidence to suggest that deep, personal change is more sustainable than other, more superficial change (Coburn, 2003). This understanding may feel rather removed from the daily concerns of many design researchers, but some sensitivity to it is essential if the interventions developed through design research are to stand a serious chance.

Who is involved?

Marsh (2004) distinguishes between three important actors in the design and implementation of educational interventions; these same groups may be involved in educational design research: decision makers, stakeholders, and influences. Decision makers are individuals or groups whose decisions largely determine what is to be taught, when, how, and by whom. In the context of schools, these include, among others, school principals, senior teachers, textbook writers, and testing agencies. In postsecondary settings, these include, among others, faculty members, administrators, legislators, instructional support staff, and accreditation agencies. Stakeholders are those who have no jurisdiction for decision making, but have a right to comment on and offer input into what happens in schools and colleges. Stakeholders include a wide variety of individuals and groups, such as education officers, parent groups or newspaper editors, taxpayers, and we add students to this list (in some countries, students actually have a say in school, even federal level decision making). Finally, influences are individuals or groups who endeavor to persuade authorities relating to some kind of ideology or interest, such as environmental lobbyists, national agencies, professional associations, or religious groups. In varying interventions, the roles of participants can change. For example, a teacher may be a decision maker in a classroom intervention, but a stakeholder in a statewide intervention. Across the literature, particular emphasis is placed on the key role of teachers and school leaders in educational innovations (Earl, Watson, & Katz, 2003; Fullan, 2000; Geijsel, Sleegers, van den Berg, & Kelchtermans, 2001; Lieberman & Pointer, 2008, 2010). Teacher participation and involvement in decision making, together with professional development and support are regarded as decisive for successful implementation. As emphasized throughout this book, active involvement of practitioners to shape design is of paramount importance to render interventions suitable for actual use (cf. Könings, Brand-Gruwel, & van Merriënboer, 2007).

When do they get involved?

In his work on diffusion of innovations, Rogers (1962, 2003) used the normal distribution of a Bell curve to identify five groups of innovation adopters. Following the normal curve, *innovators* adopt the innovation in the beginning (2.5%); *early adopters* make up for 13.5% soon thereafter; the *early majority* (34%) then follows; and after that come the *late majority* (34%); and finally the *laggards* make up for 16%. Early adopters may be among the kinds of participants who are willing to try out early product prototypes and think creatively along with designers, but it is also very important to involve representative teachers in design research, to maintain a grounded sense of how most participants respond to an intervention. In discussing his experience with different types of adopters, Bereiter (2002, p. 327) wrote:

> My own experience with innovative design research suggests that early adopters should be avoided whenever possible. They are the quickest to seize on an innovation, but they are also the quickest to abandon it in favor of the next new thing, and their approach to work with the innovation is usually superficial and unproductive.

What are their concerns?

The motives of personal development and curiosity may catalyze, but cannot sustain practitioner involvement in educational design research interventions. For interventions to be given more than a cursory trial, they must be practical (cf. Doyle & Ponder, 1978). The perceived (in)direct benefit to learners is among the strongest influences on implementing and sustaining educational interventions, but this cannot carry an intervention alone. Mobilization of values that have social attraction can be powerful to sustain interventions; these include: moral purpose, quality relationships, and quality knowledge (Fullan, 2003).

A classic lens that has been used to describe motives at play during the implementation and spread of innovations in educational settings, which can be quite useful to educational design researchers, is the Concerns-Based Adoption Model (Hall, Wallace, & Dossett, 1973), also known as C-BAM. This model assumes that a specific innovation has already been developed, and describes how the adoption process can be facilitated. It provides useful recommendations for pacing and personalizing interactions with participants, based on sensitivity to individual needs and motivations. The C-BAM stages of concern correlate closely to stages of actual use. The C-BAM work is rooted in research on the evolution of teacher concerns (cf. Fuller, 1969), and assumes that those adopting an innovation go through similar stages of: self-concern (e.g. Can I handle this? How will it affect me, my job, my future?) to task-concern (e.g. What steps am I required to do? Who else is involved in this task?) to impact-concern (e.g. What difference will this change really make? Will it be better?). The model also includes a resource system, a user system, and a (collaborative) linkage system. The first two stages are *unaware*, and *aware* of an innovation. Upon initial exposure to an innovation, participants will, to some extent, check out "(a) How congruent the innovation is with their value systems, present and possible job functions, and skills; (b) How congruent the innovation is with the institutional goals, structures and resources; and (c) How congruent any possible changes in the institution are likely to be with their personal goals." (Hall, Wallace, & Dossett, 1973, p. 14). Thereafter, participants' perceptions progress through several more stages: *exploration*; *early trial*; *limited impact*; *maximum benefit*; and *renewal*.

Understanding the concerns of those who will use interventions created through educational design research is essential to shape both design and implementation. Likewise, understanding the other constructs presented in this chapter can help shape each main phase of educational design research. In the next section, more detailed guidance is provided for attending to concerns of implementation and spread during analysis and exploration; design and construction; and evaluation and reflection.

Phase-specific considerations

As pointed out in the beginning of this chapter, the generic model for design research presented in this book represents interaction with practice, which is present from the start of the endeavor and generally increases over time.

Even though *actual* implementation and diffusion cannot take place until an intervention has been constructed, many considerations related to *planning* for actual use have been presented here. These have been offered in terms of implementation (adoption, enactment, and sustained maintenance) and spread (dissemination and diffusion). In addition, factors that influence actual use were also discussed. These included attributes of the intervention; strategies for enabling implementation and spread; context and surrounding systems; and the actors involved. Here, these perspectives are brought together with concrete considerations for the implementation and spread of design research interventions. Implications for each main phase of design research are given, along with planning considerations that can be used to stimulate thinking about actual use during each phase. These points may be most useful to ponder at the start of a new micro-cycle of research, when activities and plans are being framed.

Considering actual use during analysis and exploration

During the analysis and exploration phase, implementation and spread are anticipated. For example, information is gathered in the early stages that will help make solutions more practical (analysis). Observations of the implementation of similar solutions, previously in this context or in other contexts, are conducted (exploration). Participants in design research can be involved in this actively (e.g. if they, proactively, run the SWOT analysis), reactively (e.g. member-checking field portrait findings) or – though not our preference – indirectly (e.g. literature review to understand teacher belief and perceptions). The text below offers some important considerations for interaction with practice during the analysis and exploration phase.

Check determinants

Check current assumptions and understandings:

- What will determine adoption, enactment, and sustained maintenance in the target setting(s)?
- In relation to the problem at hand, what are the current: levels of awareness; expectations, (pedagogical) content knowledge; self-efficacy; (perceived) direct and indirect support, reinforcements, leadership, and cultural views?

Explore intervention attributes

Explore ways to render the intervention value-added and compatible, e.g.:

- What can we learn about the needs and wishes of the participants?
- What can we learn about the knowledge, skills, and attitudes of the participants?
- For this project, how wide or narrow is the jurisdiction of change?

Table 7.1 Considering implementation during analysis and exploration

	Actors	System factors	Strategies
Adoption	Who might make the decision to adopt?	What system factors have influenced adoption in the past?	What has been done in the past to influence adoption decisions, and with what results?
Enactment	Who might make the decision to enact?	What does the current system look like and how does it work?	What are the relevant knowledge, skills, and attitudes of potential enactors?
Sustained maintenance	Who might make the decision to sustain?	What system factors have influenced sustainability in the past?	Are there any actors, communities, or agencies that have previously influenced sustainability?

- What factors of the intervention matter to those adopting, implementing, and sustaining it?
- What will foster ownership in this setting?
- What strengths, weaknesses, opportunities, or threats are present in the target environment?

Anticipate implementation and spread

Table 7.1 offers questions to consider during analysis and exploration to help facilitate the implementation and spread of interventions developed through educational design research.

Considering actual use during design and construction

During the design and construction phase, plans are also made for implementation and spread. For example, practitioners may be asked to join the design team to help ensure the design is implementable (design). During prototype improvement advice may be sought from practitioners and other stakeholders on how to handle complex revision challenges (construction). Here too, participant involvement can be active (e.g. as co-designers or as lead constructors of a solution), reactive (e.g. providing critique or advice), or indirect (e.g. members of the design team advocate from practitioner perspectives; or think through the practical consequences of certain design options). The text below offers some important considerations for interaction with practice during the design and construction phase.

Table 7.2 Considering implementation during design and construction

	Actors	System factors	Strategies	Monitoring
Adoption	How can this design speak to the adopters?	How can this design align or conflict with any factors in the existing system?	Are we doing what we can to influence adoption?	Are we also addressing those things, specifically, that need to be done to constitute adoption?
Enactment	What does this design assume about the knowledge, skills, and attitudes of enactors?	What system factors might be influenced by enacting this intervention?	What (available or to-be-made) resources are we using for enactment?	What kind of variation in enactment do we consider acceptable and how can we design accordingly?
Sustained maintenance	How can this design speak to those who will decide on its continuation?	What system factors would have to change for this implementation to be sustainable?	How shall we involve certain actors, communities, or agencies who could exert a positive influence on sustainability?	Are we addressing what decision makers need to do for long-term sustainability?
Dissemination	Which broader audiences might we consider reaching with this design?	Are there mechanisms in the system that can be leveraged for dissemination?	Which dissemination strategies are known to work with these broader audiences?	How can we monitor dissemination progress?
Diffusion	What would render this design attractive to broader audiences?	Which features of the system might be especially receptive to this design?	Which diffusion strategies are known to work with these broader audiences?	How can we monitor diffusion progress?

Check determinants

Check current assumptions and understandings:

- Are we realistic and complete in accounting for those factors that will determine adoption, enactment, and sustained maintenance?
- What warrants additional investigation?
- How can these be addressed?

Explore intervention attributes

Explore ways to render the intervention value-added, clear, compatible, and tolerant, e.g.:

- How can the design of this intervention speak to those adopting, implementing, and sustaining it?
- How can this design foster ownership?
- How can this design capitalize on the strengths and opportunities, and mitigate the weaknesses and threats in the target setting?
- Are the logic model, design frameworks, and/or intervention prototypes internally consistent?
- How can the intervention be clearly communicated?
- How can the intervention be rendered tolerant to implementation variation?

Anticipate implementation and spread

Table 7.2 offers questions to consider during design and construction to help facilitate the implementation and spread of interventions developed through educational design research.

Considering actual use during evaluation and reflection

Evaluation and reflection relate to both anticipated (e.g. when initial design ideas are reviewed by experts, even before a first prototype is created), and actual implementation and spread (e.g. when prototypes are tested). This happens in various ways during evaluation and reflection. For example, perceived evidence of practicality may be gathered when evaluating designs (e.g. design brief or design specifications) and objective evidence of practicality may be gathered when evaluating constructed prototypes. In addition, critical assessment is conducted on the feasibility of the intervention and/or what can be learned from the data (reflection). Participant involvement can range from active (e.g. when they try out the intervention in their own teaching), reactive (e.g. when they comment on developer-led tryouts of the intervention) or indirect (e.g. design team tries to put themselves in the teacher's shoes when reflecting on implementation experiences). The text below offers some important considerations for interaction with practice during the evaluation and reflection phase.

Check determinants

Check current assumptions and understandings:

- What other factors determine adoption, enactment, and sustained maintenance?
- How can they be investigated?

Table 7.3 Considering implementation during evaluation and reflection

	Actors	System factors	Strategies	Monitoring
Adoption	How is this intervention perceived by those who will decide on its adoption?	Does this design align or conflict with any factors in the existing system?	What (else) can be done to influence adoption decisions?	Based on what, specifically, constitutes adoption, is there evidence that this is happening?
Enactment	Are the underlying assumptions about the knowledge, skills, and attitudes of the enactors accurate and sufficient?	What system factors are influenced by enacting this intervention?	Did the enactment resources function as planned?	What does the variation in enactment look like?
Sustained maintenance	How is this intervention perceived by those who will decide on its continuation?	What evidence suggests that any system factors that would have to change for this implementation to be sustainable can and will change?	What data about the intervention will speak to the actors, communities, or agencies that could exert a positive influence on sustainability?	To what extent are decision makers doing what is necessary for long-term sustainability?
Dissemination	How is this intervention perceived by broader audiences?	How (well) are system mechanisms being used for dissemination?	Which dissemination strategies are working (or not) and why?	How can we improve the dissemination process?
Diffusion	Is this intervention taken up by broader audiences and how?	Are there system factors that help or hinder diffusion?	Which diffusion strategies are working (or not) and why?	How can we improve the diffusion process?

Explore intervention attributes

Explore ways to test how much the intervention is value-added, clear, compatible, and tolerant, e.g.:

- To what extent does this intervention speak to the needs and wishes those adopting, implementing, and sustaining it?

- Does this intervention foster ownership?
- Does this intervention need to (better) capitalize on the strengths and opportunities, and mitigate the weaknesses and threats in the target setting?
- Do our logic model, design frameworks, and/or intervention prototypes need revision?
- What elements of the intervention seem to be clear? Engender confusion?
- What elements of the intervention do (not) sufficiently tolerate implementation variation?

Anticipate implementation and spread

Table 7.3 offers questions to consider during evaluation and reflection to help facilitate the implementation and spread of interventions developed through educational design research.

Proposing, reporting, and future directions: toward Part III

Throughout Part II of this book, the core processes involved in educational design research have been presented in relationship to the generic model presented in Chapter 3 (see Figure 3.3). Part III, the concluding part of this book, is about moving forward toward well-planned, well-described educational design research that advances the field. It fosters well-planned research through Chapter 8, which provides recommendations about how to write a design research proposal. It supports well-described educational design research through Chapter 9, which provides guidance on reporting design research. Finally, following brief reflections on this book, Chapter 10 offers considerations for what is needed to advance the field of educational design research.

Part III

Moving forward

Writing proposals for educational design research

Phillips (2006) noted that assessing research proposals in education, and especially design research proposals, is difficult for a host of reasons. This is especially because design research does not constitute what philosophers call a "natural kind." That is, while there are some common characteristics (as described in Chapter 3), there is no one thing that design studies are like. Indeed, we have endeavored to illustrate the healthy variety in educational design research throughout this book. It therefore follows that there is no one way to write a design research proposal. The task of writing a research proposal is a challenging one and, for many, this seems especially daunting when it comes to educational design research. With the ultimate aim of supporting the initiation of productive and useful design studies, this chapter shares important considerations surrounding the proposal writing process. It begins by briefly addressing the purpose and function of research proposals. Thereafter, adequate preparation for proposal writing is stressed, in terms of learning about the educational design research process and learning about the problems and phenomena to be studied. Next, perceiving a longer-term research project as a macro-cycle that consists of meso- and micro-cycles is discussed. This includes the notion that graduate student research proposals often focus on detailed description of micro-cycles or meso-cycles; whereas those that are submitted to funding agencies to obtain support for multi-year research undertakings often describe macro-cycles. Guidelines are presented for addressing the basic elements of any strong research proposal, from the perspective of integration with a necessarily iterative design process. The chapter concludes with a self-evaluation rubric for critiquing design research proposals.

Purpose and function of research proposals

Internal audiences

Research proposals are written to serve both internal and external audiences. For the internal audience (which can range from a single graduate researcher to a team of experienced researchers and practitioners), proposal writing involves deep, reasoned thinking through which research ideas are refined and plans are operationalized. Ideas are refined through the processes of: carefully crafting a clear, concise, and powerful problem statement; describing what is already known (and not) about the phenomenon at hand in the literature review; narrowing and substantiating the focus of the study in the conceptual framework; and drafting research questions that speak to the heart of the matter and can feasibly be answered. Plans are operationalized when: methods are described; sampling decisions are made; instruments are sought, conceived of, or created; procedures are delineated; data analysis techniques are chosen; and timelines are mapped.

Given the masterful orchestration required in educational design research, where both research trajectories and intervention development trajectories must be planned in sync, this is no small task. The ideas and plans described in research proposals usually mature over time, nurtured by feedback from research supervisors in the case of graduate students, and/or advisors and colleagues. New insights from literature and experience also support the maturation of design study intentions. After reaching a fairly stable state (e.g. submitted to an advisor or granting agency for review), research proposals can then serve as an initial framework for the project. Once approved, research proposals can serve as a kind of contract, making clear the goals, focus, expectations, timelines, and outputs of a study. Later, when a study is underway and reality dictates that a change of course is necessary, the research proposal can serve as a signpost during deliberation, bringing crucial questions to the fore, like: Are we considering methodological adjustments to better meet the same goals? Given our more refined understanding of the problem, would the study be more valuable if we shifted its focus? In light of budget reductions, what are the most economical forms of data collection we can use without sacrificing too much?

External audiences

For the external audience (which can include graduate advisory committees, funding agencies, schools, or other participating organizations), research proposals convincingly demonstrate that the study is worthwhile and that the researcher is competent to accomplish what is proposed. For the external audience, it must be clear that: the problem being investigated is significant enough to warrant the investigation; the study is well positioned in light of the work of others; the research framing evidences a sound understanding of both research literature and practical realities; the methods planned are suitable and feasible; and the study is likely to make a fruitful and original contribution to both theoretical understanding and educational practice. For external audiences unfamiliar with educational design research, it may be important to explain that this genre of inquiry seeks to contribute to both fundamental understanding and applied use.

Immersion first, writing second

Given the description above, it seems obvious that one cannot create a useful and convincing research proposal without careful consideration and planning. Research proposals demonstrably build on existing understanding and aspire to frame studies that are of value to others. To do this, several concerns warrant attention. While each of these may be addressed within one activity (e.g. discussions with practitioners; literature review), they are discussed separately here to emphasize three important prerequisites to proposal writing: identifying problems; probing problems; and refining methodological ideas for the study.

Identifying problems

Educational design research is a genre of inquiry concerned with solving existing problems in practice and structuring that process in such a way as to yield scientific understanding that takes into account the complex variation of the real world. Identifying problems in practice is a central, though not unique, concern in educational design research. Educational design research differs from many other types of research in that it sets out not only to understand a problem, but to solve it. The identification of problems in design research thus involves finding a problem that is worthy of investigation and capable of being solved through the research process. Specific problems may be identified by practitioners, by researchers, or through study of literature. But regardless of how the problem is first raised, verification in both literature and practice is necessary to ascertain if it is, indeed, legitimate, researchable, and research-worthy. From the theoretical perspective the problem is worth studying if doing so would address a clear gap in existing literature (legitimate); if existing methods will allow it to be studied well enough to warrant the effort (researchable); and contribute to theory development or scientific understanding related to a widely held, as opposed to idiosyncratic, concern (research-worthy). From the practical perspective, the problem is worth solving if, indeed, the real problem is identified, as opposed to a symptom (legitimate); if it can be identified in accessible contexts (researchable); and if it is severe enough that stakeholders care to invest in solving it (research-worthy).

Probing problems

Identification of problems constitutes essential, but insufficient, preparation for writing a cogent research proposal. Especially for new researchers, it is important to spend time and effort probing problems – becoming immersed in them before trying to write about which aspects warrant further study and how that can sensibly be tackled. This may be done formally or informally, but examination of the literature, discussion with experts, and dialogue with practitioners can be extremely helpful in defining the territory for a design study. For example, if the problem identified is related to the educational services of community resource centers in urban areas, literature review could certainly help to begin to build an understanding of important factors at play, but it could not provide the three-dimensional, real world understanding needed to craft a research proposal that is valuable to both science and practice. To understand the problem, it can be extremely important to see it in action, though this is obviously more feasible for some problems than others. Returning to the example above, it might not make sense for a suspicious-looking researcher to hang out at a community center in a neighborhood plagued by gang violence. But a trusted local might be able to provide information that could help build the foundation for a study. Such a professional would likely have important insights into firsthand or emic understandings about the problem, what causes it, or related issues. Probing problems helps researchers come to understand those aspects warranting deeper investigation (because they are legitimate) and, within those, sharpens the focus of the overall study (on aspects which are research-worthy).

Refining methodological ideas for the study

Preparing to write a research proposal includes learning about not only about the problem, but also learning about how problems of this type have been investigated previously. As with any sound research proposal, sufficient background work must be undertaken to explore if and how the issue at hand is researchable (cf. Gorard, Roberts, & Taylor, 2004). Here, too, literature can provide inspiring examples for approaches and lenses to use in studying a problem. In addition, practitioners can share their ways of understanding and also identify open or closed "windows of opportunity" for data collection. It can also be worthwhile to explore methodological ideas through modest preparatory studies. These may be conducted in-house or in the field, to explore how potential research scenarios play out or test the feasibility of certain instrumentation. For example, if researchers want to understand how to optimize digital lesson planning materials, they may consider the use of eye-tracking experiments to ascertain how teachers become acquainted with such materials. A preparatory study could investigate what teachers look at, when, and for how long. From this experience, researchers could gain impressions of: how powerful or limited the eye-tracking data is likely to be in light of the research questions; how easy or difficult it is to organize eye-tracking studies; and how efficient or time-consuming it is to analyze the data. This kind of understanding concerns how researchable a topic is, and can be very useful in fine-tuning a project's focus that, as discussed in the next section, may concern multiple strands of inquiry.

Positioning the study

Aligning multiple strands of inquiry

Oftentimes, educational design research projects examine multiple phenomena simultaneously, such as: the characteristics of specific learning scenarios; how they are enacted; participant responses to them; and learning gains they engender. As mentioned previously, it is not uncommon for design research to feature both investigation focused *on* an intervention and investigation conducted *through* an intervention simultaneously, or sequentially. A first step in preparing to write a design research proposal is to identify and define the strand(s) of inquiry. An example of how two strands of inquiry can be embedded into one research project is given below. One strand is focused on the intervention itself; the other strand studies phenomena engendered by the intervention. (It is also possible to have several strands of research conducted on the intervention, and/or several strands of research conducted through the intervention.)

In this example, the intervention being designed is an electronic learning environment to support pupil argumentation in middle school biology. Two interrelated, but distinct, lines of inquiry are present. Research question 1 (RQ1) pertains to student learning; and research question 2 (RQ2) pertains to characteristics of the learning environment. The sample overarching question and phase-specific sub-questions are not comprehensive, but they do offer an indication of how these strands could be aligned to inform one another, but also be of value independently:

- RQ1: How does the use of an electronic learning environment influence pupil learning of argumentation in middle school biology?
    - Analysis and exploration: What does pupil learning of argumentation in biology look like in the existing situation and why is this so?
    - Design and construction: What is already known about how to support argumentation in biology learning, especially in the presence of [specific problem-related conditions identified during analysis and exploration]?
    - Evaluation and reflection: How, in what ways, and why does pupil learning about argumentation in biology appear to be different when supported by [intervention created during design and construction] and why?
- RQ2: What is an optimal design for an electronic learning environment for middle school biology to support pupil learning of argumentation?
    - Analysis and exploration: What needs are felt for supporting pupil learning of argumentation in biology and what are the shortcomings of resources that are already available?
    - Design and construction: What is already known about designing electronic learning environments for middle school biology in general, and especially to support learning argumentation in the presence of [specific problem-related conditions identified during analysis and exploration]?
    - Evaluation and reflection: How do pupils and teachers interact with [intervention created during design and construction]; in what ways is this different from intended, with what results, and why does this seem to be the case?

Identifying micro-, meso-, and macro-cycles

Literature on design research emphasizes the need for long-term approaches featuring multiple iterations of design, development, and revision. This approach is often at odds with the short timelines of many grants, and especially graduate

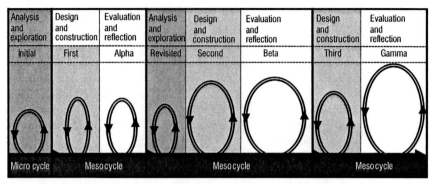

Analysis and exploration	Design and construction	Evaluation and reflection	Analysis and exploration	Design and construction	Evaluation and reflection	Design and construction	Evaluation and reflection
Initial	First	Alpha	Revisited	Second	Beta	Third	Gamma

| Micro cycle | Meso cycle | Meso cycle | Meso cycle |

Figure 8.1 An educational design research macro-cycle, consisting of micro- and meso-cycles

student capstone projects and thesis/dissertation work, which may allow only 1 or 2 years of focused research. It is extremely difficult to conduct multiple iterations of robust research and design in less than 2 years, especially when it comes to projects undertaken by one or just a few individuals. This does not mean that graduate students – many of whom must conduct their field work in less than one year – cannot conduct educational design research. Rather, it emphasizes the importance of coordinating graduate student work, in the form of micro- or meso-cycles, within larger research agendas. A first step in doing so is identifying the cycles within a larger project.

Figure 8.1 shows one example of how a long-term, multi-year educational design research project might take place. The work is conducted iteratively. Each time one of the core phases is (re-)visited, a micro-cycle takes place. In a research proposal, the micro-cycle of design and construction is usually combined with one or more empirical cycles (analysis and exploration and/or evaluation and reflection). The labels at the bottom show how individual micro-cycles or combined ones (i.e. meso-cycles) can fit into one research proposal. The two lines in the loops represent two strands of inquiry. The different size loops indicate changes in scope (e.g. time, participants); these may vary slightly for each strand.

This figure could be used to identify different cycles within a larger project, such as the above-mentioned example involving the design of an electronic learning environment for middle school biology. One line in the loops could represent work on RQ1: how the use of an electronic learning environment influences pupil learning of argumentation in biology; and the other line in the loops could represent RQ2: seeking an optimal design for the learning environment. In this example, eight individual micro-cycles are anticipated, and they are clustered into four units (one micro-cycle and three meso-cycles). The timing of certain micro-cycles, such as beta and gamma phase evaluation and reflection, would likely be steered by school calendars to enable testing of the middle school biology learning environment under representative conditions.

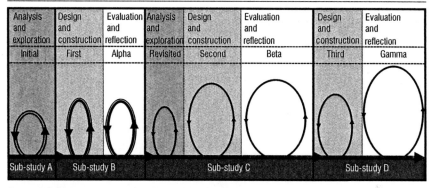

Analysis and exploration	Design and construction	Evaluation and reflection	Analysis and exploration	Design and construction	Evaluation and reflection	Design and construction	Evaluation and reflection
Initial	First	Alpha	Revisited	Second	Beta	Third	Gamma

Figure 8.2 Various options for the scope of a design research proposal

Choosing the scope for the proposal

The kind of orchestration that is required to (a) conceive of a long-term educational design research goal; and (b) designate feasible sized micro- and meso-cycles (e.g. the size of graduate student projects) usually requires a seasoned researcher to advise on the plan. A research proposal may cover a single micro-cycle, several micro-cycles (thus, a meso cycle), or the entire macro-cycle. Graduate students in course-driven programs that allow less than 2 years for field work are likely to write proposals for micro- and meso-cycles. Graduate students in field-study based programs featuring more than 2 years of field work could be more likely to write proposals for the entire macro-cycle, but likely focusing on a single strand of inquiry. University researchers might write either type, and would be more likely to include multiple strands of inquiry than graduate students would. University researcher proposals are typically influenced by both an estimation of what is needed to address the central problem (from both theoretical and practical perspectives); and the options available for getting the work done (e.g. funding, student assistants).

Figure 8.2 shows five potential options for writing research proposals based on the study shown in Figure 8.1. Many other options could also be considered. The five options shown here are:

1   One whole study: A macro-cycle proposal, where two lines of inquiry are present, but with varying emphasis across four sub-studies.
2   Sub-study A: A micro-cycle proposal, where two lines of inquiry are present.
3   Sub-Study B: A meso-cycle proposal consisting of two core processes, where two lines of inquiry are present, but one is more substantial than the other.
4   Sub-study C: A meso-cycle proposal consisting of three core processes, focusing on one line of inquiry.
5   Sub-study D: A meso-cycle proposal consisting of two core processes, focusing on one line of inquiry.

Guidelines for writing educational design research proposals

While differences between institutions and disciplines do exist, a typical research proposal includes elements such as background, problem statement, literature review, theoretical framework, methodology, data collection, data analysis, anticipated outputs, and significance of the study. Additional elements may be required such as ethical considerations, a timeline, and a budget. Educational design research proposals attend to all of these elements commonly found in most research proposals. In addition, they give tentative descriptions of the intervention to be designed, and the systematic and transparent process through which development will take place. Blending the design orientation into the proposal does more than add a few sections to the document; it has implications for the whole research process.

Deciding if and to what extent the design orientation is described in the research proposal can be a strategic choice. For example, if applying for external funding to an organization whose mission does not explicitly include development of resources for practice, it could make more sense to focus on the quest for fundamental understanding and describe comparatively little of the plans for applied use (although this will also have implications for which activities can be covered in the budget). It may be desirable or necessary to seek alternate sources for funding the work of development. Increasingly, however, research councils and advisory committees are calling for researchers to demonstrate the social relevance of their work. A design research proposal, even one that describes the research aspects more than the design aspects, should easily be able to articulate the practical relevance of the project.

Most research proposals must be limited to a few thousand words. While some ideas may be refined while writing the proposal, clear, concise writing can only be done once a strong sense of the project has started to take shape. It can be extremely useful to seek out and study good examples of proposals that have been previously approved by the same internal and/or external audiences. Often, proposals must conform to existing formats. These rarely include sections for describing the intervention to be developed or the development process. But, ideally, these will be described. Therefore, the guidelines given here demonstrate how design research proposals can be fitted into a common format. The format used here follows this structure:

1 Project overview
   a. Title
   b. Researcher name and affiliation
   c. Keywords
   d. Executive summary

2 Project description
   a. Background and problem statement
   b. Purpose, aims, and scope

   c. Literature review
   d. Theoretical framework
   e. Research questions

3 Study design
   a. Research goals and approach
   b. Methods
       i.   Participants and selection
       ii.   Instrumentation
       iii. Procedures
       iv.   Data analysis

4 Relevance
5 Dissemination
6 Limitations
7 Work plan
   a. Timeline
   b. Budget

Recommendations are given below for writing each main section in the proposal. As described in the previous section, proposals can vary extensively in terms of scope. Every research proposal is different, and researchers are encouraged to vary these sections as required to suit their own purposes, the nature of their research, and, most importantly, the questions being asked.

Project overview

The project title should clearly and succinctly describe the focus of the study. Since the focus of the study is reflected in the main research questions, a clear link should be evident between the main research question and the title. In addition to mentioning the research team and affiliation, some proposal formats require capability statements; these are often tailored, abbreviated biographies or curricula vitae that are generally added as an appendix. In the field of education, keywords are often best selected using the Educational Resources Information Center (ERIC) thesaurus. The executive summary is like an abstract of the proposal. These are easiest to write after the proposal has been constructed. A useful structure can be to incorporate approximately one sentence for each main area of the proposal.

Project description

Background and problem statement

The statement of the problem in an educational design research proposal generally identifies a gap between the existing and the desired situation. The gap is evident in both theoretical understanding and in practice. This section explores the history, origins, and/or background of the problem. It provides a succinct, convincing, and persuasive argument that this problem is significant and worth researching. This section describes the specific context of the study, possibly also describing how or why it is suitable for participation, and may clarify the role of practitioners in it. Finally, the background and problem statement also describes the broader relevance of this study by explaining how this particular context is representative of others in which similar problems are prevalent.

Purpose, aims, and scope

Building on the problem statement, this section presents a clear rationale for the study. It explains why the research is needed, and what it intends to accomplish. A brief description of the intervention (or intentions, if it does not yet exist) is given. (This may not be the case if the proposal only concerns one micro-cycle of analysis and exploration.) This section clearly delineates how the study will contribute to both theoretical understanding and to solving a problem in practice.

Literature review

The literature review presents high-quality research from credible sources to expand on the problem statement given above. Inherent in the literature review is the identification of (hypothesized) causes for the problem, as well as other information that can be used to demonstrate what is already, and what is not yet, known about the problem. In so doing, the literature review provides well-reasoned critique of existing understanding. The literature review also synthesizes the effectiveness and inadequacies of existing solutions. It may also be used to conjecture some possible directions for a potential solution.

Theoretical framework

Whereas the literature review is used to expand understanding of the *problem,* the theoretical framework depicts the literature base that is used to shape the *investigation.* It presents relevant theories and defines important constructs that will be the focus of inquiry. This section of a research proposal summarizes the "lens" through which data will be collected and analyzed. Done well, reading the theoretical framework should enable the reader to anticipate the constructs embodied in research instruments and the units of analysis to be investigated. If the researchers have already done a preliminary investigation of the problem, and/ or if design and construction have already commenced, then this section may also present initial design considerations. Depending on the relationship between the research focus and the design task, the theoretical framework for the research may be analogous to the propositions underpinning design. If so, this connection may be described.

Research questions

It is both difficult and important to formulate good research questions. While initial research questions are identified early during proposal writing, it is useful to recognize that research questions are typically refined over time, as insights progress throughout the course of a study. Research questions bridge the stated problem and the purpose of the study. Given the exploratory nature of educational design research, the main research questions tend to be open in nature. They are clearly aligned with the purpose of the study and theoretical framework preceding them; and also with the methods and instrumentation that follow. They are specific enough to be answered; and are formulated in judgment-neutral terms. Answering the research questions will help solve a real problem, while also yielding empirical findings, new hypotheses and conjectures that will advance the development of theory.

In educational design research, it is quite common to formulate a few broad, overarching research questions and then to distinguish different sets of sub-questions, for each micro-cycle. This can help clarify research and development intentions, while also allowing for the project to respond to emerging insights. Analysis and exploration questions ask about issues such as existing practices, needs, wishes, contextual factors, opportunities, and constraints. Design and construction questions seek theories, knowledge, and examples that can guide the creation of a solution to a problem. In evaluation and reflection micro-cycles of research focusing *on* interventions, the questions focus more on (characteristics of) the intervention (type). In research conducted *through* interventions, the questions relate more to phenomena engendered by the intervention.

Study design

Research goals and approach

In this section, the practical and theoretical goals are recapitulated, and, in relation to these, the overarching approach is described. The approach clearly shows how the study will make a contribution to practice (outlines a systematic, transparent process for developing an intervention) and to theoretical understanding (outlines a systematic, transparent process for empirical investigation). Ideally this description will also demonstrate how empirical findings will be used to inform development of the intervention. The basic approach described in this section will be compatible with the methods described in the subsequent section.

Methods

Many, if not most, educational design researchers employ a mixture of quantitative and qualitative methods to understand if, how, and why interventions function, under certain conditions in certain settings, and with what results. The methods section specifies who will participate, from which settings; the instruments that will be used to collect data; the procedures through which data will be collected; and techniques that will be used to analyze the data.

PARTICIPANTS AND SELECTION

This section of the proposal describes the groups of people who will participate as respondents in the study. In educational design research, this usually includes experts, teachers, learners, and other educational professionals. The description clarifies the criteria for selecting participants and the research site, and may provide justification for the choices made (e.g. the choice for working under natural conditions may preclude purposive sampling within a group of learners). It also describes any relevant triangulation of different respondent perspectives (e.g. one construct may be studied from different perspectives, such as that of the observer, the teacher, and the learner). It also describes any salient characteristics of the research setting (e.g. the socio-economic status of the community where the research will be conducted).

INSTRUMENTATION

This section describes the research instruments, insofar as they are known at the time of proposal writing. The instrument descriptions demonstrate alignment with the research questions and the concepts presented in the theoretical framework. The overall description demonstrates how triangulation of instruments will be achieved (e.g. one construct may be examined through multiple different data sources, such as observation, interview, and document analysis). Where possible individual instrument descriptions give an impression of the nature of the instrument (how many items, open or closed, administered to whom, when) and how validity and reliability will be guarded. If existing instruments are used (which, if feasible, can be very helpful, given that sound instrument development can be a lengthy process), brief commentary is warranted on their origins and quality. If new instruments are being developed (which may be necessary given the innovative nature of much design research), a sound process should be described for constructing valid and reliable measures. Instruments that will be used repeatedly (e.g. baseline measures, and pre-tests that are administered again later on) are indicated as such.

PROCEDURES

For many proposal formats, the procedures section is the most logical place to discuss the design work. While it would be difficult (and perhaps undesirable to try) to provide a comprehensive description of the *intervention* at the proposal stage, it can be useful to describe the *systematic process* through which the solution will be conceptualized and developed. Following the process described in Chapter 5, this can include the establishment of design requirements, framing of design propositions, and the careful elaboration of ideas from skeleton designs to detailed specifications, across the different micro-cycles envisioned. It can also help to describe how the process will be documented and audited, and to present any initial (integrated) design propositions that are being considered.

A description of the design procedures can also set the stage for explaining the research procedures. For example, this can help readers envision the involvement of different participants at various stages (e.g. expert appraisals earlier and learner experiences later). This section also includes a detailed account of how instruments will be administered (e.g. pairs of students will be observed;

interviews will be conducted individually, audio recordings and transcriptions will be made). Additionally, it describes how standards set by ethics committees and internal review boards will be met.

DATA ANALYSIS

This section of the proposal specifies the techniques that will be used to analyze the data. The units and methods of analysis demonstrate alignment with the questions being asked and the type of data being collected. For example, pattern coding and sequential analysis may be used with qualitative data; and statistical analyses such as ANOVA, Mann-Whitney or T-tests may be run with quantitative data.

Relevance

Educational design research is conducted with the dual aims of contributing to theoretical understanding and to practice; both the scientific and practical relevance are described in this section. The scientific contribution is discussed in terms of how this study will help to close gaps in existing literature. The practical contribution describes how implementation of the intervention will benefit the particular context in question, as well as (potentially) serve other settings. If the research activities themselves will offer a practical contribution to the participants involved (e.g. promoting reflection and fostering professional development), these may also be mentioned here.

Dissemination

In this section, anticipated reporting outputs are described, such as publications in research journals; publications in practitioner journals; and project reports to the sponsor. In addition, ideas or plans concerning the spread of the intervention are presented. This could include, for example, a conference or a workshop where the intervention developed (and possibly similar ones) are showcased by the development team, or demonstrated by practitioners.

Limitations

This section briefly acknowledges methodological limitations as well as constraints of the study (e.g. limited time or personnel). In light of what is both feasible and sound, it justifies particular choices in the research plan and clarifies how the study will be of value, despite the limitations.

Work plan

Timeline

The timeline given in the research proposal should be realistic. Attention to careful planning of micro-cycle work, including fine-tuning data collection plans and instruments, is important. It should allow sufficient time to collect data in the field and to reduce and analyze it. Specific periods in the timeline should be delineated for interim reporting (usually between micro-cycles) and final reporting. The timeline must be realistically aligned with data collection opportunities (e.g. learner interviews are not planned during summer holidays).

Budget

Not all proposal formats require a budget, though considering the costs associated with a project can be informative, even when not required. The budget must account for both research and development costs. Researcher, developer, and support personnel time is usually measured in terms of days. Participant time is usually accounted for in terms of honoraria and/or days (e.g. for which days substitute teachers must be arranged so regular teachers can be engaged in research-related tasks). Publication and dissemination costs generally include building and maintaining a project website, as well as any conference or workshop activities, to be hosted and/or attended. For conferences, workshops, team meetings, and advisory board meetings, travel and subsistence costs should be allotted. Finally, educational design research projects also incur material expenses (e.g. for computers, software, equipment, and printing).

Proposal presentation

The proposal should be presented in a scholarly tone, addressing a research audience. In most cases, it should be written in professional, third-person voice. The style of writing should be clear and coherent, with well-phrased sentences and carefully chosen words. Sentence structure should flow smoothly and the paragraph sequence should be logical and easy to follow. The sources used throughout the document must be high quality, relevant, and traceable. Appropriate citation style (e.g. APA) should be followed in both the body of the text and the reference list. Attending to the mechanics of the proposal will increase its face validity. Good use of headings and subheadings can dramatically increase the readability of the document. Terms should be defined where appropriate and used correctly and consistently throughout. The document should have no capitalization, punctuation, or spelling errors.

Rubric for evaluating educational design research proposals

Edelson (2006) points out several specific considerations that pertain to proposals that endeavor to conduct research within the context of design work. He notes that the driving questions behind many studies mirror that of innovative design: What alternatives are currently available? How can alternatives be established and maintained? He also describes several issues that design research proposals should address: the work must yield insights into an important need or problem, e.g.

a new or elaborated theory; the proposed design must be grounded in prior research or sound theory; it must have a plan for systematic documentation; it must incorporate feedback into a plan for iterative design and development; and it must allow for a process of generalization.

Building Edelson's recommendations and those presented in the previous sections, this chapter closes with a self-evaluation rubric that combines elements of a common research proposal with those that attend specifically to research embedded in design trajectories. In creating research proposals, as well as with many other forms of (academic) writing, critical self- and peer review are important forms of evaluation before submitting a proposal to an external committee or examiner for appraisal. Shown in Table 8.1, the elements in this rubric offer useful starting points, but of course specific requirements and guidelines may vary with different organizations.

As stated earlier in this chapter, once a research proposal has been deemed satisfactory, it can serve as a framework, or organizer, for conducting the design study. Another benefit of a well-written proposal is that it can help frame reports of design research. Some elements (e.g. literature review, theoretical framework, methods) can form the building blocks for various types of reports. The next chapter provides considerations for reporting educational design research.

Table 8.1 Self-evaluation rubric for a proposal to conduct educational design research

	Description	✓	Comments
Content			
Background and problem statement	The problem is clearly and succinctly described		
	The problem is related to substantial societal or educational need(s)		
	Practitioner participation is clarified		
	The local and broader context is briefly described		
Purpose, aims, and scope	The proposal presents a clear rationale for the study		
	The proposal states relevant goals and objectives		
	The proposal encompasses a salient intervention		
	The proposal addresses practical and scientific contributions		
Literature review	Provides well-reasoned critique of relevant literature		
	Synthesizes effectiveness and inadequacies of existing solutions		
	Presents research of high quality and credible resources		
	Clarifies relevant constructs		
Theoretical framework	Synthesizes relevant theories		
	Informs and sets framework for instrumentation and data analysis		
	May articulate relationship to design propositions		
Research questions	Research questions are strongly linked to theoretical framework		
	Research questions are specific enough to be answered		
	Research questions address an authentic problem	✓	
	Answers to the research questions could support theory building		
	Research questions are aligned with research purpose, methods, and instruments		
	Research questions are judgment neutral		

	Description	✓	Comments
Content			
Research goals and approach	The proposed study specifies its theoretical and practical goals		
	The research design supports the goals of the study		
	Initial ideas about the proposed intervention are described		
	A feasible design process is described		
	A reasonable sequence of micro-cycles is planned		
	The design of the research is consistent with the methodological orientation of the study		
Methods	The research site is described clearly		
	The participants are adequately described		
	The criteria for selecting participants is described		
	The instruments are described		
	The instruments are aligned with research questions		
	Data collection procedures are described		
	The data analysis techniques are described		
Relevance	Contributions to local and broader educational contexts are stated, and aligned with original problem statement		
	Contributions to theory development are clear		
Dissemination	Reporting on the findings and outputs are described for the theoretical contribution		
	Ideas or plans for (potential) spread are discussed for the practical contribution		
Limitations of the study	Methodological limitations are discussed		
	Constraints of the study (e.g. time, personnel) are addressed		
Work plan	The timelines given are realistic		
	The plans demonstrate realistic expectations of cooperating participants (schools, teachers, children, etc.)		
	The proposed budget (where applicable) is comprehensive and realistic		

Continued...

Table 8.1 continued...

	Description	✓	Comments
Presentation			
Tone	Addresses research audience		
	Professional; third-person voice		
Clarity and coherence	Word choice is precise		
	Sentences are well phrased		
	Sentences flow smoothly from one to the next		
	Paragraph sequence is logical and easy to follow		
References	The majority of sources are of appropriate relevance and quality		
	APA guidelines are followed in the body of the text		
	APA guidelines are followed in the reference list		
Mechanics	Readability of document layout is high, including good use of headings		
	Words and terms are defined where appropriate; used correctly		
	Capitalization and punctuation are properly used		
	The document is free of spelling errors		

Chapter 9

Reporting educational design research

Design research is conducted with two main goals: creating an intervention that solves problems in practice, and producing theoretical understanding. Reporting on design research can raise awareness about an intervention, but is primarily a means for sharing understanding. In addition, the actual reporting process itself – critical reflection that occurs with fingertips at keyboard – is frequently an important time for insights to be refined, and connections to literature to be made. Finally, the process of subjecting reports to peer review can provide a useful sounding board regarding the utility and value of the theoretical and practical ideas both guiding and resulting from the research. This chapter discusses the process of reporting educational design research. It begins by describing two common dilemmas: having too much to report, and finding ways to structure reports that align with standardized formats. Thereafter, attention is given to internal and external audiences of professionals (including practitioners, specialists, and policy makers) and researchers. Building on both discussions, the chapter concludes with three broad recommendations for addressing the aforementioned dilemmas: chose the scope, refine the message, and seek inspiring examples.

Common educational design research reporting concerns

Too much story to tell

Design research projects tend to be long-term endeavors, and have been known to involve massive amounts of data collection. In the words of Dede (2004, p. 7), "everything that moved within a 15-foot radius of the phenomenon was repeatedly interviewed, videotaped, surveyed and so-forth ..." Design researchers have commented that reporting can be problematic because of the scope of many research projects (Reeves, Herrington, & Oliver, 2005). Books offer opportunities for providing more detailed accounts of design research projects, but are less common, perhaps for the simple reason that they are substantially less valued among most university tenure and promotion committees. Journal papers and conference presentations have word count and time slot limitations that render the task of sharing the planning, methods, results, and implications of educational design research studies difficult, to say the least. Design researchers frequently struggle with questions like: Which size story can be told? Where to find interested audiences? How much of a story is useful? Whose story or whose perspective should be shared? Other struggles relate to the level of detail with which the context should be described; the explicitness of design propositions; or what additional information is required for readers to be able to generalize the findings to their own situation.

Alignment with standardized research reports

Some design researchers have expressed difficulty aligning reports of design studies with the expectations of what research reports usually look like (Reeves, Herrington, & Oliver, 2005). For example, it can be difficult to figure out how and where to describe the intervention, and very few formats obviously allow for detailed description of how interventions are designed. Indeed, not all audiences value such information equally. When it comes to scientific journals, very few seek to publish design narratives, though *Educational Technology Research & Development* and *Educational Designer* are two notable exceptions.

It has also been suggested that design research may not align to standard criteria for scientific publication because, in its quest for being relevant, design research may be less rigorous (Kelly, 2004). But rigor and relevance are not mutually exclusive (Reeves, 2011), although they can stand in one another's way. Design studies, like all scientific work, must provide adequate warrants for their knowledge claims (cf. Shavelson, Phillips, Towne, & Feuer, 2003). While design researchers may choose to make some trade-offs, such as giving up control of variables in exchange for ecological validity, they must also understand that sacrificing methodological rigor depletes the value and relevance of its theoretical contribution. In the words of Charles Desforges (2001, p. 2), former Director of the Teaching and Learning Research Programme of the Economic and Social Research Council in the United Kingdom, "The status of research deemed educational would have to be judged, first in terms of its disciplined quality and secondly in terms of its impact. Poor discipline is no discipline. And excellent research without impact is not educational."

Understanding different audiences

Reporting educational design research can attend to both practical goals of informing intervention development and theoretical goals of creating new understanding. Different kinds of audiences may be interested in learning about educational design research, each from their own perspectives. This section first discusses an important concept related to understanding different audiences: commissive space. Thereafter, the goals and needs associated with reporting to three kinds of groups are discussed: internal audiences; external professional audiences; and external research audiences.

Commissive space

To write effectively for a particular audience, it is important to understand what that audience values and expects. This is true for all audiences, and is particularly relevant to reporting the findings from educational design research to other researchers. This is because researchers often have very deep-seated notions about the nature of scientific inquiry, and can balk at reports that seem to conflict with what they deem important. In reporting educational design research, it can be useful to demonstrate commonalities, rather than highlight differences between what Kelly (2006) refers to as the commissive space of educational design research and that of other approaches in the social sciences.

Kelly's notion of commissive space has to do with commitments to certain assumptions about, in this case, the nature of scientific research. Simply put, it could be summarized as one's perception of the "rules of the game." When everyone accepts the same basic rules of the game, they are working within the same commissive space; yet without the same rules, it is nearly impossible to engage in productive debate. For example, the commissive space of those who view randomized controlled trials using only quantitative methods as the gold standard of all research and those interested in design research is likely to have relatively little common ground. This allows very little room for productive debate, and the result can rather quickly be flat out rejection as soon as one member violates the "rules of the game" or commitments to assumptions within the other's commissive space. While design researchers violate many of the assumptions of the randomized field trials commissive space (Kelly, 2006), most share the same basic assumptions of, for example, the mixed methods commissive space. By reporting sound educational design research in high-quality journals, the commissive space of design research can be made more transparent, exposed for both skeptics and supporters alike.

As in any kind of discussion, identifying and honoring the commissive space of the various kinds of participants can be an important step in initiating dialogue, for example through publication in a research journal. This does not mean being untrue to the story a particular design study has to tell; but it does mean considering which aspects may be more or less valued by others, and making strategic decisions about which elements of the story to include or exclude. In any good research reporting, it is necessary to convince the audience that the work adds to the existing body of knowledge through careful and convincing descriptions. Bringing new perspectives to a journal can be refreshing, but disregarding what is valued by the readership for that journal will likely result in rejection.

Internal audiences

Reports of design research can serve several goals when written for internal audiences. First, writing internal reports can prompt reflection. In this way, the reporting process itself can be insightful and thereby help to direct the development of the intervention as well as further theoretical understanding.

Second, reporting to internal audiences can be a form of documenting events, allowing for transparent justification (and, later, recall) of design decisions. Third, an internal research report can serve as an important discussion tool within a design research team. Creating and reflecting on reports of design research can help team ideas to gel, or help identify poorly aligned understandings and perspectives (e.g. "this is a very different interpretation from what I thought we discussed").

Internal publications may be written in a scholarly, or a more colloquial tone; and for efficiency purposes, they generally assume rather high degrees of prerequisite knowledge. For example, internal publications may briefly summarize, but not detail, elements that are considered to be common knowledge within a team (e.g. limited discussion of design propositions). Generally, fellow team members will read research reports, which can range from formalized to quite sketchy, from a more formative perspective (e.g. to inform consideration of how to move forward) or a more summative perspective (e.g. to decide if this project warrants continuation, or if it is ready for public exposure).

External professional audiences

Educational professionals, including practitioners, specialists, and policy makers, are an extremely important audience for educational design research reports. Indeed, if educational design research is ever to have the level of impact that it promises, then professionals must be regularly informed of the progress and results of educational design research projects. Reports for this audience may be written with the goals of inspiring and/or informing others. Authorities who set or influence priorities for funding, for example government policy makers and granting agency personnel, are part of this audience. These groups have a powerful say in what kinds of research are supported; and, through them, so does society at large. But educational researchers often fail to communicate clearly with these influential groups (Whitty, 2006). To a large extent, this may stem from traditions of producing thick, book-like documentation which evidences little appreciation for the real concerns of the readers.

Reports written for these audiences may contain certain levels of prerequisite knowledge, depending on the medium used (e.g. content knowledge may be assumed when writing for a subject-based practitioner journal). Practitioners are generally most interested in the implications of educational design research work for their own teaching, such as descriptions of the interventions created (e.g. What does the intervention look like? Would it be useful for me? Can I gain access or participate?), though research results are not unimportant (How can I use this new information? Would this intervention be practical and effective enough to justify getting involved?). Ideally, the professionals who are actually involved in an educational design research project share joint authorship on at least papers intended for teachers, administrators, school board members, parents, students, and the public at large, if not on other publications.

Reports for professional audiences may be published though a variety of media, including professional journals, websites, and newspapers. In some fields (e.g.

environmental engineering), it is much more common for researchers to take the microphone on television or radio talk shows, or to write editorials in local or national newspapers. Noting what seems to be an increase in societal decision making based on opinion and emotion rather than evidence (cf. Fresco, 2011), it seems that both research and practice would benefit from well-informed societal discussion about educational issues, which could be promulgated if educational researchers in general and educational design researchers in particular were more attentive to these audiences.

External research audiences

A main goal of reporting research to fellow researchers is to share emerging theoretical understanding. But while scientific audiences value knowledge sharing (one-way communication), they tend to thrive on debate (two-way communication). Creating and discussing research reports is also a main vehicle for stimulating the researcher–researcher interaction (e.g. experienced at conferences, or through peer refereeing) that is needed to push ideas from internal thoughts to valuable conceptualizations. Scientific reports of design research can have the goals of describing designed interventions, and the ideas underpinning them, as well as the results and implications of empirical testing. It is primarily on the basis of published scientific reports that case-to-case and analytic generalization takes place. Most journals, many conferences, and some book ventures employ a peer review process to guard the rigor and relevance of the work being reported. Although the peer review process is hardly perfect and needs significant improvements (Mandviwalla, Patnayakuni, & Schuff, 2008; McCarty, 2002), it ultimately serves both author and reader, and is an essential pillar of support for scientific research and development.

External publications for a scientific audience employ a scholarly, distanced tone. Because they are intended for a wide audience, some, but not many, assumptions can be made about prerequisite knowledge. For example, understanding of research methodology can be assumed when writing for an academic journal, but understanding of a design research approach cannot. Careful, detailed accounts of design study propositions, interventions, and findings allow others to understand, question and possibly even build on the theoretical understanding produced. Researchers value transparency in reporting; this allows for readers to assess for themselves the trustworthiness of the findings. Lincoln and Guba (1985) declared that trustworthiness involves establishing credibility, transferability, dependability, and confirmability. They proposed that these criteria are analogous to more well-known criteria, typically used to describe quantitative research. Credibility has parallels with internal validity, relating to the "truth" of the findings. It can be enhanced in educational design research, for example, by describing prolonged engagement during intervention testing. Transferability is similar to external validity, and shows that the findings can be informative for other contexts. This can be done, for example, through thick descriptions. Dependability is similar to reliability, as it shows that the findings are consistent and could be repeated. In design research, this might be done by using the same set of design propositions or the same intervention more than once. Confirmability relates to objectivity, and deals with the extent to which the findings of a study are shaped by the respondents and not researcher bias, motivation, or self-interest. This may be addressed, for example, through triangulation of data collection methods. Understanding and explicating these aspects of a design study can be one way to demonstrate commonalities between the aforementioned commissive space of design research, and that of other approaches to scientific inquiry.

Ideally, a group of educational design researchers addressing a particular set of problems will come to form a learning community. This is easy to see in the example of the community of scholars interested in enhancing STEM (science, technology, engineering, and mathematics) education in the USA through the development of immersive digital learning environments working on projects such as Quest Atlantis (Barab, Gresalfi, & Ingram-Goble, 2010), River City (Ketelhut, Nelson, Clarke, & Dede, 2010), and Whyville (Neulight, Kafai, Kao, Foley, & Galas, 2007). Sasha Barab, Chris Dede, and Yasmin Kafai, along with numerous colleagues, graduate students, and practitioners appear to have formed a powerful research and development community through their application of educational design research methods to challenges related to STEM education and their focus on pushing the state-of-the-art of multi-user virtual environments for learning. No doubt these researchers and their collaborators sometimes must compete for the same resources from the National Science Foundation and other agencies, but at the same time they have also contributed to each other's work. Moreover, they have all helped to refine the educational design research approach itself (cf. Barab & Squire, 2004; Dede, 2005; Kafai, 2005).

Writing recommendations

Choose the scope

As mentioned earlier in this chapter, educational design researchers often want to tell the whole story all at once. This may be possible in books, is rarely the case with journal articles, and virtually impossible in popular media. Breaking educational design research findings into interesting and informative chunks is usually necessary. This requires the ability to "see" different "stories" within the research. This may have been done at the time a study was conceptualized (see also Chapter 8) or it may be done after it has taken shape. Either way, it can be useful to look at the research in terms of: (a) individual micro-cycles; or (b) specific themes across several cycles. As each micro-cycle (analysis and exploration; design and construction; or evaluation and reflection) contains its own cogent reasoning and its own (albeit humble) contribution to theory and practice, it may be possible to report on each micro-cycle separately. This was the case with the second example given in Chapter 2, concerning para-teacher professional development in Indian slums. From that study, one article was published about the needs and context analysis; one article described the conceptual model underpinning the designed intervention; and three articles discussed three different cycles of evaluation, respectively. Some studies, however, lend themselves more naturally to reporting across several cycles. To do this, well-defined themes (or, in larger projects, sub-themes) determine the scope. The story may then be told more or less chronologically, although that is not always the most useful sequence. Thematic reporting across cycles was used with the first example of an educational design research study given in Chapter 2, on strategies for developing preschooler oral language skills. From that study, one article was published on the intervention and research findings, while another article gave a critical account of the educational design research process.

Refine the message

Educational design researchers usually have many stories to tell. From a single study, there may be stories of design trajectories and intervention characteristics; stories of learning, engagement, and student outcomes; or stories of teacher expertise and researcher–practitioner collaboration. Crafting a powerful message often has more to do with judiciously excluding information than it does with figuring out what to include. In so doing, two main issues warrant consideration: the audience and the core message. As described above, reports of educational design research can be of interest to practitioners, specialists, policy makers, researchers, or the general public. Consider what background knowledge can reasonably be expected from the audience of a particular piece and, if needed, test those assumptions before writing (e.g. ask several people who are not closely involved in the research to review the paper). It can be useful to literally visualize someone from the audience during writing and consider their reactions as sentences are crafted and the story unfolds. It is also important to identify which pieces of the story the audience needs to understand the core message, and which ones are extraneous or even distracting. Chances are reasonable that (a) not all data collected within one micro-cycle or across one theme are pertinent to a specific message; and (b) certain data or insights are more powerful than others. Omitting weak data sources or poorly justified design considerations can bring more powerful ones to the fore, and allow in-depth reporting of those that really matter. Finally, it can be useful to recognize that educational design researchers, many of whom grow rather attached to their designed interventions, must sometimes struggle to focus on telling a coherent story to readers, and not reporting on only what is important to them personally.

Seek inspiring examples

The educational design research community can learn from one another in many ways. While the content of research reports is of course extremely important, much can be learned from studying the format. It can be extremely useful to peruse papers that are methodologically similar for good ideas on concise, efficient presentation of, for example, (integrated) design propositions; intervention descriptions; research designs; data; or emerging (theoretical and/or practical) insights. Given the connection to designed interventions, it can be informative to supplement design research papers with linked resources. For example, *Educational Designer* is an open access journal that welcomes critical reflection on and rich exemplification of designed interventions, and especially the grounds for design evolution (e.g. What insights prompted which changes to interventions or their underlying ideas?).

Good examples of design study reports can be helpful in shaping one's own publications. They can also inspire new ideas for conceptualizing and executing design research. Conceptualizing design research, including new directions for this genre of inquiry, is discussed in the next chapter.

Chapter 10

Looking back and looking ahead

This book has been written to support researchers, and especially doctoral students, in conducting educational design research. Ideally, the ideas presented in these pages provide an enhanced foundation for further discussion and more widespread adoption of this genre of inquiry. This chapter briefly recapitulates some key concepts raised throughout the book, which may be the subject of future discourse. It also considers new directions and potential contributions that might be tackled through this approach.

Looking back: this book in review

Part I

The first three chapters built the foundation for the remainder of the book. The origins and centrality of the dual goals of seeking theoretical understanding through the development of solutions to real problems were discussed. Educational design research was characterized as being theoretically oriented, interventionist, collaborative, responsively grounded, and iterative. Across rich variation of interpretations of this approach, two main orientations were distinguished: research conducted *through* interventions and research conducted *on* interventions, both of which are often seen during the lifespan of single projects. The theoretical contributions of educational design research were discussed in terms of empirical findings, hypotheses, conjectures, and theoretical principles. These may be used for descriptive, explanatory, predictive and/or prescriptive/normative purposes; and they may hold local, middle-range or broad, applicability. Four, very different, examples of educational design research undertakings were described, along with their theoretical and practical contributions. The ways in which the fields of instructional design and curriculum development have influenced our conceptualization of educational design research were described, along with lessons learned from existing models portraying this kind of study. Rooted in these understandings, the first part of the book culminated with the presentation and discussion of a generic model for conducting educational design research.

Part II

The generic model presented in Chapter 3 set the stage for the second part of the book, which discussed the main processes involved in educational design research. It was stressed that these processes are generally evident in most design studies, but that the sequence, duration, and frequency varies with each project. Three core phases were discussed, each of which: involves interaction with practice; can feed into another phase; and can be viewed as a micro-cycle with its own cogent chain of reasoning and action. Throughout each of these phases, the value of approaching the work using the mindsets of both detective and inventor were noted. The first phase discussed was that of analysis (featuring initial orientation, literature review, and field-based investigation) and exploration (involving site visits, professional meetings, and networking). This phase yields a descriptive and explanatory definition of the problem; long-range goals; initial design propositions; and partial design requirements. The second phase described was that of design (exploring solutions through the generation, consideration and checking of ideas, and mapping solutions from design requirements and propositions through a skeleton design to detailed design specifications) and construction (creating and revising initial prototypes). This phase yields products that describe design ideas, as well as products that embody design ideas. The third phase described was that of evaluation (which entails an empirical cycle of testing) and reflection (which can be organic or structured). This phase yields theoretical understanding and recommendations for (refining) applied use. Each of these phases involves interaction with practice, and this was discussed in terms of the implementation and spread of interventions developed through design research. After describing the mindset of planning for actual use, implementation (adoption, enactment, and sustained maintenance) and spread (dissemination and diffusion) were described before attention was given to important factors that shape these processes: intervention attributes; strategies for change; the context, including its surrounding system; and the actors involved. Finally, considerations were given for implementation and spread during each of the three main phases of educational design research.

Part III

The third part of the book has considered the advancement of educational design research. Attention was given to writing proposals for studies that use this approach. This discussion addressed: the purpose and functions of research proposals; the need for immersion in phenomena before being able to write proposals about them; different ways to position (sub-) studies in research proposals; and guidelines for proposal writing, including a rubric for self-evaluation of research proposals. Attention was also given to reporting design research. This included common reporting concerns, the different audiences of educational design research, and, with these in mind, various writing recommendations were offered.

Looking ahead: the future of educational design research

Challenges to be tackled

We have argued throughout this book that educational design research holds great potential for developing theoretical understanding that can be put to applied use. But there are many challenges to be tackled if this potential is to be realized; this discussion focuses on three that we consider to be among the most substantial now. First, we must acknowledge that the twin pursuit of theory building and practical innovation is extremely difficult. In fact, some thoughtful scholars question whether it is even feasible, especially given the inherent challenges to guarding methodological rigor (e.g. Phillips & Dolle, 2006). While we remain convinced that the pursuit of theoretical understanding and practical applications can commence simultaneously, even synergistically, more high-quality examples of such work are greatly needed.

Second, in refining understanding of how to conduct educational design research, it may be useful to explore field-specific interpretations and approaches. As mentioned in Chapter 2, design research has been active for over 20 years in the fields of curriculum; learning and instruction; media and technology; and professional development. To some extent, the methods of empirical testing may be further developed within specific fields. For example, design researchers can learn from each other by sharing and critiquing specific techniques to evaluate educational media and technology, which tend to differ substantially from those used to evaluate teacher professional development. To a greater extent, the methods of educational and instructional design stand to be refined through exchange of field-specific work. For example, while implementation and spread are taken into consideration from the start of any educational design research project, this may be undertaken differently in various fields. Design research that strives toward large-scale curriculum reform would likely engage various key actors in the educational system (policy makers, textbook publishers, assessment bureaus, professional developers) to help frame the project, or at least in the initial analysis. By contrast, a project that strives to create specific learning materials would be more likely to consider the existing system as a given, and tailor design to fit the curriculum frameworks, assessment modes, and other elements already in place. The International Society for Design and Development in Education and the Learning Design Grid are two of the few organizations today whose mission is to promote excellence in educational design. While they welcome educational designers from different fields and foster cross-pollination of ideas across educational design fields, these organizations actively support within-field collaboration that can advance understanding about the design of, for example, assessment structures, professional development, or technology-rich learning materials.

Third, the design research approach affords outstanding opportunities to further develop theoretical understanding in several key areas that are currently under-researched, including: intervention theory; implementation theory;

and educational design theory. While existing design research has yielded contributions to theoretical understanding about the design of some intervention types, this work is limited to date. Developers of many intervention types have descriptive and explanatory theories to guide their work, but often lack predictive and prescriptive theories to sufficiently inform design. A notable exception can be seen with one specific intervention type: computer supported collaborative learning (CSCL) environments. Many recent studies have yielded findings and principles that provide a sound basis for the development of CSCL environments (Dillenbourg, Järvelä, & Fischer, 2009; Stahl, Koschmann, & Suthers, 2006). Often, they have employed an educational design research approach (cf. Roschelle, Rafanan, Estrella, Nussbaum, & Claro, 2010). A worthy challenge facing educational design researchers is to further the development of predictive and prescriptive theories concerning additional intervention types.

Design research inherently involves the study of implementation, but relatively few design studies to date have capitalized on this opportunity to advance implementation theory. In a similar vein, relatively few design research efforts have documented or tested the design process well enough to advance the field of educational design. While design narratives can inform our collective craft wisdom, it would seem that most educational design research could benefit from more robust theoretical grounding for steering specific design processes. For example, the ideas presented in this book have been strongly influenced by theory, and are also largely based on experience; but they have not yet been subjected to rigorous testing and refinement. We aim to tackle this challenge in the coming years, and hope that this task interests other scholars, as well.

Socially responsible research

Writing in the journal, *Nature*, Gibbons (1999, p. 11) said:

> Under the prevailing contract between science and society, science has been expected to produce "reliable" knowledge, provided merely that it communicates its discoveries to society. A new contract must now ensure that scientific knowledge is "socially robust", and that its production is seen by society to be both transparent and participative.

Gibbons (1999) points out that (a) the basic conditions and processes that have underpinned the production of "reliable knowledge" are not necessarily compromised by the shift to "socially robust knowledge;" (b) reliable knowledge has always only been reliable within boundaries; and (c) there is no one set of practices that describe, much less lead to, good science. He calls upon scientists in all fields, natural and well as social, to go beyond their traditional search for "reliable knowledge" to seek "socially robust knowledge," that is, knowledge that would have more reliable impact on the problems faced by society at large. It would seem that educational design research inherently seeks socially robust knowledge, alongside reliable knowledge. As such, it may be viewed as a socially responsive form of inquiry.

Gibbons, Limoges, Nowotny, Shwartman, Scott, and Trow (1994) distinguish two forms of knowledge production: Mode 1 and Mode 2. Mode 1 knowledge production is primarily directed by university researchers. Within this relatively impermeable structure, specific problems and investigations are defined and vetted. The resulting knowledge is general and transferable. The spread of knowledge is hierarchical and linear, from researchers (sometimes through intermediaries) to practice. In contrast, Mode 2 knowledge production is not hierarchically organized, and the problems are defined and solved in practice. The resulting knowledge is practical and context-specific. The knowledge produced through these two modes is valued in different ways by different actors (Bartels, 2003).

While design research clearly has a Mode 1 agenda, we see opportunity and also evidence for Mode 2 knowledge production as well (e.g. McKenney, 2005). Some design researchers view this contribution more along the lines of a fringe benefit. For us, it is part of a socially responsible mandate. If we truly want to contribute to improving education and are honest about the pace and mechanisms through which Mode 1 knowledge production takes place, then we need to take seriously the production of knowledge that resides in the minds of those who participate in the enterprise. In this, we imply a range of participants, most notably educational professionals, but also the researchers and experts whose intimate knowledge of the situation at hand help craft and refine solutions in context.

We do not expect design research to dramatically change the field of education any time soon. Instead, we maintain humble expectations about the extent to which research can truly inform and improve educational practice. From the stance of the realistic optimist, we acknowledge that, in the best of cases, it takes years or decades for theoretical understanding to be able to have any impact on practice. But we also acknowledge that educational design research has more to offer to practice. When the research activities themselves are shaped to be of practical value, through the intervention designed and/or the participant learning that ensues, research makes a clear and immediate contribution to practice. Though the scale of these contributions may be modest, they may help demonstrate the value of educational research, something which has been questioned repeatedly (Kaestle, 1993; Oancea, 2005).

The educational design research community

The call for educational researchers to make strategic choices and work collaboratively to develop, share, and build on insights is being made across approaches (cf. Schoenfeld, 2009b) and with specific regard to design research (Barab & Squire, 2004; Nieveen, McKenney, van den Akker, 2006). Burkhardt (2006) writes about what is needed to build the design research community (he uses the term "engineering research") and bring about greater acceptance of the approach and use of its products, in terms of interventions and theoretical understanding. He calls for the development of skills, among intervention-testing professionals, designers, and researchers. In addition, he makes the case for the need to influence governments (who allocate funding) and industry (notably, companies that produce educational materials). Burkhardt further indicates that major changes will need to come in academia, stating that "Currently, the *academic value system in education*, which controls academic appointments and promotions, is actively hostile to engineering research" (2006, p. 144, emphasis in original text). Instead, Burkhardt describes several Nobel Prize winners for design and development and concludes that educational design research candidates should be assessed on the basis of their: impact on practice; contribution to theoretical understanding; and improvement in either research and/or design methodology.

Through our teaching, mentoring, and the publication of this book, we work toward developing the skills necessary for design research to be adopted both widely and well. We seek to influence governments, industry, and academia – though this is a slow and often frustrating process. But in the meantime, let us not wait for the academic value system to catch up with what society has already deemed important. Let us, as a community, choose to prioritize impact on practice as we already do the advancement of theory, knowledge, and methodology. Positive impact on practice is not a fringe benefit – it is the hallmark of socially responsible research.

The time for educational design research is upon us

Nowotny, Scott, and Gibbons (2001, 2003) conclude that the aforementioned Mode 2 does not apply to knowledge production alone, but that there is also a Mode 2 society, and that the traditionally well-drawn distinctions between science and society are opening up. Society is speaking back. This is happening though increased societal participation in the mechanisms that guide research, including the many panels set up to assess the social relevance of government-funded research. There is also a stronger climate of accountability. Society's voice is also being heard through the increase of researcher engagement with practice; this includes gradual, but increasing, funding to support such interaction. In addition, media coverage on policies that help or hinder socially relevant research that involves collaboration with practice (cf. Viadero, 2009) has increased in recent years.

Society is not just demanding participation. "Society is ... demanding innovation in a variety of ways ... altering what problems researchers work on, how they do so and with whom" (Gibbons, 2000, p. 161). Society, it seems, is demanding Mode 2 knowledge. Educational design researchers clearly can foster the development of Mode 2 knowledge, particularly by mediating a dialogue between knowledge production and knowledge use. The interventions we design play a crucial role in this, as do the choices we make about how to engage with practice during the endeavor. When we accept the needs and wishes of practice, not only as being heard, but as transformational in steering our research agendas, we also increase the chance that the theoretical and practical products of design research will, indeed, mature and be used over time.

Reflecting on current conceptualizations of educational design research and considering ways forward, it seems appropriate to raise questions about where we, those who practice design research, stand on the issues related to knowledge production and knowledge use. Various authors have addressed the importance of seriously considering the social agenda in design research (Barab, Dodge, Thomas, Jackson, & Tuzun, 2007; Brown, 1992; Reeves, 2011). To some extent, there is room for personal choice in the matter. But as Gibbons (1999, 2000) has pointed out, society is speaking back. Educational design research is an outstanding way to demonstrate how researchers are listening.

Appendix
Related reading

Educational design research models and frameworks

Bannan-Ritland, B. & Baek, J. (2008). Investigating the act of design in design research: The road taken. In A. E. Kelly, R. A. Lesh & J. Y. Baek (Eds.), *Handbook of design research methods in education* (pp. 299–319). London: Routledge.

Barab, S. & Squire, K. (2004). Design-based research: Putting a stake in the ground. *Journal of the Learning Sciences*, 13(1), 1–14.

Ejersbo, L., Engelhardt, R., Frølunde, L., Hanghøj, T., Magnussen, R., & Misfeldt, M. (2008). Balancing product design and theoretical insight. In A. E. Kelly, R. A. Lesh & J. Y. Baek (Eds.), *The handbook of design research methods in education* (pp. 149–163). London: Routledge.

Gravemeijer, K. & Cobb, P. (2006). Outline of a method for design research in mathematics education. In J. van den Akker, K. Gravemeijer, S. McKenney & N. Nieveen (Eds.), *Educational design research* (pp. 17–51). London: Routledge.

Jonassen, D. H., Cernusca, D., & Ionas, G. (2007). Constructivism and instructional design: The emergence of the learning sciences and design research. In R. Reiser & J. Dempsey (Eds.), *Trends and issues in instructional design and technology* (pp. 45–52). Upper Saddle River, NJ: Pearson Education.

McKenney, S., Nieveen, N., & van den Akker, J. (2006). Design research from the curriculum perspective. In J. van den Akker, K. Gravemeijer, S. McKenney & N. Nieveen (Eds.), *Educational design research* (pp. 67–90). London: Routledge.

Reeves, T. C. (2006). Design research from the technology perspective. In J. van den Akker, K. Gravemeijer, S. McKenney & N. Nieveen (Eds.), *Educational design research* (pp. 86–109). London: Routledge.

Reinking, D. & Bradley, B. A. (2008). *Formative and design experiments: Approaches to language and literacy research.* New York: Teachers College Press.

van den Akker, J., Gravemeijer, K., McKenney, S. & Nieveen, N. (Eds.), (2006). *Educational design research.* London: Routledge.

Wang, F. & Hannafin, M. (2005). Design-based research and technology-enhances learning environments. *Educational Technology Research and Development*, 53(4), 5–23.

Online resources

http://projects.coe.uga.edu/dbr/index.htm

Conducting and writing a literature review

Fink, A. (2009). *Conducting research literature reviews*. London: Sage.

Hart, C. (2002). *Doing a literature review: Releasing the social science research imagination*. London: Sage.

Jesson, J. & Matheson, L. (2011). *Doing your literature review: Traditional and systematic techniques*. London: Sage.

Machi, L. & McEvoy, B. (2009). *The literature review: Six steps to success*. Thousand Oaks, CA: Corwin Press.

Ridley, D. (2008). *The literature review: A step-by-step guide for students*. Thousand Oaks, CA: Sage.

Online resources

http://www.gwu.edu/~litrev/

http://libguides.library.cqu.edu.au/content.php?pid=9872&sid=64803

Creating research instruments

Bradburn, N. M., Sudman, S., & Wansink, B. (2004). *Asking questions: The definitive guide to questionnaire design – For market research, political polls, and social and health questionnaires*. San Francisco, CA: Jossey-Bass.

Colton, D. & Covert, R. (2007). *Designing and constructing instruments for social research and evaluation*. San Francisco, CA: Jossey-Bass.

DeVellis, R. (2011). *Scale development*. London: Sage.

Dillman, D. A., Smyth, J. D., & Christian, L. M. (2009). *Internet, mail, and mixed-mode surveys: The tailored design method* (3rd ed.). New York: Wiley.

Gubrium, J. & Holstein, J. (2002). *Handbook of interview research: Context and method*. London: Sage.

Online resources

http://www.surveysystem.com/sdesign.htm

http://www2.acs.ncsu.edu/upa/assmt/resource.htm

http://www.transformingassessment.com/

Project management

Greer, M. (2000). *The manager's pocket guide to project management*. Amherst, MA: HRD Press.

Kerzner, H. (2009). *Project management: A systems approach to planning, scheduling, and controlling* (10th ed.). New York: Wiley.

Mantel, S.J., Meredith, J. R., Shafer, S. M., & Sutton, M. M. (2010). *Project management in practice* (4th ed.). New York: Wiley.

Weiss, J. & Wysocki, R. (1992). *Five-phase project management: A practical planning and implementation guide*. New York: Basic Books.

Online resources

http://michaelgreer.biz/
http://www.microsoft.com/project/
http://www.smartsheet.com/
http://projectwizards.net/en/

Planning, data collection, and analysis

Creswell, J. (2011). *Educational research: Planning, conducting, and evaluating quantitative and qualitative research* (4th ed.). London: Sage.
Creswell, J. & Plano Clark, V. L. (2011). *Designing and conducting mixed methods research* (2nd ed.). London: Sage.
Denzin, N. & Lincoln, Y. (2005). *The SAGE handbook of qualitative research design: Qualitative, quantitative, and mixed methods* (3rd ed.). London: Sage.
Gorard, S. (2008). *Quantitative research in education*. London: Sage.
Merriam, S. (2009). *Qualitative research: A guide to design and implementation*. San Francisco, CA: Jossey-Bass.
Miles, M., & Huberman, M. (1994). *Qualitative data analysis*. London: Sage.
Muijs, D. (2010). *Doing quantitative research in education with SPSS*. London: Sage
Patton, M. Q. (2001). *Qualitative research and evaluation methods* (3rd ed.). London: Sage.
Robson, C. (2011). *Real world research*. Malden, MA: Blackwell Publishers.

Online resources

http://www.socialresearchmethods.net/

Educational design

Dick, W., Carey, L., & Carey, J. O. (2011). *The systematic design of instruction* (7th ed.). New York: Allyn & Bacon.
Morrison, G. R., Ross, S. M., Kalman, H., & Kemp, J. E. (2011). *Designing effective instruction* (6th ed.). New York: Wiley.
Posner, G. & Rudnitsky, A. (2005). *Course design: A guide to curriculum development for teachers* (7th ed.). New York: Allyn & Bacon.
Smith, P. L. & Ragan, T. J. (2004). *Instructional design*. New York: Wiley.
Wiles, J. W. & Bondi, J. C. (2010). *Curriculum development: A guide to practice* (8th ed.). Upper Saddle River, NJ: Prentice Hall.

Online resources

http://www.instructionaldesign.org/
http://www4.uwsp.edu/education/lwilson/curric/

Product or program evaluation

Flagg, B. N. (1990). *Formative evaluation for educational technologies.* Hillsdale, NJ: Lawrence Erlbaum Associates.
Patton, M. Q. (2008). *Utilization-focused evaluation.* London: Sage.
Patton, M. Q. (2011). *Developmental evaluation: Applying complexity concepts to enhance innovation and use.* New York: The Guilford Press.
Reeves, T. C. & Hedberg, J. G. (2003). *Interactive learning systems evaluation.* Englewood Cliffs, NJ: Educational Technology Publications.
Russ-Eft, D. & Preskill, H. (2009). *Evaluation in organizations: A systematic approach to enhancing learning, performance, and change.* New York: Basic Books.

Online resources

http://www.cdc.gov/eval/resources/index.htm

Implementation and spread

Ellsworth, J. (2000). *Surviving change: A survey of educational change models.* Englewood Cliffs, NJ: Educational Technology Publications.
Evans, R. (2001). *The human side of school change: Reform, resistance, and the real-life problems of innovation.* San Francisco, CA: Jossey-Bass.
Fullan, M. (1993). *Change forces: Probing the depths of educational reform.* London: RoutledgeFalmer.
Fullan, M. (1999). *Change forces: The sequel.* London: Taylor and Francis Group.
Fullan, M. (2007). *The new meaning of educational change* (4th ed.). New York: Teachers College Press.
Fullan, M. (2011). *Change leader: Learning to do what matters most.* San Francisco, CA: Jossey-Bass.
Hall, G. & Hord, S. (2010) *Implementing change: Patterns, principles, and potholes.* Upper Saddle River, NJ: Prentice Hall.
Havelock, R. (1971). *Planning for innovation through dissemination and utilization of knowledge.* Ann Arbor, MI: Center for Research on Utilization of Scientific Knowledge.
Reigeluth, C. & Garfinkel, R. (1994). *Systemic change in education.* Englewood Cliffs, NJ: Educational Technology Publications.

Online resources

http://smhp.psych.ucla.edu/qf/systemicchange.html
http://www.edutopia.org/

References

Anderson, T. H., West, C. K., Beck, D. P., Macdonell, E. S., & Frisbie, D. S. (1997). Integrating reading and science education: On developing and evaluating WEE Science. *Journal of Curriculum Studies, 29*(6), 711–733.

Baker, L. (1991). Metacognition, reading, and science education. In C. M. Santa & D. E. Alvermann (Eds.), *Science learning: Processes and applications* (pp. 2–13). Newark, DE: International Reading Association.

Bannan-Ritland, B. (2003). The role of design in research: The integrative learning design framework. *Educational Researcher, 32*(1), 21–24.

Bannan-Ritland, B. & Baek, J. Y. (2008). Investigating the act of design in design research: The road taken. In A. E. Kelly, R. A. Lesh & J. Y. Baek (Eds.), *Handbook of design research methods in education* (pp. 299–319). London: Routledge.

Barab, S. A., Dodge, T., & Gee, J. P. (2009). *The worked example: Invitational scholarship in service of an emerging field.* Paper presented at the annual meeting of the American Educational Research Association, San Diego, CA, April. Retrieved from http://inkido.indiana.edu/research/onlinemanu/papers/workedexample.pdf

Barab, S., Dodge, T., Thomas, M., Jackson, C. & Tuzun, H. (2007). Our designs and the social agendas they carry. *Journal of the Learning Sciences, 16*(2), 263–305.

Barab, S. A., Gresalfi, M. S., & Ingram-Goble, A. (2010). Transformational play: Using games to position person, content, and context. *Educational Researcher, 39*(7), 525–536.

Barab, S. & Squire, K. (2004). Design-based research: Putting a stake in the ground. *Journal of the Learning Sciences, 13*(1), 1–14.

Bartels, N. (2003). How teachers and researchers read academic articles. *Teaching and Teacher Education, 19*(7), 737–753.

Bartholomew, L., Parcel, G., Kok, G., & Gottleib, N. (2006). *Planning health promotion programs: An intervention mapping approach.* San Francisco, CA: Jossey-Bass.

Bell, P. (2004). On the theoretical breadth of design-based research in education. *Educational Psychologist, 39*(4), 243–253.

Bereiter, C. (2002). Design research for sustained innovation. *Cognitive Studies, Bulletin of the Japanese Cognitive Science Society, 9*(3), 321–327.

Bers, M. (2001). Identity construction environments: Developing personal and moral values through the design of a virtual city. *Journal of the Learning Sciences, 10*(4), 365–415.

Bielaczyc, K. (2006). Designing social infrastructure: Critical issues in creating learning environments with technology. *Journal of the Learning Sciences, 15*(3), 301–329.

Boschman, F., McKenney, S., & Voogt, J. (2011). *Exploring practical knowledge of teachers as designers of ICT-rich learning environments for early literacy development: Unraveling a messy construct.* Paper presented at the annual Onderwijs Research Dagen [Educational Research Conference], June 8–10, Maastricht, The Netherlands.

Bradley, B. (2004). *A formative experiment to enhance verbal interactions in a preschool classroom.* Doctoral dissertation. University of Georgia.

Bradley, B. & Reinking, D. (2011a). A formative experiment to enhance teacher-child language interactions in a preschool classroom. *Journal of Early Childhood Literacy, 11*(3), 362–401.

Bradley, B. & Reinking, D. (2011b). Enhancing research and practice in early childhood through formative and design experiments. *Early Childhood Development and Care, 181*(3), 305–319.

Branch, R. M. (2009). *Instructional design: The ADDIE approach.* New York: Springer.

Bransford, J. D., Brown, A. L., & Cocking, R. R. (2000). *How people learn: Brain, mind, experience, and school.* Washington, DC: National Academy Press.

Bransford, J., Sherwood, R., Hasselbring, T., Kinzer, C., & Williams, S. (1990). Anchored instruction: Why we need it and how technology can help. In D. Nix & R. Spiro (Eds.), *Cognition education and multimedia: Exploring ideas in high technology* (pp. 115–141). Hillsdale, NJ: Lawrence Erlbaum Associates.

Bransford, J. D., Vye, N. J., Stevens, R., Kuhl, P., Schwartz, D., Bell, P., et al. (2005). Learning theories and education: Toward a decade of synergy. In P. Alexander & P. Winne (Eds.), *Handbook of educational psychology* (Vol. 2) (pp. 209–244). Mahwah, NJ: Lawrence Erlbaum Associates.

Brewer, M. (2000). Research design and issues of validity. In H. T. Reis & C. M. Judd (Eds.), *Handbook of research methods in social and personality psychology* (pp. 3–16). Cambridge, UK: Cambridge University Press.

Broekkamp, H. & Hout-Wolters, B. H. A. M. (2007). The gap between educational research and practice: A literature review, symposium, and questionnaire. *Educational Research and Evaluation, 13*(3), 203–220.

Brown, A. L. (1992). Design experiments: Theoretical and methodological challenges in creating complex interventions in classroom settings. *Journal of the Learning Sciences, 2*(2), 141–178.

Brown, A. L. & Campione, J. (1996). Psychological theory and the design of innovative learning environments: On procedures, principles, and systems. In L. Schauble & R. Glaser (Eds.), *Innovations in learning* (pp. 289–325). Mahwah, NJ: Lawrence Erlbaum Associates.

Brown, J. S., Collins, A., & Duguid, P. (1989). Situated cognition and the culture of learning. *Educational Researcher, 18*(1), 32–42.

Bryant, D. M., Burchinal, M., Lau, L. B., & Sparling, J. J. (1994). Family and classroom correlates of Head Start children's developmental outcomes. *Early Childhood Research Quarterly, 9*(3–4), 289–309.

Burkhardt, H. (1987). On specifying a national curriculum. In I. Wirszup & R. Streit, (Eds.), *Developments in school mathematics worldwide* (pp. 3–30). Reston, VA: National Council of Teachers of Mathematics.

Burkhardt, H. (2006). From design research to large-scale impact: Engineering research in education. In J. van den Akker, K. Gravemeijer, S. McKenney & N. Nieveen (Eds.), *Educational design research* (pp. 121–150). London: Routledge.

Burkhardt, H. (2009). On strategic design. *Educational Designer, 1*(3). Retrieved from http://www.educationaldesigner.org/ed/volume1/issue3/article9/index.htm

Burkhardt, H. & Schoenfeld, A. (2003). Improving educational research: Toward a more useful, more influential, and better-funded enterprise. *Educational Researcher, 32*(9), 3–14.

Carin, A. A. & Sund, R. B. (1985). *Teaching modern science* (4th ed.). Columbus, OH: Merrill.

Cervetti, G. & Barber, J. (2008). Text in hands-on science. In E. Hiebert & M. Sailors (Eds.), *Finding the right texts: What works for beginning and struggling readers* (pp. 89–108). New York: Guilford.

Cervetti, G., Barber, J., Dorph, R., Goldschmidt, P., & Pearson, D. (under review). The impact of an integrated approach to science and literacy in elementary school classrooms.

Cervetti, G., Bravo, M., Hiebert, E., Pearson, D., & Jaynes, C. (2009). Text genre and science content: Ease of reading, comprehension and reader preference. *Reading Psychology, 30*(6) 487–511.

Cervetti, G., Pearson, D., Barber, J., Hiebert, E., & Bravo, M. (2007). Integrating literacy and science: The research we have, the research we need. In M. Pressley, A. K. Billman, K. H. Perry, K. E. Reffitt & J. M. Reynolds (Eds.), *Shaping literacy achievement: Research we have, research we need* (pp. 157–174). New York: Guilford.

Cervetti, G., Pearson, D., Bravo, M., & Barber, J. (2006). Reading and writing in the service of inquiry-based science. In R. Douglas, P. Klentschy & K. Worth (Eds.), *Linking science and literacy in the K-8 classroom* (pp. 221–244). Arlington, VA: NSTA Press.

Charters, W. (1923). The Los Angeles high school curriculum. *The School Review 31*(2), 95–103.

Clark, D. (2004). Hands-on investigation in Internet environments: Teaching thermal equilibrium. In M. Linn, E. Davis & P. Bell (Eds.), *Internet environments for science education* (pp. 175–200). Mahwah, NJ: Lawrence Erlbaum Associates.

Clarke, J. & Dede, C. (2009). Design for scalability: A case study of the river city curriculum. *Journal of Science Education and Technology, 18*(4), 353–365.

Cobb, P., Confrey, J., diSessa, A., Lehrer, R., & Schauble, L. (2003). Design experiments in educational research. *Educational Researcher, 32*(1), 9–13.

Cobb, P. & Gravemeijer, K. (2008). Experimenting to support and understand learning processes. In A. E. Kelly, R. A. Lesh & J. Y. Baek (Eds.), *Handbook of design research methods in education* (pp. 68–95). London: Routledge.

Coburn, C. (2003). Rethinking scale: Moving beyond numbers to deep and lasting change. *Educational Researcher, 32*(6), 3–12.

Cognition and Technology Group at Vanderbilt. (1990). Anchored instruction and its relationship to situated cognition. *Educational Researcher, 19*(6), 2–10.

Cognition and Technology Group at Vanderbilt. (1992a). The Jasper experiment: An exploration of issues in learning and instructional design. *Educational Technology Research and Development, 40*(1), 65–80.

Cognition and Technology Group at Vanderbilt. (1992b). The Jasper series as an example of anchored instruction: Theory, program description and assessment data. *Educational Psychologist*, 27, 291–315.

Cognition and Technology Group at Vanderbilt. (1993). The Jasper experiment: Using video to provide real-world problem-solving contexts. *Arithmetic Teacher*, 40(8), 474–478.

Cognition and Technology Group at Vanderbilt. (1997a). *The Jasper Project: Lessons in curriculum, instruction, assessment, and professional development*. Mahwah, NJ: Lawrence Erlbaum Associates.

Cognition and Technology Group at Vanderbilt. (1997b). The Jasper series: A design experiment in complex, mathematical problem solving. In J. Hawkins & A. M. Collins (Eds.), *Design experiments: Integrating technologies into schools*. New York: Cambridge University Press.

Collins, A. M. (1992). Towards a design science of education. In E. Scanlon & T. O'Shea (Eds.), *New directions in educational technology* (pp. 15–22). Berlin: Springer.

Collins, A. M., Joseph, D., & Bielaczyc, K. (2004). Design research: Theoretical and methodological issues. *Journal of the Learning Sciences*, 13(1), 15–42.

Connell, J. & Shafer, L. (1989). *Structured rapid prototyping: An evolutionary approach to software development*. Englewood Cliffs, NJ: Yourdan Press.

Corrigan, S., Loper, S., and Barber, J. (2010). *Cui bono? How learning progressions stand to benefit curriculum developers and education researchers*. Paper presented at the annual meeting of the American Educational Research Association, April 30 – May 4, Denver, Colorado.

Cronbach, L. J. (1975). Beyond the two disciplines of scientific psychology. *American Psychologist*, 35, 116–127.

Cross, N. (1990). The nature and nurture of design ability. *Design Studies*, 11(3), 127–140.

Crouch, C. H. & Mazur, E. (2001). Peer instruction: Ten years of experience and results. *American Journal of Physics*, 69(9), 970–977.

Cuban, L. (1986). *Teachers and machines: The classroom use of technology since 1920*. New York: Teachers College Press.

Cviko, A., McKenney, S., & Voogt, J. (2011). *Teachers as (re-)designers of an ICT-rich learning environment for early literacy*. Paper presented at the annual European Conference for Educational Research, September 13–16, Berlin.

Cviko, A., McKenney, S., & Voogt, J. (2011). Teachers enacting a technology-rich curriculum for emergent literacy. *Educational Technology Research and Development*. Advance online publication. Doi: 10.1007/s11423-011-9208-3.

Davis, E. & Krajcik, J. (2005). Designing educative curriculum materials to promote teacher learning. *Educational Researcher*, 34(3), 3–14.

Dede, C. (2004). If design-based research is the answer, what is the question? *Journal of the Learning Sciences*, 13(1), 105–114.

Dede, C. (2005). Why design-based research is both important and difficult. *Educational Technology*, 45(1), 5–8.

Desforges, C. (2001). Familiar challenges and new approaches: Necessary advances in theory and methods in research on teaching and learning. The Desmond Nuttall/ Carfax Memorial Lecture, British Educational Research Association (BERA)

Annual Conference, Cardiff, August. Retrieved from http://www.tlrp.org/acadpub/Desforges2000a.pdf

Design-Based Research Collective. (2003). Design-based research: An emerging paradigm for educational inquiry. *Educational Researcher, 32*(1), 5–8.

De Groot, A. D. (1969). *Methodology. Foundations of inference and research in the behavioral sciences.* The Hague, Paris: Mouton & Co.

De Vaney, A. (1998). Can and need educational technology become a postmodern enterprise? *Theory into Practice, 37*(1), 72–80.

De Vries, B. & Pieters, J. M. (2007). Knowledge sharing at conferences. *Educational Research and Evaluation, 14*(3), 237–249.

De Vries, B., van der Meij, H., Boersma, K., & Pieters, J. (2005). Embedding e-mail in primary schools: Developing a tool for collective reflection. *Journal of Educational Computing Research, 32*(2), 167–183.

Dewey, J. (1900). *The school and society.* Chicago, IL: University of Chicago Press.

Dickinson, G. & Summers, E. J. (2010). (Re)Anchored, video-centered engagement: The transferability of preservice training to practice. *Contemporary Issues in Technology and Teacher Education, 10*(1). Retrieved from http://www.citejournal.org/vol10/iss1/science/article1.cfm

Dillenbourg, P., Järvelä, S., & Fischer, F. (2009). The evolution of research on computer supported collaborative learning: From design to orchestration. In N. Balacheff, S. Ludwigsen, T. de Jong, A. Lazonder & S. Barnes (Eds.), *Technology-enhanced learning: Principles and products* (pp. 3–19). The Netherlands: Springer.

Dix, K. (2007). DBRIEF: A research paradigm for ICT adoption. *International Education Journal, 8*(2), 113–124.

Doyle, W. & Ponder, G. (1978). The practicality ethic in teacher decision-making. *Interchange, 8*(3), 1–12.

Drent, M., Meelissen, M.R.M., & van der Kleij, F.M. (2010). *The contribution of TIMSS to theories of educational effectiveness: A systematic review of the literature.* Paper presented at the 4th IEA International Research Conference, University of Gothenburg, Sweden. Retrieved from http://www.iea-irc.org/index.php?id=timss

Driscoll, M. P. (2005). *Psychology of learning for instruction* (3rd ed.). Boston, MA: Pearson Allyn and Bacon.

Driscoll, M. P. (2007). Psychological foundations of instructional design. In R. Reiser & J. Dempsey (Eds.), *Trends and issues in instructional design and technology* (pp. 36–44). Upper Saddle River, NJ: Pearson Education.

Earl, L., Watson, N., & Katz, S. (2003). *Large-scale education reform: Life cycles and implications for sustainability.* Reading, UK: Centre for British Teachers.

Eash, M. (1991). Curriculum components. In A. Lewy (Ed.), *The international encyclopedia of curriculum* (pp. 71–73). Oxford, UK: Pergamon Press.

Edelson, D. (2001). Learning-for-use: A framework for the design of technology-supported inquiry activities. *Journal of Research in Science Teaching, 38*(3), 355–385.

Edelson, D. C. (2002). Design research: What we learn when we engage in design. *Journal of the Learning Sciences, 11*(1), 105–122.

Edelson, D. (2006). Balancing innovation and risk: Assessing design research proposals. In J. van den Akker, K. Gravemeijer, S. McKenney & N. Nieveen (Eds.), *Educational Design Research* (pp. 100–106). London: Routledge.

Eisner, E. (1979). *The educational imagination.* New York: Macmillan.

Eisner, E. (1994). *The educational imagination* (2nd ed.). New York: Macmillan.

Ejersbo, L., Engelhardt, R., Frølunde, L., Hanghøj, T., Magnussen, R., & Misfeldt, M. (2008). Balancing product design and theoretical insight. In A. E. Kelly, R. A. Lesh & J. Y. Baek (Eds.), *The handbook of design research methods in education* (pp. 149–163). Mahwah, NJ: Lawrence Erlbaum Associates.

Enright, K. A. (2011). Language and literacy for a new mainstream. *American Educational Research Journal, 48*(1), 80–118.

Evans, R. (2001). *The human side of school change: Reform, resistance, and the real-life problems of innovation.* San Francisco, CA: Jossey-Bass.

Firestone, W. A. (1993). Alternative arguments for generalizing from data as applied to qualitative research. *Educational Researcher, 22*(4), 16–23.

Fishman, B. & Krajcik, J. S. (2003). What does it mean to create sustainable science curriculum innovations? *Science Education, 87*(4), 564–573.

Fresco, L. (2011). *Duurzame ontwikkeling: Feiten versus meningen [Sustainable development: Facts versus opinions].* Presentation given at the annual Kohnstam lecture series. March 23, Amsterdam.

Fullan, M. (1982). *The meaning of educational change.* New York: Teachers College Press.

Fullan, M. (1991). *The new meaning of educational change.* London: Cassell Educational Limited.

Fullan, M. (2000). The return of large-scale reform. *Journal of Educational Change, 1*, 1–23.

Fullan, M. (2003). *Change forces with a vengeance.* London: RoutledgeFalmer.

Fullan, M. & Pomfret, A. (1977). Research on curriculum and instruction implementation. *Review of Educational Research, 47*(2), 335–397.

Fuller, F. (1969). Concerns of teachers: A developmental conceptualization. *American Educational Research Journal, 6*(2), 207–226.

Gagné, R. M. (1965). *The conditions of learning.* New York: Holt, Rinehart & Winston.

Gagné, R. M. (1997). *The conditions of learning and theory of instruction.* New York: Holt, Rinehart and Winston.

Gagné, R. M, Wager, W. W., Golas, K., & Keller, J. M. (2004). *Principles of instructional design* (5th ed.). Belmont, CA: Wadsworth Publishing.

Geijsel, F., Sleegers, P., van den Berg, R., & Kelchtermans, G. (2001). Conditions fostering the implementation of large-scale innovation programs in schools: Teachers' perspectives. *Educational Administration Quarterly, 37(1)*, 130–166.

Gibbons, M. (1999). Science's new social contract with society. *Nature, 402*, 11–18.

Gibbons, M. (2000). Mode 2 society and the emergence of context-sensitive science. *Science and Public Policy, 27*(3), 159–163.

Gibbons, M., Limoges, C., Nowotny, H., Shwartman, S., Scott, P., & Trow, M. (1994). *The new production of knowledge: The dynamics of science and research in contemporary societies.* London: Sage.

Glaser, R. (1976). Components of a psychology instruction: Towards a science of design. *Review of Educational Research, 46*(1), 1–24.

Goldschmidt, P. (2010). *Evaluation of Seeds of Science/Roots of Reading: Effective tools for developing literacy through science in the early grades.* Los Angeles, CA: National Center for Research on Evaluation, Standards, and Student Testing (CRESST).

Goodlad, J., Klein, M., & Tye, K. (1979). The domains of curriculum and their study. In J. Goodlad & Associates (Eds.), *Curriculum inquiry: The study of curriculum practice* (pp. 43–76). New York: McGraw-Hill.

Gorard, S., Roberts, K., & Taylor, C. (2004). What kind of creature is a design experiment? *British Educational Research Journal, 30*(4), 577–590.

Gravemeijer, K. & Cobb, P. (2006). Outline of a method for design research in mathematics education. In J. van den Akker, K. Gravemeijer, S. McKenney & N. Nieveen (Eds.), *Educational design research* (pp. 17–51). London: Routledge.

Green, J. (2000). The role of theory in evidence-based health promotion practice. *Health Education Research, 15*(2), 125–129.

Gustafson, K. & Branch, R. (1997). *Survey of instructional development models.* Syracuse, NY: ERIC Clearinghouse on Information and Technology.

Gustafson, K. L. & Branch, R. M. (2002). *Survey of instructional development models* (4th ed.). Syracuse, NY: ERIC Clearinghouse on Information & Technology.

Guthrie, J. T. & Ozgungor, S. (2002). Instructional contexts for reading engagement. In C. Collins Block & M. Pressley (Eds.), *Comprehension instruction: Research-based best practices* (pp. 275–288). New York: Guilford Press.

Hake, R. R. (2008). Design-based research in physics education research: A review. In A. E. Kelly, R. A. Lesh & J. Y. Baek (Eds.), *Handbook of design research methods in education* (pp. 493–508). New York: Routledge.

Hall, G. E. & Hord, S. M. (2010). *Implementing change: Patterns, principles, and potholes.* Upper Saddle River, NJ: Prentice Hall.

Hall, G. E. & Loucks, S. F. (1978). Teacher concerns as a basis for facilitating and personalizing staff development. *Teacher's College Record, 80*(1), 36–53.

Hall, G. E., Wallace, R. C., & Dossett, W. A. (1973). *A developmental conceptualization of the adoption process within educational institutions.* Austin, TX: The Research and Development Center for Teacher Education.

Hammer, D. K. & Reymen, I. M. M. J. (2002). *The role of emotion in design reflection.* Paper presented at the 3rd International Conference on Design and Emotion, Loughborough, UK. Retrieved from http://doc.utwente.nl/58076/1/role_of_emotion.pdf

Hannafin, M. J., Hannafin, K. M., Land, S., & Oliver, K. (1997). Grounded practice and the design of constructivist learning environments. *Educational Technology Research and Development, 45*(3), 101–117.

Hannafin, M. J. & Hill, J. (2007). Epistemology and the design of learning environments. In R. Reiser & J. Dempsey (Eds.), *Trends and issues in instructional design and technology* (pp. 53–61). Upper Saddle River, NJ: Pearson Education.

Hargreaves, A. & Fink, D. (2006). *Sustainable leadership.* San Francisco, CA: Jossey-Bass.

Havelock, R. (1969). *A comparative study of the literature on the dissemination and utilization of scientific knowledge.* Ann Arbor, MI: Center for Research on Utilization of Scientific Knowledge.

Havelock, R. (1971). *Planning for innovation through dissemination and utilization of knowledge.* Ann Arbor, MI: Center for Research on Utilization of Scientific Knowledge.

Herrington, A., Herrington, J., & Mantei, J. (2009). Design principles for mobile learning. In J. Herrington, A. Herrington, J. Mantei, I. Olney & B. Ferry (Eds.), *New technologies, new pedagogies: Mobile learning in higher education* (pp. 129–

138). Wollongong, Australia: University of Wollongong. Retrieved from http://ro.uow.edu.au/

Herrington, J., McKenney, S., Reeves, T. C., & Oliver, R. (2007). Design-based research and doctoral students: Guidelines for preparing a dissertation proposal. In C. Montgomerie & J. Seale (Eds.), *Proceedings of World Conference on Educational Multimedia, Hypermedia and Telecommunications 2007* (pp. 4089–4097). Chesapeake, VA: Association for the Advancement of Computing in Education.

Herrington, J. & Oliver, R. (2000). An instructional design framework for authentic learning environments. *Educational Technology Research and Development, 48*(3), 23–48.

Hoadley, C. (2004). Methodological alignment in design-based research. *Educational Psychologist, 39*(4), 203–212.

Jackson, P. W. (Ed.) (1992). *Handbook of research on curriculum.* New York: Macmillan.

Janssen, F. J. J. M., Tigelaar, D. E. H., & Verloop, N. (2009). Developing biology lessons aimed at teaching for understanding: A domain-specific heuristic for student teachers. *Journal of Science Teacher Education, 20*(1), 1–20.

Johnson, S. (2010). *Where good ideas come from: The natural history of innovation.* New York: Riverhead Books.

Jonassen, D. (1999). Designing constructivist learning environments. In C. M. Reigeluth (Ed.) *Instructional-design theories and models: A new paradigm of instructional theory* (pp. 215–239). Mahwah, NJ: Lawrence Erlbaum Associates.

Jonassen, D., Cernusca, D., & Ionas, G. (2007). Constructivism and instructional design: The emergence of the learning sciences and design research. In R. Reiser & J. Dempsey (Eds.), *Trends and issues in instructional design and technology* (pp. 45–52). Upper Saddle River, NJ: Pearson Education.

Joseph, R. & Reigeluth, C. M. (2005). Formative research on an early stage of the systemic change process in a small school district. *British Journal of Educational Technology, 36*(6), 937–956.

Joseph, R. & Reigeluth, C. M. (2010). The systemic change process in education: A conceptual framework. *Contemporary Educational Technology, 1*(2) 97–117.

Kaestle, C. F. (1993). The awful reputation of education research. *Educational Researcher, 22*(1), 23, 26–31.

Kafai, Y. B. (2005). The classroom as living laboratory: Design-based research for understanding, comparing, and evaluating learning science through design. *Educational Technology, 45*(1), 28–34.

Kali, Y. (2006). Collaborative knowledge-building using the Design Principles Database. *International Journal of Computer Support for Collaborative Learning, 1*(2), 187–201.

Kali, Y. (2008). The Design Principles Database as means for promoting design-based research. In A. E. Kelly, R. A. Lesh & J. Y. Baek (Eds.), *Handbook of design research methods in education* (pp. 423–438). London: Routledge.

Kali, Y. & Linn, M. C. (2008). Technology-enhanced support strategies for inquiry learning. In J. M. Spector, M. D. Merrill, J. J. G. van Merriënboer & M. P. Driscoll (Eds.), *Handbook of research on educational communications and technology* (3rd ed.), (pp. 145–161). New York: Lawrence Erlbaum Associates/Routledge.

Kali, Y. & Ronen-Fuhrmann, T. (2011). Teaching to design educational technologies. *The International Journal of Learning and Technology, 6*(1), 4–23.

Kant, E. (1781/2008). *Critique of pure reason*, trans. Norman Kemp Smith. London: Macmillan.

Kellogg Foundation (2004). *Logic model development guide*. Battle Creek, MI: Kellogg Foundation. Retrieved from www.wkkf.org.

Kelly, A. E. (2003). Research as design. *Educational Researcher, 32*(1), 3–4.

Kelly, A. E. (2004). Design research in education: Yes, but is it methodological? *Journal of the Learning Sciences, 13*(1), 115–128.

Kelly, A. E. (2006). Quality criteria for design research: Evidence and commitments. In J. van den Akker, K. Gravemeijer, S. McKenney & N. Nieveen (Eds.), *Educational design research* (pp. 107–118). London: Routledge.

Kelly, A. E., Lesh, R. A., & Baek, J. Y. (Eds.), (2008). *Handbook of design research methods in education*. London: Routledge.

Kelly, K. (2010). *What technology wants*. New York: Penguin Group.

Kennedy, M. M. (1979). Generalizing from single case studies. *Evaluation Quarterly, 3*, 661–678.

Kennedy, M. M. (1997). The connection between research and practice. *Educational Researcher, 26*(7), 4–12.

Ketelhut, D. J., Nelson, B., Clarke, J., & Dede, C. (2010). A multi-user virtual environment for building higher order inquiry skills in science. *British Journal of Educational Technology, 41*(1), 56–68.

Kim, H. & Hannafin, M. (2008). Grounded design of web-enhanced case-based activity. *Educational Technology Research & Development, 56*(2), 161–179.

Kirschner, P., Beers, P., Bosjuizen, H., & Gijselaers, W. (2008). Coercing shared knowledge in collaborative learning environments. *Computers in Human Behavior, 24*, 403–420.

Kirschner, P., Carr, C., van Merriënboer, J., & Sloep, P. (2002). How expert designers design. *Performance Improvement Quarterly, 15*(4), 86–104.

Klein, F. (1991). A conceptual framework for curriculum decision making. In F. Klein (Ed.), *The politics of curriculum decision making: Issues in centralizing the curriculum* (pp. 24–41). Albany, NY: State University of New York Press.

Klopfer, E. & Squire, K. (2008). Environmental detectives – The development of an augmented reality platform for environmental simulations. *Educational Technology Research and Development, 56*(2), 203–228.

Könings, K., Brand-Gruwel, S., & van Merriënboer, J. (2005). Towards more powerful learning environments through combining the perspective of designers, teachers and students. *British Journal of Educational Psychology, 75*(4), 645–660.

Könings, K., Brand-Gruwel, S., & van Merriënboer, J. (2007). Teacher perspectives on innovations: Implications for educational design. *Teaching and Teacher Education, 23*, 985–997.

Kozma, R. (2007). One Laptop Per Child and premature scaling. *OLPC News*. Retrieved from http://www.olpcnews.com

Krathwohl, D. R. (1993). *Methods of educational and social science research: An integrated approach*. New York: Longman.

Kubitskey, B. & Fishman, B. (2005). *Untangling the relationships between professional development, enactment, student learning and teacher learning through multiple case studies*. Paper presented at the annual meeting of the American Educational Research Association, April 11–15, Montreal.

Lagemann, E. C. (2002). *An elusive science: The troubling history of education research.* Chicago, IL: University of Chicago Press.

Larson, S. & Dearing, J. (2008). Design research and the diffusion of innovations. In A. E. Kelly, R. A. Lesh & J. Y. Baek (Eds.), *Handbook of design research methods in education* (pp. 512–533). London: Routledge.

Lasry, N., Mazur, E., & Watkins, J. (2008). Peer instruction: From Harvard to the two-year college. *American Journal of Physics, 76*(11), 1066–1069.

Laurel, B. (2003). *Design research: Methods and perspectives.* Cambridge, MA: MIT Press.

Lawrence Hall of Science. (2010). *Seeds of Science/Roots of Reading: Research and development for accommodation of English language learners.* Berkeley, CA: Lawrence Hall of Science.

Lawshe, C. H. (1975). The quantitative approach to content validity. *Personnel Psychology, 28,* 563–575.

Lehrer, R. (2009). Designing to develop disciplinary dispositions: Modeling natural systems. *American Psychologist, 64*(8), 759–771.

Lehrer, R. & Schauble, L. (2004). Modeling natural variation through distribution. *American Educational Research Journal, 41*(3), 635–679.

Lewis, C., Perry, R., & Murata, A. (2006). How should research contribute to instructional improvement? The case of lesson study. *Educational Researcher 35*(3), 3–14.

Lieberman, A. & Pointer, D. (2008). Teacher learning: The key to educational reform. *Journal of Teacher Education, 59*(3), 226–234.

Lieberman, A. & Pointer, D. (2010). Making practice public: teacher learning in the 21st century. *Journal of Teacher Education, 61*(1–2), 77–88.

Lincoln, Y. S. & Guba, E. G. (1985). *Naturalistic inquiry.* Newbury Park, CA: Sage Publications.

Linn, M. C., Davis, E. A., & Bell, P. (Eds.) (2004). *Internet environments for science education.* Mahwah, NJ: Lawrence Erlbaum Associates.

Linn, M. C. & Hsi, S. (2000). *Computers, teachers, peers: Science learning partners.* Mawah, NJ: Lawrence Erlbaum Associates.

Loucks-Horseley, S., Hewson, P., Love, N., & Stiles, K. (1998). *Designing professional development for teachers of science and mathematics.* Thousand Oaks, CA: Corwin Press.

Lumsdaine, E., Lumsdaine, M., & Shelnutt, J. (1999). *Creative problem solving and engineering design.* New York: McGraw-Hill.

Mandviwalla, M., Patnayakuni, R., & Schuff, D. (2008). Improving the peer review process with information technology. *Decision Support Systems, 46*(1), 29–40.

Marsh, C. J. (2004). *Key concepts for understanding curriculum* (3rd ed.). London: RoutledgeFalmer.

Marsh, C. J. & Willis, G. (2007). *Curriculum: Alternative approaches, ongoing issues.* Upper Saddle River, NJ: Pearson.

Mayer, R. E. (2009). *Multimedia learning* (2nd ed.). New York: Cambridge University Press.

Mayeske, G. W. & Lambur, M. T. (2001). *How to design better programs: A staff centered stakeholder approach to program logic modeling.* Crofton, MD: Program Design Institute.

Mazur, E. (1996). Science lectures: A relic of the past? *Physics World, 9,* 13–14.

Mazur, E. (1997). *Peer instruction: A user's manual.* Upper Saddle River, NJ: Prentice Hall.

McCarty, R. (2002). Science, politics, and peer review: An editor's dilemma. *American Psychologist, 57*(3), 198–201.

McDonnell, L. (2008). Thoughts on research quality while cleaning my office. *Educational Researcher, 37*(7), 448–449.

McFarland, M. (2000). *The Papers of Wilbur and Orville Wright, Including the Chanute-Wright Letters.* New York: McGraw-Hill Professional.

McKenney, S. (2001). *Computer based support for science education materials developers in Africa: Exploring potentials.* University of Twente, Enschede, The Netherlands. Retrieved from http://doc.utwente.nl/75705/

McKenney, S. (2005). Technology for curriculum and teacher development: Software to help educators learn while designing teacher guides. *Journal of Research on Technology in Education, 28*(2), 167–190.

McKenney, S., Nieveen, N., & van den Akker, J. (2006). Design research from the curriculum perspective. In J. van den Akker, K. Gravemeijer, S. E. McKenney & N. Nieveen (Eds.), *Educational Design Research* (pp. 67–90). London: Routledge.

McKenney, S. & van den Akker, J. (2005). Computer-based support for curriculum designers: A case of developmental research. *Educational Technology Research & Development, 53*(2), 41–66.

McKenney, S. & Voogt, J. (2009). Designing technology for emergent literacy: The PictoPal initiative. *Computers & Education, 52,* 719–729.

McKenney, S & Voogt, J. (2010). Technology and young children: How 4–7 year olds perceive their own use of computers. *Computers in Human Behavior, 26,* 656–664.

McKenney, S. & Voogt, J. (in press). Teacher design of technology for emergent literacy: An explorative feasibility study. *Australasian Journal of Early Childhood.*

McLaughlin, M. & Mitra, D. (2001). Theory-based change and change-based theory: Going deeper going broader. *Journal of Educational Change, 2*(4), 301–323.

Merrill, D. (2007). First principles of instruction: A synthesis. In R. Reiser & J. Dempsey (Eds.), *Trends and issues in instructional design and technology* (pp. 62–71). Upper Saddle River, NJ: Pearson Education.

Merrill, M. D. (1994). *Instructional design theory.* Englewood Cliffs, NJ: Educational Technology Publications.

Merton, R. K. (1957). *Social theory and social structure.* New York: Free Press.

Middleton, J., Gorard, S., Taylor, C., & Bannan-Ritland, B. (2008). The "compleat" design experiment: From soup to nuts. In A. E. Kelly, R. A. Lesh & J. Y. Baek (Eds.), *Handbook of design research methods in education* (pp. 21–46). Routledge: London.

Mishra, P. & Koehler, M. (2006). Technological pedagogical content knowledge: A framework for teacher knowledge. *Teachers College Record, 108*(6), 1017–1054.

Münsterberg, H. (1899). *Psychology and life.* New York: Houghton Mifflin.

Nelson, B., Ketelhut, D. J., Clarke, J., Bowman, C., & Dede, C. (2005). Design-based research strategies for developing a scientific inquiry curriculum in a multi-user virtual environment. *Educational Technology, 45*(1), 21–27.

Neulight, N., Kafai, Y., Kao, L., Foley, B., & Galas, C. (2007). Children's participation in a virtual epidemic in the science classroom: Making connections to natural infectious diseases. *Journal of Science Education and Technology, 16*(1), 47–58.

Neumeier, M. (2008). *The Designful Company: How to build a culture of nonstop innovation*. Berkeley, CA: Peachpit Press.

Newman, D. (1990). Opportunities for research on the organizational impact of school computers. *Educational Researcher, 19*(3), 8–13.

Nieveen, N. (1997). *Computer-based support for curriculum developers: A study on the potential of computer support in the domain of formative curriculum evaluation.* Doctoral dissertation. Enschede, The Netherlands: Twente University.

Nieveen, N. (1999). Prototyping to reach product quality. In J. van den Akker, R. Branch, K. Gustafson, N. Nieveen & T. Plomp (Eds.), *Design approaches and tools in education and training* (pp. 125–136). Dordrecht: Kluwer Academic Publishers.

Nieveen, N., McKenney, S., & van den Akker, J. (2006). Educational design research: The value of variety. In J. van den Akker, K. Gravemeijer, S. McKenney & N. Nieveen (Eds.), *Educational design research* (pp. 151–158). London: Routledge.

Nonaka, I. & Takeuchi, H. (1995). *The knowledge-creating company: how Japanese companies create the dynamic of innovation*. Oxford, UK: Oxford University Press.

Nowotny, H., Scott, P., & Gibbons, M. (2001). *Re-thinking science: Knowledge and the public in an age of uncertainty*. London: Polity Press.

Nowotny, H., Scott, P., & Gibbons, M. (2003). "Mode 2" revisited: The new production of knowledge. *Minerva, 41*, 179–194.

Oancea, A. (2005). Criticisms of educational research: Key topics and levels of analysis. *British Educational Research Journal, 31*(2), 157–183.

O'Connor, E. E., Dearing, E., & Collins, B. A. (2011). Teacher–child relationship trajectories: Predictors of behavior problem trajectories and mediators of child and family factors. *American Educational Research Journal, 48*(1), 120–162.

Oh, E. (2011). *Collaborative group work in an online learning environment: A design research study*. Doctoral dissertation. Athens, GA: The University of Georgia.

Oh, E., Liu, Y., & Reeves, T. C. (2009). *Conducting design research as doctoral students: Process and lessons learned*. Paper presented at the 2009 annual conference of Association for Educational Communications and Technology, Louisville, KY.

Padilla, M. J., Muth, K. D., & Lund Padilla, R. K. (1991). Science and reading: Many process skills in common? In C. M. Santa & D. E. Alvermann (Eds.), *Science learning – Processes and applications* (pp. 14–19). Newark, DE: International Reading Association.

Palincsar, A. S. & Magnusson, S. J. (2001). The interplay of firsthand and text-based investigations to model and support the development of scientific knowledge and reasoning. In S. Carver & D. Klahr (Eds.), *Cognition and instruction: Twenty-five years of progress* (pp. 151–194). Mahwah, NJ: Lawrence Erlbaum Associates.

Palincsar, A. S., Magnusson, S. J., Collins, K. M., & Cutter, J. (2001). Promoting deep understanding of science in students with disabilities in inclusion classrooms. *Learning Disabilities Quarterly, 24*(1), 15–32.

Pappas, C. C., Varelas, M., Barry, A., & Rife, A. (2002). Dialogic inquiry around information texts: The role of intertextuality in constructing scientific understandings in urban primary classrooms. *Linguistics and Education, 13*(4), 435–482.

Patton, M. Q. (2001). *Qualitative research and evaluation methods*. Thousand Oaks, CA: Sage.

Pearson, D., Moje, E., & Greenleaf, C. (2010). Literacy and science: Each in the service of the other. *Science, 328*, 459–463.

Pellegrino, J. W. & Brophy, S. (2008). From cognitive theory to instructional practice: Technology and the evolution of anchored Instruction. In D. Ifenthaler, P. Pirnay-Dummer & J. M. Spector, J. (Eds.), *Understanding models for learning and instruction: Essays in honor of Norbert M. Seel* (pp. 277–303). New York: Springer.

Pellegrino, J. W., Hickey, D., Heath, A., Rewey, K., Vye, N. J., & the CTGV. (1991). *Assessing the outcomes of an innovative instructional program: The 1990–1991 implementation of "The Adventures of Jasper Woodbury Program"* (Tech. Rep. No 91-1). Nashville, TN: Vanderbilt University, Learning & Technology Center.

Phillips, D. C. (2006). Assessing the quality of design research proposals: Some philosophical perspectives. In J. van den Akker, K. Gravemeijer, S. McKenney & N. Nieveen (Eds.), *Educational Design Research* (pp. 93–99). London: Routledge.

Phillips, D. C. & Dolle, J. R. (2006). From Plato to Brown and beyond: Theory, practice, and the promise of design experiments. In L. Verschaffel, F. Dochy, M. Boekaerts & S. Vosniadou (Eds.), *Instructional psychology: Past, present and future trends. Sixteen essays in honour of Erik De Corte* (pp. 277–292). Oxford, UK: Elsevier Science Ltd.

Piaget, J. & Inhelder, B. (1969). *The psychology of the child.* New York: Basic Books.

Plomp, T. (2009). Educational design research: An introduction. In T. Plomp & N. Nieveen (Eds.), *An introduction to educational design research: Proceedings of the seminar conducted at the East China Normal University, Shanghai* (pp. 9–35). Enschede, The Netherlands: SLO – The Netherlands Institute for Curriculum Development.

Plomp, T. & Nieveen, N. (Eds.), (2009). *An introduction to educational design research: Proceedings of the seminar conducted at the East China Normal University, Shanghai.* Enschede, The Netherlands: SLO – The Netherlands Institute for Curriculum Development.

Posner, G. (2004). *Analyzing the curriculum.* New York: McGraw-Hill.

Posner, G. & Rudnitsky, A. (1978). *Course design: A guide to curriculum development for teachers.* New York: Longman.

Posner, G. & Rudnitsky, A. (2005). *Course design: A guide to curriculum development for teachers* (7th ed.). New York: Allyn & Bacon.

Prado, M. M. & Gravoso, R. S. (2011). Improving high school students' statistical reasoning skills: A case of applying anchored instruction. *Asia-Pacific Education Researcher, 20*(1), 61–72.

Procee, H. (2006). Reflection in education: A Kantian epistemology. *Educational Theory, 56*(3), 237–253.

Procee. H. & Visscher-Voerman, I. (2004). Reflecteren in het onderwijs: Een kleine systmatiek. *Velon, 25*(3), 37–44.

Quintana, C., Reiser, B., Davis, E., Krajcik, J., Fretz, E., Duncan, R., Kyza, E., Edelson, D., & Soloway, E. (2004). A scaffolding design framework for software to support science inquiry. *Journal of the Learning Sciences, 13*(3), 337–386.

Raval, H. (2010). *Supporting para-teachers in an Indian NGO: The plan–enact–reflect cycle.* Doctoral dissertation. Enschede, The Netherlands: Twente University.

Raval, H., McKenney, S., & Pieters, J. (2010). A conceptual model for supporting para-teacher learning in an Indian NGO. *Studies in Continuing Education, 32*(3), 217–234.

Raval, H., McKenney, S., & Pieters, J. (2011a). A needs and context analysis for teacher learning in an Indian NGO. *International Journal of Training and Development*. Advance online publication. Doi: 10.1111/j.1468-2419.2011.00393.x.

Raval, H., McKenney, S., & Pieters, J. (2011b). Institutionalizing planning, enactment and reflection of daily lessons through appropriate organizational restructuring. *The Asia-Pacific Educational Researcher*, 20(3), 438–455.

Raval, H., McKenney, S., & Pieters, J. (under review). Supporting para-teachers by regularizing and strengthening planning, enactment and reflection of daily lessons.

Raval, H., McKenney, S. & Pieters, J. (under review). Summative evaluation of para-teacher support for remedial teaching in Indian slums.

Reason, P. (2001). Learning and chance through action research (pp. 182-194). In J. Henry (Ed.), *Creative Management* (2nd ed.). London: Sage.

Reeves, T. C. (2000). Socially responsible educational technology research. *Educational Technology*, 40(6), 19–28.

Reeves, T. C. (2006). Design research from the technology perspective. In J. van den Akker, K. Gravemeijer, S. McKenney & N. Nieveen (Eds.), *Educational Design Research* (pp. 86–109). London: Routledge.

Reeves, T.C. (2011). Can educational research be both rigorous and relevant? *Educational Designer*, 1(4). Retrieved from http://www.educationaldesigner. org/ed/volume1/issue4/article13/index.htm

Reeves, T. C. & Carter, B. J. (2001). Usability testing and return-on-investment studies: Key evaluation strategies for web-based training. In B. Khan (Ed.), *Web-based training* (pp. 547–557). Englewood Cliffs, NJ: Educational Technology Publications.

Reeves, T. C. & Hedberg, J. (2003). *Interactive learning systems evaluation*. Englewood Cliffs, NJ: Educational Technology Publications.

Reeves, T. C., Herrington, J., & Oliver, R. (2005). Design research: A socially responsible approach to instructional technology research in higher education. *Journal of Computing in Higher Education*, 16(2), 97–116.

Reigeluth, C. M. (Ed.), (1999). *Instructional-design theories and models: A new paradigm of instructional theory*. Mahwah, NJ: Lawrence Erlbaum Associates.

Reigeluth, C. M. & Carr-Chellman, A. (Eds.), (2009). *Instructional-design theories and models, volume III: Building a common knowledge base*. New York: Routledge.

Reigeluth, C. M. & Frick, T. W. (1999). Formative research: A methodology for improving design theories. In C. M. Reigeluth (Ed.), *Instructional-design theories and models: A new paradigm of instructional theory* (Vol. II). Mahwah, NJ: Lawrence Erlbaum Associates.

Reinking, D. & Bradley, B. A. (2008). *Formative and design experiments: Approaches to language and literacy research*. New York: Teachers College Press.

Reinking, D. & Watkins, J. (1996). *A formative experiment investigating the use of multimedia book reviews to increase elementary students' independent reading*. Reading research Report No. 55 (Also available as ERIC Document # 398 570). Athens, GA: National Reading Research Center, The University of Georgia.

Reiser, R. A. & Dempsey, J. V. (2012). *Trends and issues in instructional design and technology* (3rd ed.). Upper Saddle River, NJ: Pearson Education.

Reymen, I. M. M. J., Hammer, D. K., Kroes, P. A., van Aken, J. E., Dorst, C. H., Bax, M. F. T., & Basten, T. (2006). A domain-independent descriptive design model and its application to structured reflection on design processes. *Research in Engineering Design, 16*(4), 147–173.

Richey, R. & Klein, J. D. (2007). *Design and development research: Methods, strategies, and issues.* Mahwah, NJ: Lawrence Erlbaum Associates.

Richey, R. & Nelson, W. (1996). Developmental research. In D. Jonassen (Ed.), *Handbook of research for educational communications and technology* (pp. 1213–1245). New York: Macmillan.

Riley, B. (2003). Dissemination of heart health promotion in the Ontario Public Health System: 1989–1999. *Health Education Research, 18*(1), 15–31.

Rogers, E. M. (1962). *Diffusion of innovations.* New York: Free Press

Rogers, E. M. (2003). *Diffusion of innovations* (5th ed.). New York: Free Press.

Romme, A. G. L. (2003). Making a difference: Organization as design. *Organization Science, 14,* 558–573.

Roschelle, J., Bakia, M., Toyama, Y., & Patton, C. (2011). Eight issues for learning scientists about education and the economy. *Journal of the Learning Sciences, 20*(1), 3–49.

Roschelle, J., Rafanan, K., Estrella, G., Nussbaum, M., & Claro, S. (2010). From handheld collaborative tool to effective classroom module: Embedding CSCL in a broader design framework. *Computers & Education, 55*(3), 1018–1026.

Ross, S. M., Morrison, G. R., Hannafin, R. D., Young, M., van den Akker, J., Kuiper, W., Richey, R. C., & Klein, J. D. (2008). Research designs. In J. Spector, M. Merrill, J. van Merriënboer & M. Driscoll (Eds.), *Handbook of research on educational communications and technology* (3rd ed.), (pp. 715–761). New York: Lawrence Erlbaum Associates/Routledge.

Sandoval, W. A. (2004). Developing learning theory by refining conjectures embodied in educational designs. *Educational Psychologist, 39*(4), 213–223.

Sanny, R. & Teale, W. (2008). Using multimedia anchored instruction cases in literacy methods courses: Lessons learned from pre-service teachers. *Journal of Literacy & Technology, 9*(1), 2–35.

Schoenfeld, A. H. (2006). Design experiments. In J. L. Green, G. Camilli, P. B. Ellmore & A. Skukauskaite (Eds.), *Handbook of complementary methods in education research* (pp. 193–206). Washington, DC: American Educational Research Association.

Schoenfeld, A. H. (2007). Method. In F. Lester (Ed.), *Handbook of research on mathematics teaching and learning* (2nd ed., pp. 69–107). Charlotte, NC: Information Age Publishing.

Schoenfeld, A. H. (2009a). Bridging the cultures of educational research and design. *Educational Designer, 1*(2). Retrieved from http://www.educationaldesigner. org/ed/volume1/issue2/article5/index.htm

Schoenfeld, A. H. (2009b). Instructional research and the improvement of practice. In J. D. Bransford, D. J. Stipek, N. J. Vye, L. M. Gomez & D. Lam (Eds.), *The role of research in educational improvement* (pp. 161–188). Cambridge, MA: Harvard Education Press.

Schön, D. (1983). *The reflective practitioner: How professionals think in action.* New York: Basic Books.

Schubert, W. H. (1986). *Curriculum: Perspective, paradigm, and possibility.* New York: Macmillan.

Schubert, W., Lopez Schubert, A., Thomas, T., & Carroll, W. (2002). *Curriculum books: The first hundred years*. New York: Peter Lang.

Shavelson, R., Phillips, D. C., Towne, L., & Feuer, M. (2003). On the science of education design studies. *Educational Researcher, 32*(1), 25–28.

Shiflet, A. B. & Shiflet, G. W. (2006). *Introduction to computational science: Modeling and simulation for the sciences*. Princeton, NJ: Princeton University Press.

Smith, G. F. (1998). Idea-generation techniques: A formulary of active ingredients. *The Journal of Creative Behavior, 32*(2), 107–133.

Snow, C. E. (1983). Literacy and language: Relationships during the preschool years. *Harvard Educational Review, 53*(2), 165–189.

Snyder, J., Bolin, F., & Zumwalt, K. (1992). Curriculum implementation. In P. Jackson (Ed.), *Handbook of research on curriculum* (pp. 402–435). New York: Macmillan.

Spector, J. M., Merrill, M. D., van Merriënboer, J. J. G., & Driscoll, M. (Eds.), (2008). *Handbook of research on educational communications and technology*. New York: Lawrence Erlbaum Associates/Routledge.

Spencer, H. (1859). What knowledge is of most worth? *Westminster Review*.

Stahl, G., Koschmann, T., & Suthers, D. (2006). Computer-supported collaborative learning: An historical perspective. In R. K. Sawyer (Ed.), *Cambridge handbook of the learning sciences* (pp. 409–426). Cambridge, UK: Cambridge University Press.

Stenhouse, L. (1975). *An introduction to curriculum research and development*. London: Heinemann.

Stokes, D. (1997). *Pasteur's quadrant: Basic science and technological innovation*. Washington, DC: Brookings Institution Press.

Stoof, A., Martens, R., & Merriënboer, J. (2007). Web-based support for constructing competence maps: Design and formative evaluation. *Educational Technology Research & Development, 55*(4), 347–368.

Swan, M. (2007). The impact of task-based professional development on teachers' practices and beliefs: A design research study. *Journal of Mathematics Teacher Education, 10*(4–6), 217–237.

Sweller, J., van Merrienboer, J., & Paas, F. (1998). Cognitive architecture and instructional design. *Educational Psychology Review, 10*(3), 251–296.

Taba, H. (1962). *Curriculum development: Theory and practice*. New York: Harcourt, Brace & World.

Tabak, I. (2004). Reconstructing context: Negotiating the tension between exogenous and endogenous educational design. *Educational Psychologist, 39*(4), 225–233.

Thijs, A. (1999). *Supporting science curriculum reform in Botswana: The potential of peer coaching*. Doctoral dissertation. University of Twente: Enschede, The Netherlands.

Thijs, A. & van den Akker, J. (1997). *Peer coaching as a promising component of science teachers inservice training?* Paper presented at the SAARMSE annual conference, January 23–26, Johannesburg.

Thijs, A. & van den Akker, J. (2009). *Curriculum in development*. Enschede, The Netherlands: SLO – The Netherlands Institute for Curriculum Development.

Thijs, A. & van den Berg, E. (2002). Peer coaching as part of a professional development program for science teachers in Botswana. *International Journal of Educational Development, 22*(1), 55–68.

Thompson, M. & Wiliam, D. (2008). Tight but loose: A conceptual framework for scaling up school reforms. In E. Wylie (Ed.). *Tight but loose: Scaling up teacher professional development in diverse contexts* (pp. 1–45). Princeton, NJ: Educational Testing Service.

Tilson, J., Billman, A., Corrigan, S., & Barber, J. (2011). Two for one: Assessing science and literacy using writing prompts. In P. Noyce & D. T. Hickey (Eds.), *New frontiers in formative assessment*. Cambridge, MA: Harvard Education Press.

Tinto, V. (2010). From theory to action: Exploring the institutional conditions for student retention. In J. C. Smart (Ed.), *Higher education: Handbook of theory and research* (Vol. 25, pp. 51–89). New York: Springer.

Tondeur, J., Valke, M., & van Braak, J. (2008). A multidimensional approach to determinants of computer use in primary education: teacher and school characteristics. *Journal of Computer Assisted Learning, 24,* 494–506.

Torrance, H. (2008). Building confidence in qualitative research: Engaging the demands of policy. *Qualitative Inquiry, 14*(4), 507–527.

Tyler, R. (1949). *Basic principles of curriculum and instruction.* Chicago, IL: University of Chicago Press.

van den Akker, J. (1998a). *De uitbeelding van de curriculum [The enactment of curriculum].* Inaugural address. Enschede, The Netherlands: University of Twente.

van den Akker, J. (1998b). The science curriculum: Between ideals and outcomes. In B. Fraser & K. Tobin (Eds.), *International handbook of science education* (pp. 421–447). Dordrecht: Kluwer Academic Publishers.

van den Akker, J. (1999). Principles and methods of development research. In J. van den Akker, R. Branch, K. Gustafson, N. Nieveen & T. Plomp (Eds.), *Design approaches and tools in education and training* (pp. 1–14). Dordrecht: Kluwer Academic Publishers.

van den Akker, J. (2003). Curriculum perspectives: An introduction. In J. van den Akker, W. Kuiper & U. Hameyer (Eds.), *Curriculum landscapes and trends* (pp. 1–10). Dordrecht: Kluwer Academic Publishers.

van den Akker, J. (2010). Building bridges: How research may improve curriculum policies and classroom practices. In S. Stoney (Ed.), *Beyond Lisbon 2010: Perspectives from research and development for education policy in Europe* (CIDREE Yearbook 2010). Slough, UK: National Foundation for Educational Research.

van den Akker, J., McKenney, S., & Nieveen, N. (2006a). Introduction to educational design research. In J. van den Akker, K. Gravemeijer, S. McKenney & N. Nieveen (Eds.), *Educational design research* (pp. 67–90). London: Routledge.

van den Akker, J., Gravemeijer, K., McKenney, S., & Nieveen, N. (2006b). *Educational design research.* London: Routledge.

van Heuvelen, A. (1995). Experiment problems for mechanics. *Physics Teacher, 33*(3), 176.

van Merriënboer, J. (1997). *Training complex cognitive skills: A four-component instructional design model for technical training.* Englewood Cliffs, NJ: Educational Technology Publications.

van Merriënboer, J., Clark, R., & de Croock, M. (2002). Blueprints for complex learning: The 4C/ID-model. *Educational Technology, Research and Development, 50*(2), 39–64.

van Merriënboer, J. & Kirschner, P. (2007). *Ten steps to complex learning: A systematic approach to four-component instructional design.* London: Lawrence Erlbaum Associates.

van Strien, P. J. (1975). Naar een methodologie van het praktijkdenken in de sociale wetenschappen [Towards a methodology of professional practice in the social sciences]. *Nederlands Tijdschrijft voor de Psychologie, 30,* 601–619.

van Strien, P. J. (1997), Towards a methodology of psychological practice: The regulative cycle. *Theory & Psychology, 7*(5): 683–700.

Vesper, J., Herrington, J., Kartoglu, U., & Reeves, T. C. (2011). *The application of expert review as a formative evaluation strategy within an educational design research study.* Paper presented at E-Learn 2011, World Conference on E-learning in Corporate, Government, Healthcare, & Higher Education, October 18–21, Honolulu, HI, USA.

Viadero, D. (2009). New head of U.S. research agency aims for relevance. *Education Week, 29*(13), 10.

Visscher-Voerman, I. (1999). *Design approaches in education and training.* Doctoral dissertation. University of Twente, Enschede, The Netherlands.

Visscher-Voerman, I. & Gustafson, K. L. (2004). Paradigms in the theory and practice of education and training design. *Educational Technology Research and Development, 52*(2), 69–89.

Wagner, J. (1997). The unavoidable intervention of educational research: A framework for reconsidering researcher–practitioner cooperation. *Educational Researcher, (26)*7, 13–22.

Walker, D. (1971a). A naturalistic model for curriculum development. *The School Review, 80*(1), 51–65.

Walker, D. (1971b). A study of deliberation in their curriculum projects. *Curriculum Theory Network, 7,* 118–134.

Walker, D. (1982). Curriculum theory is many things to many people. *Theory into Practice 21*(1), 62–65.

Walker, D. (1990). *Fundamentals of curriculum.* San Diego, CA: Harcourt, Brace Jovanovich.

Walker, D. (1992). Methodological issues in curriculum research. In P. W. Jackson (Ed.), *Handbook of research on curriculum* (pp. 98–118). New York: Macmillan.

Walker, D. (2006). Toward productive design studies. In J. van den Akker, K. Gravemeijer, S. McKenney & N. Nieveen (Eds.), *Educational design research* (pp. 8–13). London: Routledge.

Wang, F. & Hannafin, M. (2005). Design-based research and technology-enhanced learning environments. *Educational Technology Research and Development, 53*(4), 5–23.

Wang, J. & Herman, J. (2005). *Evaluation of Seeds of Science/Roots of Reading Project: Shoreline Science and Terrarium Investigations.* Los Angeles, CA: National Center for Research on Evaluation, Standards, and Student Testing (CRESST).

Wang, Q. (2001). *Computer support for multimedia curriculum design.* Doctoral dissertation. Enschede, The Netherlands: University of Twente.

Whitty, G. (2006). Education(al) research and education policy making: Is conflict inevitable? *British Educational Research Journal, 32*(2), 159–176.

Williams, M. (2004). *Exploring the effects of a multimedia case-based learning environment in pre-service science teacher education in Jamaica.* Doctoral dissertation. Enschede, The Netherlands: University of Twente.

Wylie, E. (2008). *Tight but loose: Scaling up teacher professional development in diverse contexts* (Ed.). Princeton, NJ: Educational Testing Service.

Yin, R. (1989). *Case study research: Design and methods* (2nd ed.). Newbury Park, CA: Sage.

Young, M. (1993). Instructional design for situated learning. *Educational Technology Research and Development, 41*(1), 43–58.

Zhao, Y., Pugh, K., Sheldon, S., & Byers, J. L. (2002). Conditions for classroom technology innovations. *Teachers College Record, 104*(3), 482–515.

Zulkardi, Z. (2002). *Developing a learning environment on RME for student teachers in Indonesia.* Doctoral dissertation. Enschede, The Netherlands: University of Twente.

Index